James Baldwin
and the Short Story

James Baldwin and the Short Story

Ethics, Aesthetics, Psychogeography

BENEDICT USHEDO

☙PICKWICK *Publications* · Eugene, Oregon

JAMES BALDWIN AND THE SHORT STORY
Ethics, Aesthetics, Psychogeography

Copyright © 2018 Benedict Ushedo. All rights reserved. Except for brief quotations in critical publications or reviews, no part of this book may be reproduced in any manner without prior written permission from the publisher. Write: Permissions, Wipf and Stock Publishers, 199 W. 8th Ave., Suite 3, Eugene, OR 97401.

Pickwick Publications
An Imprint of Wipf and Stock Publishers
199 W. 8th Ave., Suite 3
Eugene, OR 97401

www.wipfandstock.com

PAPERBACK ISBN: 978-1-5326-1738-6
HARDCOVER ISBN: 978-1-4982-4205-9
EBOOK ISBN: 978-1-4982-4204-2

Cataloging-in-Publication data:

Names: Ushedo, Benedict, author.

Title: James Baldwin and the short story : ethics, aesthetics, psychogeography / Benedict Ushedo.

Description: Eugene, OR: Pickwick Publications, 2018. | Includes bibliographical references and index.

Identifiers: ISBN: 978-1-5326-1738-6 (paperback). | ISBN: 978-1-4982-4205-9 (hardcover). | ISBN: 978-1-4982-4204-2 (ebook).

Subjects: LCSH: Baldwin, James, 1924–1987—Criticism and interpretation. | American fiction—History and criticism. | Ethics in literature.

Classification: PS3552 A45 Z84 2018 (print). | PS3552 (ebook).

Manufactured in the U.S.A.   03/16/18

Contents

Preface | vii

1 Ethics, Selfhood, and Textuality | 1
2 Myth and the Scapegoat Rhetoric | 30
3 Tragedy: A Method of Inquiry | 59
4 Contrast Experience: Threshold to Creativity | 90
5 Music and Revelation | 118
6 Conclusion: A Spiritual Autobiography | 152

Works and Interviews by James Baldwin | 159
General Bibliography | 161
Index | 177

Preface

This study of James Baldwin's short stories focuses on the interplay of reason and intuition within the process of interpretation. It draws on the protest of theological criticism against a narrow understanding of critical theory fostered by the thinking that literature is "autonomous" and that objectivity implies that the critic has to approach texts as an emotional blank slate. The study demonstrates the capacity of literature to elicit specific ethical and theological responses. I will argue that even where a literary work does not seem to exhibit a theme immediately relevant to ethical inquiry, it remains doubtful whether an analysis of such a text can be effective if it is left neutral or purely descriptive. The underlying assumption is that the power of language constantly stimulates the development of sensibilities and reflections on texts—be they "sacred" or "secular." Hence, it is contended that interpretation necessarily demands the making of choices or the preference of one system of value over another.

More specifically, and against the background of the mindset engendered in James Baldwin by his encounter with religion and subsequent experience as a child preacher, this study examines the range of issues that echo in *Going to Meet the Man*, his collection of short stories. My claim is that the stories are autobiographically driven. To support this line of thought and the related proposition that the stories feed into ethical themes relevant to self-knowledge, vicarious suffering, love and forgiveness, their effectiveness as transformative and revelatory texts is highlighted. By drawing on short story theories and challenging the view that short stories are no more than miniature pieces merely echoing "major" works of their authors, it is further argued that the genre can be profoundly forceful and effective in the articulation of complex human issues.

The study reveals that since a short story seems to "demand" to be read in "one sitting," it has the tendency to be intensely dramatic, and like biblical parables, capable of effecting an immediate change of perspective in the reader. This study shows also that the theological and ethical import of the Baldwin stories is amplified by their ability to accumulate moral tension as they elicit the participation of the reader in an imaginative quest for a better world. A brief conclusion clarifies why Baldwin's autobiographical memory—influenced by borrowing and rereading of the master narratives of biblical literature—equips him with refreshing vocabularies that facilitate the transformation of personal and social problems into a spiritual odyssey that point to a moral vision with universal significance.

1

Ethics, Selfhood, and Textuality

> ...my own interests led me to see literary situations as cultural situations, and cultural situations as great elaborate fights about moral issues...
>
> —Lionel Trilling, *Beyond Culture*

THE FUNCTIONING OF LITERATURE

I will focus on the themes which are specifically highlighted in the short stories of James Baldwin in the collection *Going to Meet the Man*.[1] The discussion will be undertaken within the wider context of the writer's novels and non-fictional writings in appreciation of the autobiographical as well as the ethical and theological dimensions in the stories. It will be demonstrated that his art grew from his early exposure to the Bible through the religious, cultural values and images of America as he knew and understood the country.

The study goes against the grain of many critics who unduly emphasize Baldwin as a political author thereby coming to much narrower conclusions about his vision. It is inspired by the conviction that there is a symbiotic relationship between literature, theology, and the arts given

---

1. Baldwin, *Going to Meet the Man*.

that the relevance of any narrative is determined by the extent to which the "facts" of the story as evocations of human experience are organized to inform, edify or challenge its audience. A work of fiction can also be entertaining and even deconstructive as it transmits its messages. It is the nature of fiction to operate in a universe of the author's own making. As we shall discover, Baldwin wrote directly from autobiographical experiences which gave him the raw materials for his art. Like many writers of fiction, he used language with regard to what he knew, felt, and believed about the world in which he lived and he did not conform to the restrictions of any specific literary paradigm.[2] This framework provides ample opportunities for creativity on the parts of both reader and writer, including both the advantages and disadvantages of their backgrounds.[3]

Baldwin was very much aware that works of fiction are transformative; they help people to think clearly and feel more deeply as well as judge—for good or ill. Their transforming and revelatory powers are evident in the capacity of fiction persuasively to invite imaginative participation as well as to draw attention to alternative visions of life. What is remarkable about these alternative visions is that they "are less equivocal and easier to see than they are within the drudgery and pain of our own ordinary lives."[4] Literature functions also by facilitating a sympathetic understanding of other people, and the motivations behind their actions and reactions as

---

2. While stressing the freedom of the poet (creative writer) J. L. Lucaites and C. M. Condit write in "Re-constructing Narrative Theory," 90: "possibility, not probability, and internal consistency, not external validity, are the criteria for judging poetic narratives." They add that the poet is even free to restrict attention to either content, context, or to the implied reader. Cf. also Novitz, "Art Narrative and Human Nature," 61.

3. A hermeneutic system does not fully determine meaning. Rather, it supplies the rules for making sense out of the observed phenomena in texts. This is particularly significant in cases where the literary text is ambiguous or allows gaps which create room for a diversity of views such that "the same story can be actualised in a variety of ways by different readers." Cf. Goldingay, "How Far Do Readers Make Sense? Interpreting Biblical Narratives," 6; and Berlin, "Role of the Text in the Reading Process," 6. One can also add here that to the radical deconstructionists, the emphasis is more on the notion of "text" rather than on literary "work." This approach is meant to erase any suggestion that a text is a product of an intentional human agent. It also allows the text to become a field within which there circulate forces, energies, or warring components. Hence, not only is a text to be interpreted but subjects who perform the interpretation are themselves textual constructs. But as Abrams points out, "every textual particular, in order to be interpreted requires a context; but every context, when called into play, is itself a text needing to be interpreted." Cf. Abrams, "Transformation of English Studies," 120.

4. Wallace, "Faith and Fiction," 393.

well as the choices they make. This makes it particularly useful for Christian religious discourse in as much as Christian Scriptures deal also with the human condition.[5]

In its relationship with theological ethics, literature tends to break down barriers and establishes a plurality that rejects the distinction between "sacred" and "secular." It is concerned with issues of freedom, the liberation of values, and the endless, democratic exercise of reading. As David Jasper has suggested, the fear of relativism cannot be ruled out in theological criticism, but the approach only amounts to a shift from the authority of the text to the authority of the interpreting community where communication occurs. The shift depends neither on the privileging of text, nor on the particular texts as the final arbiter on matters of faith. On the contrary, theological criticism is idealistic, fragile, and open to change since "literary value is not the property of an object or of a subject but, rather, the product of the dynamic of a system."[6] Hence, the interaction of literature with Scripture responds to the immediacy of human creativity.[7] Equally characteristic of theological criticism is the fact that literature is used to maintain the vitality of the biblical text, its narrative and its lyrics, while resisting conclusion or dogma defined by the endless search for a final word on the Bible. The outlook allows for the assumption that the text is always more than we can say about it. In this regard, the metaphorical quality of texts provide platforms for new adventures of understanding and imagination—giving energy to that which theology and its orthodoxy tend to ossify.

The vitality that is embodied in this approach to texts and contexts inspires artists and creative writers to respond to "sacred texts" like the Bible in an acknowledgment of dissimilar sociopolitical agendas, and to explore the complexities in the human condition. In this regard, works that

---

5. Romantic literary theories in Germany in the eighteenth century, for instance, thought of art as something produced by persons of rare imaginative sensibilities. At this period, the artist was generally thought of as a secular "Christ figure, doomed to know the truth that might redeem his society and to die for his allegiance to that truth, to die isolated and misunderstood, offering a redemption that the culture is too crass to accept. The poet's only hope for resurrection is literary immortality, the approbation of poets in subsequent generations." Cf. Wallace, "Faith and Fiction," 385.

6. Herrnstein-Smith, *Contingencies of Values*, 15–16.

7. Because of what David Rutledge terms the "numinous force," which wells up within art and literature, they invite theological analysis within the tradition of criticism, and at the same time counter-reading. Cf. Rutledge, "Faithful Reading," 270; Jasper, *Rhetoric, Power and Community*, 127.

fictionalize biblical characters and narratives often succeed in articulating the timelessness of human experience. Revitalized by the notion of intertextuality, works of fiction echo, rewrite, or are otherwise intertwined with biblical texts or other non-biblical co-texts in acknowledgment of the fact that theology entertains open-ended narratives.[8] The dynamics of intertextuality ensure also that stories and images trigger insights which move beyond existing theological frameworks.

This state of affairs engenders a plurality of interpretation given that at no point can one claim to have arrived at the final conclusion. Thus, the power of the images in art and fiction reside in endless resistance to definition and refusal to be pigeonholed.[9] Carried to its conclusion, creative reading through literature and the arts has the capacity to disturb the narrative order in biblical stories and challenge the institutions and the theology which govern orthodox interpretations of canonical texts. It equally means that the "shepherd" image of the theologian, supposedly best positioned to dispense true knowledge to the "sheep" of his flock, will become suspect since such conception of an all-knowing guru of the Christian "tradition" often degenerates into an idealisation of the past, a situation which the postmodern condition resists.[10]

THE CHALLENGE OF THE BALDWIN SHORT STORIES

The challenge of this study does not lie in a search for theological and/or ethical propositions since the stories are neither prescriptive nor do they necessarily aim at providing answers. Yet the themes embedded in them will be studied with a view to finding out the questions they stimulate. Moreover, even though it can be argued, as biographers tend to do, that Baldwin abandoned formal religion (at least intellectually) in the course of his life, the stories will be researched to determine how they draw upon the

---

[8] As widely accepted intertextuality can come about through overt citation and allusions or through the fact of the text in question forming a network with other texts. Cf. Jasper, *Rhetoric, Power and Community*, 127. See also Moore, *Post-structuralism and the New Testament*, 130.

[9] This outlook is future-oriented. It presupposes that tradition is, in essence, meaningful only if it prepares the individual to be ready for wider horizons. Cf. De Schrijver, "Hermeneutics and Tradition," 33.

[10] See Jasper, *Rhetoric, Power and the Community*, 33. Jasper does not see any opposition between the instability, plurality and indeterminacy characteristic of the postmodern times and the "real presence" (of the Divine) engendered by aesthetic experience.

master narratives of biblical literature and generate refreshing vocabularies that "reread" and transform personal and societal problems into a spiritual autobiography. It is equally of paramount interest to explore how the stories elicit creative thinking as well as facilitate an appreciation of the practical implications of the clash of values implicit or explicit in them. It is against this background that we shall understand how the stories, read in terms of Baldwin's priorities, are able to blend ethics and aesthetics such that they not only function as "revelatory text" but also constitute, in some sense, a bridge toward the transcendent. Attempts will be made to examine how each of the stories through its literary form and religious connotations, enhances the possible choice of one ethical position over another.

Each of the stories in this collection has its own peculiarities. All of them are, however, held together by the interplay of metaphors which Baldwin uses to blend the secular, the ethical and the religious in language. Thematic analysis that is derived from the rhetorical features and structures of the stories will be used to carry out close readings. Themes tie the stories to other cultural discourses found in American history, literature, philosophy and theological mindset, all of which, we shall argue, seek to grapple with how things ought to be or might have been.[11] This is very much in keeping with how Catherine Wallace, literary critic and theologian, perceives the calling of the poet and creative writer. According to her, the vocation of the poet: "is to take all muddled disruptive incoherence of real fact and actual memory—whether communal or personal—and then select and arrange, reform and recast them into coherent aesthetic whole that tell the visionary trust that fact alone cannot reveal."[12]

My claim is that the Baldwin short stories capture his world view made more manifest in his major works. The nature of the short story genre makes this possible. The short story functions to provide, in synthesis, what may need long and extended analysis in a novel in affirmation of the fact that the hermeneutical possibilities in a short story can be very complex.[13]

---

11. This has practical significance, for in Aristotelian terms, ethics has less to do with knowing what goodness essentially is than knowing how one is to become a good person. Cf. Parker, *Ethics, Theory and the Novel*, 37, with reference to Thomson, *Ethics of Aristotle*, 90–91.

12. Cf. Wallace, "Faith and Fiction," 398.

13. Moravia, "Short Story and the Novel," 147–50. See Nadine Gordimer's remark to the effect that short story writers have learnt to do without lengthy explanations of what went before, and how characters, will appear, think, behave and comprehend "tomorrow." Gordimer, "Flash of the Fireflies," 180.

Thus, in novels, characters may, for instance, begin young and then, grow old. They might move from scene to scene, from place to place.[14] It is this development of character, requiring elaborate constructions, that is a central factor in many novels.[15] On the other hand, in short stories, time need not move (in time or in space), except by an infinitesimal fraction. The characters themselves need not move, nor need they grow old. For instance, "Previous Condition"[16] works through flashbacks and flash forward, bringing isolated pieces of information to bear in the protagonist's present life. The story is not weighed down by lengthy explanations and elaborate character sketches. Rather, "revelatory moments" on which the short story genre thrives are used to exhibit insightful portraits.[17] Each of the characters, in his or her own way, was presented as having been confronted with moments where ethical choices were made, with the result that each of them proved to be a victim of social conditions.

The way Baldwin structures "Previous Condition" brings the structure of biblical parables[18] to mind in that the story does function as a "generative metaphor," that is, a means of seeing one thing in terms of another.[19] Thus, afraid of losing her means of livelihood if she allowed a black tenant to live in her house, the landlady in "Previous Condition" ejected Peter, an

14. Moravia, "Short Story and the Novel," 147–50.
15. Cf. Lohafer, *Coming to Terms with the Short Story*, 33.
16. Baldwin, *Going to Meet the Man*, 79–99.
17. See Detweiler and Meeter, *Faith and Fiction*, xxxi.

18. It is also important to stress here that while regarding the literary designs in modern fiction as parabolic, the contexts in which modern parables are received have to be taken into account given that diversity of techniques and themes are constantly changing. This perspective is much in accord with the temporality of existence which demands that humans give forms to new systems and meanings, which have the potentialities to resonate beyond the times. See Champion, "Parable as an Ancient and a Modern Form," 29–35; and Kermode, *Genesis of Secrecy*, 28. Refer also to De Schrijver, "Hermeneutics and Tradition," 33.

19. Although there is no universal agreement on the precise definition of metaphor, contemporary insight owes much to Aristotle whose understanding boils down to the notion that metaphor consists in giving a name to something that belongs to something else. In this regard, the transference from the literal to the figurative could either be from genus to species or from species to genius, or from species to species, or on the ground of analogy. Cf. Kjargaard, *Metaphor and Parable*, 11. It is a process that shows how abstract concepts such as time, states and causation are made use of in everyday language. Cf. Lakoff, "Contemporary Theory of Metaphor," 203–8. Metaphor becomes generative when it goes beyond points of grammar and functions as a process by which new visions of the world are articulated. See Schon, "Generative Metaphor," 137.

unsuccessful black musician. Taken at face value, she had nothing against black people but she was too scared to go against the general social convention that did not tolerate black tenants. Jules, Peter's friend, was presented as someone frustrated by his inability to be of further help to Peter. Like the landlady, he was not prepared to defy social convention; the best he could do was merely to suggest that Peter should lie low and avoid being noticed in a white neighborhood. Ida, a white woman friend of Peter, represents the figure of a victim who has little control of her circumstances. Even so, control was exercised, or misused one might suggest, with the result that she married for money while keeping lovers. For his part, Peter the main character has no control over his life whatsoever. Ironically, his ejection from a white neighbourhood affects a new beginning.

It is in this sense that the story that began with racial discrimination provides a platform for a discourse on human loneliness; each of the four named characters is eventually forced to recognise his or her human limitation in the face of obstacles or moments in which human vulnerability is made manifest. Like the parables of Jesus, "Previous Condition" functions along the line of everyday experiences, assuming neither belief nor unbelief on the parts of the audience.[20] Nonetheless, moments of decision are thrown to the reader such that the story becomes quasi-revelatory.[21] Peter eventually receives the grace that enables him to stop acting—a free and unsuspected gift that appeared through the commonplace atmosphere of a bar—enabling him also to initiate the act of reconciliation between himself and a woman whose friendship he had spurned earlier.

LIFE HISTORY

Available literature and my own research indicate that James Arthur Baldwin's own life is well reflected in a sequence of the short stories.[22] He was

---

20. Cf. Hendrickx, *Parables of Jesus*, 3. Cf. also Wilder, *Early Christian Rhetoric*, 84, where a moralizing approach to the parables of Jesus is rejected.

21. Cf. Syreeni, "Metaphorical Appropriation," 324; and Jones, *Art and Truth of the Parables*, 129–30. It comes out clearly also that Robert Detweiler's understanding of the idea of revelation is quite apposite at this juncture. For him, revelation is but the culmination of unconscious experiences, a disclosure of the self to the self. Detweiler, *Faith and Fiction*, 302.

22. In the course of the research into the Baldwin mindset, I have drawn on full-length biographies such as Eckman, *Furious Passages of James Baldwin*, and Campbell, *Talking at the Gates*. Mosher, "James Baldwin Blues," 112–24, has also been a useful

born in Harlem, New York, on 2 August 1924 by a single mother, Emma Berdis Jones. When James was older, his mother married a David Baldwin, an itinerant preacher from Louisiana. James grew up as the caretaker of his younger siblings while his parents worked. He was an avid reader, and depended initially on the two Harlem public libraries and later borrowing from other New York libraries. Baldwin's writing talent was discovered early, and his teachers were quite encouraging. They sometimes requested special assignments from him. At Frederick Douglass Junior High School, he edited the school newspaper, the *Douglass Pilot*, to which he contributed several articles. At De Witt Clinton High School, he published a number of stories in the school newspaper. His childhood and teenage years were far from happy.[23] For instance, the man he took to be his father could not hide his hatred for James. He let it be known that James was ugly and bore the mark of the devil. He refused to recognize the boy's intelligence or the approval of his white teachers. The older Baldwin was a religious fanatic who imposed a rigorous code of conduct on his children. Away from home, James found himself the target of police as well as unscrupulous neighbours. Moreover, the poverty, the filth and hopelessness that hovered all around were mind-boggling.[24] Baldwin was later to "escape" into the Church. On one occasion during a religious service, he began to have an unusual feeling. Before he knew it, he was on his feet:

> singing and clapping and, at the same time, working out in my head the plot of a play I was working on then; the next moment, with no transition, no sensation of falling, I was on my back, with the lights beating down into my face and all the vertical saints stood above me. I did not know what I was doing so low, or how I got there. And the anguish that filled me cannot be described. It moved in me like one of those floods that devastate countries . . . All I really remember is the pain, the unspeakable pain; it was a though I were yelling up to Heaven and Heaven would not hear me. And if Heaven would not hear me, if love could not descend

---

source. So has Harris' contribution in *Oxford Companion to African American Literature*, 44–46. There are a number of collections of essays that contain invaluable biographical information. Worthy of special mention are Standley and Burt, *Critical Essays on James Baldwin*; Kinnamon, *James Baldwin*; Leeming, *James Baldwin*; Bloom's "Introduction" in *James Baldwin*; and Lynch, "Just Above My Head," 284–98.

23. On his childhood Baldwin writes: "The story of my childhood is the usual bleak fantasy, and we can dismiss it with the restrained observations that I certainly would not consider living it again." See his *Notes of a Native Son*, 11.

24. Baldwin, *Fire Next Time*, 27.

from Heaven—to wash me, to make me clean—then utter disaster was my portion...[25]

He was in this state throughout the night. At daybreak, the worshippers congratulated him for having been "saved." Although he was not exactly sure what they meant, he did feel exhausted and, curiously released from guilt feelings. Not long afterwards, he was drawn into preaching. Being a preacher at fourteen brought an exciting new status. But this also meant that he began to pay less attention to his own reading and writing.

After a year as a child preacher, his faith began to crumble. Having mixed with people of diverse faiths in his senior school, he began to be suspicious of religious injunctions as he perceived them in his church. It occurred to him that being a preacher was no different from being an actor in a theatre. Moreover, his privileged position as "young Brother Baldwin" not only brought him "behind the scenes" but also taught him how the illusion of working up oneself and a congregation was effected.[26] In addition, he was not particularly impressed with the quality of life of the ministers whose hypocrisy he came to see at close quarters. He also began to think that there should be more to religion than just trying to avoid hellfire.[27]

Considering the events leading up to and including Baldwin's conversion and subsequent revolt against the Church, it would seem that what Henri Ellenberger terms "creative illness" can be helpful in understanding the evolution of Baldwin's literary creativity. Such illness may take the form of a neurosis, or a psychosis. It can be a one-off event or a series of events. Whatever form it takes, it almost always ends with a feeling of exultation, a spiritual and intellectual discovery and, ultimately, a shift of interest.[28]

---

25. Ibid., 40–41. For biblical references that meet this understanding of ritual purity, see Num 19:7; Ps 51:1–14; Acts 2:38, 22:16; Heb 9:10; and 1 Pet 3:21.

26. Baldwin, *Fire Next Time*, 48.

27. Ibid., 45.

28. Ellenberger, "Concept of Creative Illness," 443. See also Pickering, *Creative Malady*, 17: "an illness that is not debilitating or disabling, or threatening to life, may provide the ideal circumstances for creative work." See also Ellenberger, *Discovery of the Unconscious*, 447. Creative illness can equally manifest itself in the form of literary aridity "caused by something other than exhaustion; it is then the development through which the writer succeeds in bringing to the surface of his mind a world of images and thoughts buried in the depths of the unconscious; this development is terribly painful and thus constitutes the creative illness." Ellenberger, "Concept of Creative Illness," 449. It can then result in the transformation of personality which sometimes leads to a feeling of having discovered a grandiose truth." *Discovery of the Unconscious*, 450. Refer also to Pickering, *Creative Malady*, 19.

This sort of malady is present in the cases of psychoanalysts like Freud (1856–1939), the philosopher Friedrich Nietzsche (1844–1900), and creative writers such as Jean-Paul Sartre (1905–1980), Fyodor Mikhailovich Dostoevsky (1821–1881), and William Blake (1757–1827). While Baldwin used writing as a way of escaping the poisoned atmosphere in his home as well as the lovelessness in the Church, ironically, the same creative process functions also as an instrument of self-discovery and a tool for chastising his social environment.[29]

After graduating from school, Baldwin worked briefly for a construction company. He later moved to Greenwich Village, where he began exploring his writing potential more seriously, and eventually began his first novel. Racial and personal encounters led him to consider leaving the United Stated of America for his own good. France did provide the psychological space he needed but it was not without tensions. On his arrival in France, he soon realized that France was not perfect; it was no less racist than the America he had run away from. Nonetheless, his literary career blossomed during this period of his life. Although he was out of America physically, Baldwin was constantly using American settings to address social issues. His favourite themes include the failure of the promise of American democracy, questions of racial and sexual identity, the failure of the Christian Church, difficult family relationships, insensitive legal systems and inequalities, as well as obstacles to individual fulfillment. Biographical sketches of Baldwin indicate that the author was often suicidal during his years in France. He was an indefatigable partygoer, with an almost infinite capacity to consume liquor. Yet for all his weaknesses, he never failed to receive well-deserved acknowledgments for his novels, essays, and other creative works.

Although Baldwin's sexual tendencies are not significant for this study, it is worth pointing out that before his departure for France, his biographers note that he seriously considered marriage. He eventually terminated the wedding plans and threw the engagement rings into the Hudson River. Critics and biographers generally think that this was the last occasion he gave serious thoughts to a heterosexual relationship. With time, his relationships become decidedly homosexual, an aspect of his personality that is helpful in understanding novels such as *Giovanni's Room* and *Just Above My Head*, among others. By the late 1970s to mid-1980s his career had attained

---

29. Cf. Storr, *Dynamic of Creation*, 92, for insight into how the effort to control oneself and one's environment through the creative process can become an obsession.

new heights veering toward the academe. He eventually accepted various lecturing commitments, including an arrangement as a visiting professor at the University of Massachusetts at Amherst. He also accepted teaching posts at Bowling Green State University and the University of California at Berkeley. He died of cancer on 1 December 1987.

BALDWIN AND HIS CRITICS

Religious reading of James Baldwin by critics is at best, inadequate, and at worst, ignored. In cases where attempts are made to evaluate religious themes in his works, two lines of approaches seem to dominate. There are those commentators who see in his writings a "progressive negativity," a sort of cynicism that began with his revolt against organized religion at the age of seventeen culminating in his remark that "whoever wishes to become a truly moral being . . . must first divorce himself of all the prohibitions, crimes and hypocrisy of the Christian Church."[30] Along this line of thinking is the notable fact that many characters in his fiction and drama have a very negative image of God. In *Giovanni's Room*, for instance, one character spits at a crucifix in disgust at God, while in the play *Blues for Mister Charlie* a number of characters cannot hide their disdain for a God who seems quite indifferent to human suffering. The character of Lorenzo typifies such attitudes when he confesses: "this damn almighty God who don't care what happens to no body . . . If I could get my hands on Him, I'd pull Him out of heaven and drag Him through this town at the end of a rope."[31]

Critics who find in Baldwin's writing only a revolt against religion draw some support also from what Michael F. Lynch perceives as a general African American problematic relationship with Christianity.[32] This relationship is not unconnected with the tendency in fundamentalist Christians throughout the ages, to emphasize the immutability of the divine law read into the curse of Ham, the supposedly black son of Noah (Gen 9:25) as the excuse for slavery. It is a line of thought closely associated with segregationists in the United States of America right through the slave times

---

30. Baldwin, "Down at the Cross," 57.

31. Baldwin, *Blues for Mister Charlie*, as cited in Lynch, "James Baldwin's Quest for Belief," 289. Other Baldwin characters who are not at peace with God can be found in works such as *Go Tell It on the Mountain*, *Another Country* and *If Beale Street Could Talk*.

32. Lynch, "Just Above My Head," 289.

up to the civil rights era.[33] That such apartheid exegesis which sanctions "man's inhumanity to man" was championed over and above the theology of "neighbourly love" by professed Christians obviously proved problematic for Baldwin. On a more practical level, Baldwin was scandalized by the ease with which Christian missionaries mixed their activities with politics to the point where the spreading of the gospel was used as a justification for colonisation.[34]

There are, on the other hand, some analysts who are of the opinion that Baldwin's fascination with religion never wavered even if such faith was not always anchored in a formal endorsement of a particular denomination. Although even casual readers do not have any difficulty agreeing with Baldwin's confession regarding the influence of the Bible, and the preacher rhetoric of the Harlem storefront Church on his career, there remains a surprising paucity of studies on his personalist and private religious perspectives. Michael Lynch's grasp of this situation is worthy of attention.[35] Part of the explanation, he says, lies in the fact that many researchers do not appreciate the dialectics of Baldwin's mindset. In consequence, the political realities and the spiritual visions which he attempted to reconcile are misrepresented.[36] This seems to explain why many of the Baldwin critics do not, for instance, see that the revolt against God displayed by some of his fictional characters is not meant to deny God *per se*. On the contrary, such hostility and questioning of the goodness and justice of God in the face of evil are directed at emphasizing the characters' yearnings for an almighty being and underline Baldwin's own way of theologizing.[37]

33. In "Color, Conscience and Crucifixion," 37, Charles H. Nichols recalls the remark of a South Carolina legislator who, in 1850, insisted that "every distinction should be created between the white and the Negro to make the latter feel the superiority of the former." Beyond this historical fact, Nichols adds that trying to understand how characters are portrayed in fiction can equally be helpful in having an idea of the mainstream Christian social attitudes of one American ethnic group toward the other.

34. Baldwin pictures the process of colonisation as one that usually begins with the missionaries, clutching the Bible while the indigenous people, thought of as pagans, had the land. Being "saved" then meant that the new converts gave up their land in exchange for the Bible. Cf. Baldwin, "Down at the Cross," 46–47.

35. Studies by Michael F. Lynch which typify a tendency toward a theological reading of Baldwin includes "Just Above my Head," and "Beyond Guilt and Innocence," *Obsidian II: Black Literature in Review*, 1–19; "Glimpse of the Hidden God," 181–95; and "The Everlasting Father," 156–75.

36. Baldwin, "Autobiographical Notes," 13.

37. Lynch, "*Just Above My Head*," 285.

Ethics, Selfhood, and Textuality

THE AFRICAN-AMERICAN CHURCH IN HISTORY

This study does not deny Baldwin's profound awareness of political issues. However, its focus is mainly upon the private world of the short stories seen against the background of the author's own life and personal experience, rather than upon the public aspects to which most critics give attention. Nonetheless, in these introductory pages, it is important to establish the culture against which his personal experiences were worked out as an expression of universal human experience. To facilitate a deeper appreciation of this culture, it seems necessary to examine the background and historical development of the form of Christianity Baldwin had to deal with. This will facilitate an appreciation of the history of the black American family and experience from the time of slavery, through emancipation, racial segregation and the disappointment that migration to cities did not lead to the realisation of dreams. This historical background will also throw light on how the black church functions to help in "maintaining a sense of communal identity in the face of socially and psychologically destructive pressures."[38]

Before the middle of the seventeenth century, there were some doubts among slaveowners as to whether or not the reception of the Christian sacraments altered the social condition of the slaves. But following an English Law of 1667 which clarified the situation, there emerged in the slavemasters the feeling that it was, indeed, good for the slaves to be converted to Christianity. The reasoning was that "the deeper the piety of the slave, the more valuable will he be in every respect."[39] Moreover, recent studies indicate that Churches in particularly Catholic areas of the United States insisted on Christian marriages amongst slaves although this did not prevent the slave owners from selling a wife and a husband to different buyers as market forces demanded. In 1838, for instance, when the Jesuits, the Catholic religious order which was running the college that became Georgetown University in Washington DC ran into financial difficulties, they sold 272 African American men, women and children to various sugar plantations in the south of the United States.[40]

---

38. Courage, "Baldwin's *Go Tell It on the Mountain*," 415; and Motlhabi, "Historical Origins of Black Theology," 41–45.

39. See Cone, *Spirituals and the Blues*, 23, with reference to Harding, "Religion and Resistance among Antebellum Nigroes 1800-1960," 181. For comment, see Gollwitzer, "Why Black Theology?," 160. Gollwitzer stresses that the self-interest of slave masters rather than Christian brotherhood, was the motive for the conversion of slaves.

40. Cf. Buttlar, "Problems of African American History," 25. See Swarns, "272 Slaves

Against this historical background, one can put in proper context why the American slaves at this time, succumbed to the little consolation there was in the religion of their masters. With neither a language nor a social structure which they could call their own and coupled with incessant relocation of people, religion became the only source of hope and stability. It was evident, however, that the ever-present reality of dehumanisation and suffering exposed the new converts to a preoccupation with the theology of death and eternal life—beyond their time and space.[41] It needs to be pointed out here that while slave masters saw the advantages of allowing their wards to become Christians, there was some degree of discomfort regarding the establishment of independent churches for slaves. It was feared that the gathering of unsupervised slaves in a religious service might prove a fertile ground for the rebellious among them.[42]

As time went on, some black Church congregations did emerge, although historical evidence shows that it was the American Civil War coupled with the abolition of slavery that created the atmosphere for the establishment of autonomous black Churches in a formal sense. Soon enough, some of the ex-slaves began to use their new-found freedom as a platform for political agitation. On the other hand, those who remained in the churches of the white ex-masters wanted equality within the congregations. Understandably, such agitations often led to the expulsion of black Church members who were then forced to establish new churches. It is worth noting here that with the abolition of slavery, researchers in African American Church history are persuaded that a number of former slave owners did make financial contributions toward the establishment of churches exclusively for black members.

Freedom, a major theme in the Baldwin mindset and as a universal ideal, was for the ex-slave, a dream realized. It emphasized the reality that self-determination and equality were of the essence of Christianity.[43] The atmosphere in the churches provided a formal setting where leadership opportunities were available for the charismatic individual, and where ordinary people could develop their talents. As G. Clarke Chapman explains, members drew inspiration upon the continual remembrance of years of

---

Were Sold to Save Georgetown." See also Wilder, "War and Priests."

41. This frame of mind has to be understood against the background of what experience taught the slaves about the futility of rebellion. Cone, *Black Theology*, 3, 90.

42. Ibid., 101.

43. Cone, *Black Theology*, 94.

oppression, their preachers and the anonymous singers of slavery days as well as distinguished leaders.[44] Thus, the church environment provided a platform where former slaves could articulate their own individual identity in an atmosphere of liberty.

But hostility in the wider society could not be easily wished away, nor did emancipation lead to economic independence. In fact, a statement by what was then the National Committee of the Negro Churchmen published in the *New York Times* of 31 July 1966 reads in part: "in 1963, slaves were made legally free as individuals, but the real question, regarding personal and group power to maintain that freedom was pushed aside. Power for many rural people meant land and tools to work the land . . . but this power was not made available."[45]

The statement of the church leaders added that lack of economic empowerment that followed emancipation led to the migration of many black families to urban areas in a quest for employment. Thus, with neither jobs nor means of livelihood, poverty became the lot of many families who had also to contend with segregation and all its implications.

For our purpose, two tendencies are discernible from this socio-economic situation. Broadly speaking, such conditions reinforced the grounds for recourse to religion as a place of shelter on the one hand, and on the other hand, religion became a platform for articulating sociopolitical issues. For the politically radical among black religious leaders, emphasis on heavenly rewards became suspect. Rather, they thought that "eschatology has to be related to history, to what God has done, is doing and will do for his people."[46] James H. Cone explains that such a look at past history helps one to understand the ugliness of the present while a perspective on the future should not be in expectation of future reward from God. It should, instead, be a means of articulating dissatisfaction with prevailing ills in the society.[47] For the black Christians of simpler disposition, however, racism seemed to have destroyed earthly hope and as they saw it, all that could be dreamt of was a sort of eschatology that could be attained through a fundamentalist understanding of Christian piety.

---

44. Chapman, "Black Theology," 194.

45. Statement by the National Committee of Negro Churchmen, "Black Power," July 31, 1966, in Wilmore and Cone, *Black Theology*, 26.

46. See Cone, *Black Theology*, 126.

47. Ibid.

James Baldwin and the Short Story

ONTOLOGICAL GAP

There is no gainsaying the fact that the short story genre is almost always seen as a marginal art form as compared with the novel.[48] They are often considered "shadow" pieces of major works already published or being awaited.[49] The novel, on the other hand, creates the simple impression of an "all-embracing big event" that aims at saying everything. The technique of the short story writer's art brings to mind the techniques in drama and film, both of which pay specific attention to form within closely determined structures. In his essay "The Modern Short Story: Retrospect," (1976), H. E. Bates demonstrates how this works, adding that each movement in film and short story tend to imply something that is not stated. Each seems to send signals on a certain emotional wavelength which the audiences pick up.[50] Thus, in a short story, as in poems, a great deal of inferring may be necessary to expose the "ontological gap" that emerges due to the inability of language to capture reality in all its ramifications.[51]

In line with this understanding, the following examination of "The Rockpile" and "The Outing" are used as specific examples to demonstrate how the short story genre functions as well as show the way in which Baldwin uses the stories to articulate complex issues that demanded lengthy and detailed discussions in other fictional and non-fictional writings. "The Rockpile" and "The Outing" are especially relevant in deepening our understanding of the aspects of the African American Church that comes under Baldwin's scrutiny. Each of the two stories has its own artistic integrity. However, for the purpose of highlighting the differences between the technique of the short story and that of the novel, the two stories are examined here as co-texts of *Go Tell It on the Mountain* rather than as "remnants" of the novel.[52]

---

48. The essays collected in May, *Short Story Theories*, are quite accomplished in their articulation of how the genre functions.

49. Issues relating to the theories of short stories are well articulated in May, *Short Story Theories*.

50. See Bates "Modern Short Story," 7.

51. Lohafer, *Coming to Terms with the Short Story*, 52–53.

52. One other instance of how themes in one work of Baldwin echo in another is evidenced in "Sonny's Blues" and the novel *Just Above My Head*. Among other things, both works explore the relationship between brothers. A biographer notes that the "brother motif" in these works take much of its energy and vocabularies from the close relationship between James Baldwin himself and his own younger brother, David Baldwin. See Leeming, *James Baldwin*, 135.

Narrative World

Johnnie, Gabriel and Elizabeth Grimes all feature as the main characters within the novel, *Go Tell It on the Mountain*, as well as the short stories. The central question which scholars see in the novel revolves around the issue of how one can attain true functionality as a human being.[53] Baldwin approaches this issue by examining an African-American family beginning from the time of slavery. The novel introduces a fourteen-year-old schoolboy, John Grimes. He is praised by white school teachers and principals. However, his father, Gabriel Grimes, cannot stand the fact that John is an illegitimate son although the boy is brought up to believe that Gabriel Grimes, his mother's husband, is his true father. With time, John grows up to become aware of the mutual hatred between himself and the man he calls his father. John's upbringing is such that even before he consciously became a fully fledged member of his parents' church, he had been burdened with a scrupulous conscience and is constantly aware of the presence of sin and sinners all around him. This fact fills him with fear and embarrassment.[54] One of his earliest memories, for instance, is that of his family going to church on Sundays while

> sinners along the avenue watched them—men still wearing their Saturday-night clothes, wrinkled and dusty now, muddy-eyed and muddy-faced; and women with harsh voices and tights, bright dresses, cigarettes between their fingers or held tightly in the corners of their mouths. They talked and laughed and fought together and the women fought like the men.[55]

The scorn Gabriel pours on John generated corresponding hatred in John and more than that in his brother Roy. Roy, headstrong, responds to their father's domineering love with rebellion and disdain for the man's religious zeal.[56]

In the "The Outing," a description of the annual Fourth of July picnic organized by the Harlem Mount of Olives Pentecostal Assembly community, Baldwin touches, in a more succinct way, on a number of issues that

---

53. Kent, "Baldwin and the Problem of Being," 17. See also Möller, *Theme of Identity*, 1–2.

54. Lunden, "Progress of a Pilgrim," 12.2

55. Baldwin, *Go Tell It on the Mountain*, 13.

56. Ibid., 130. See also Fabre, "Fathers and Sons," 126–27; and Courage, "Baldwin's *Go Tell It on the Mountain*," 417.

echo in *Go Tell It on the Mountain*. The picnic involves a boat trip up the Hudson River to a Bear Mountain, a holiday resort. On the day of the journey, Gabriel and Elizabeth Grimes, and their son Johnnie (John) can hardly suppress their excitement, but not their younger boy, Roy. Like Johnnie, he is ever ill at ease in the company of his father, Gabriel, who he is sure to encounter during the day's boat trip. While the ride is in progress, the exhibitionist tendencies of the church members are given full reign.

Gabriel Grimes uses every opportunity at his disposal to put his favourite son in a good light, despite the fact that the boy, Roy, is not particularly enamoured of him. Gabriel tells a Mrs Jackson that Roy "came to the Lord" about a month previously and that he has even brought a convert into the Christian fold, a point the boy and his friends thought laughable.[57] Quite unkindly, Gabriel succeeds in humiliating Johnnie, his less favoured son. As he, for instance, meets him in the company of his friends and the said Mrs Jackson, Gabriel, offers this advice to his listeners: "don't let Johnnie talk fresh to you."[58] While leaving the company, he adds: "You kids enjoy yourselves"; but to Johnnie he says: "don't get into no mischief, you hear me?" Visibly embarrassed, the boy replies: "Don't worry about me, Daddy. Roy'll see to it that I behave."[59]

While the older male children map out plans on how to present a birthday gift to one of the girls in the group without drawing undue attention to themselves, the older adults on the boat discuss about impending religious services and revivals as they act out their vanity. A Church elder urges the children to "make a noise for the Lord."[60]

At noon, the picnickers have their lunch. This is followed by a religious service over which their leader, Father James, presides. A young man named Elisha plays the piano. The children are not unaffected by the atmosphere. As the service proceeds, the mien of the Grimes boys—Johnnie and Roy—and their friend, David Jackson, undergo a change. They kneel down in prayer, letting the music and dance seep through them as some members of the group, the "saints," begin to "testify." At the Bear Mountain, venue of the picnic, the older male children succeed in presenting a birthday present to Silvia, the girl they admire. She is the teenage daughter of one of the Church elders. At six in the evening, the whole group prepare to return

---

57. Baldwin, "Outing," 31.
58. Ibid., 30.
59. Ibid., 31.
60. Ibid., 34.

home, after the day's recreation. As the group walk toward the boat, chatting, Johnnie thought to himself: "good Lord, . . . don't they ever mention anything but sin?"[61]

Paternal Disapproval

"The Rockpile" is another story in which Gabriel Grimes, his wife Elizabeth, and their sons Johnny and Roy feature as characters. It is a story so rich that one cannot but suggest that, despite its shortness, it is able to present substantial insights into plot, individual characters and themes. It describes how the children in a Harlem neighbourhood enjoy playing on and around a mysterious pile of rocks jutting out of the ground near the Grimes' family home. John, the protagonist of the story, unlike Roy, his more boisterous brother, is afraid of the rockpile and all those children who play there. Their parents, in fact, forbid them from playing outside the home for fear of getting involved in the "wickedness of the street."[62] As the story goes, each Sunday morning John and Roy sit on the fire escape and watch the forbidden street below where "men and women, boys and girls, sinners all, loitered." Young as they are, John and Roy are conscious of the "sins" and wickedness of the street and their own unworthiness as sinful creatures of their God. Thus, the atmosphere of guilt and sinfulness pervades the Grimes' family home such that simple childlike fantasies incite a fear of damnation and hellfire.

One day Roy sneaks out of the house to join his friends who are playing on the pile of rocks in a nearby street. Soon enough, he is injured on the forehead just above the eye by an empty can thrown by a playmate. A passer-by picks up the injured boy and carries him to his mother and a visiting family friend, Sister McCandless. First-aid treatment is soon administered. A few hours later, Gabriel Grimes—the father of the house—returns from work. He is understandably angry that his favourite son is injured. And quite unreasonably and true to character, he blames everybody for letting Roy out of the house in the first place. His wife, Elizabeth, exonerates herself, pointing out that Roy is particularly headstrong because Gabriel himself tends to be too affectionate towards him. For his part, John is too timid and scared to defend himself from any accusation of negligence. Save

---

61. Ibid., 53.
62. Baldwin, "Rockpile," 12.

for his mother's protective reaction toward him when Gabriel directs his anger at him, John says very little.

What seems to be the obvious theme in the story is that of despair over Gabriel Grimes' overbearing attitude toward his wife and John his son. Baldwin does not make this point too obviously. He merely lets the reader peep into the mind of Gabriel Grimes as his children are described in the story. In the end, the reader understands that John is an illegitimate child in the family, born "nameless and a stranger, living, unalterable testimony to his mother's days in sin."[63] This literary technique of economizing words typifies the desire of the short story writer to be frugal with words, thereby focusing upon a limited and specific moment of time for artistic effects.[64] This enables the reader's imagination to fill in the gaps in the light of personal insights.[65] The facts of John's illegitimacy and his mother's "days in sin" are used to highlight the background out of which the characters are acting or reacting. Other incidents do no more than cast light on the activities of the characters, thereby functioning as incidentals on which plot hinges. Thus, in line with the thought of Norman Friedman, the significance of the protagonist's action usually depends upon the fate which the writer has mapped out. John, the protagonist, for instance, is presented as helpless and timid in the face of Gabriel, his father. The writer also includes events which are both important and sufficient to motivate and make words, action or inactions appropriate.[66]

Although there are some literary works in which nothing significant would be gained or lost by specifically identifying the narrators from whose points of view the stories are told,[67] the perspective from which the reader is represented with the characters, actions, setting and events in a story is another fundamental principle operating in the structure of short stories.[68]

---

63. Ibid., 18. As it were, Johnny is to Gabriel, a living symbol of Elizabeth's past immorality. See Fabre, "Fathers and Sons," 122.

64. Bader, "Structure of Modern Short Story," 110.

65. Strong, "The Story," 281–82 as quoted in Bader, "The Structure of the Modern Short Story," 110. The short story, in this sense, seems romantic and individualistic. See O'Connor, *Lonely Voice*, 21.

66. Friedman, "What Makes a Short Story Short," 134.

67. Walton, *Mimesis as Make-Believe*, 367. See also Shlomith Rimmon-Kenan who explains that points of view could be external or internal. It is external when an author distances himself or herself from the narrative but internal if the story is told from the perspective of a character within the story. See Rimmon-Kenan, *Narrative Fiction*, 71–85.

68. Abrams, *Glossary of Literary Terms*, 144–45.

In the context of "The Rockpile" the all-knowing narrator is able to enter into the minds of the characters and to reveal their thoughts and emotions. This is, at times, done with a certain degree of distance and at other times, with emotional involvement as he tries to adopt the multiple viewpoints of various characters.[69] While being economical in choice of words and presentations of events, the narrator of the story drops hints here and there about the timidity of John and the boisterousness of his brother, Roy.

In the light of the foregoing, one can suggest that what can be said about the novel *Go Tell It on the Mountain* as an articulation of the "failure of love"[70] in the African-American family does apply to "The Outing" and "The Rockpile." As an exploration of African-American Christianity, each of the three works can be read as critiques of any fundamentalist inspirational worship that is characterized by obsession with the immediacy of God and his Christ. Such views of Christianity have the tendency to induce morbid fear of death, distrust of human finitude and a suffocating awareness of sin. However, considering the historical origins of the Pentecostal churches, it becomes clear why it was easy for the churches to exploit the emotions of its members. The Churches drew on members' fears of racial injustices, poverty and all sorts of social horrors which they explained in the light of analogies with the Jews of old: likening their social situation to those in bondage to a hard taskmaster and who are waiting for a liberator to lead them into the Promised Land.[71] Ironically, and true to their own theodicy, church members never blamed their social conditions on God. Fashioning their own explanation, the Christian community of Harlem see the real world as evil and set much store on heavenly reward in the afterlife.[72] Analysts are generally united in the conclusion that this preoccupation with a celestial reward for injustices on earth has both a metaphysical and political significance. Not only does it make their lives here on earth quite meaningful, it equally turns them into a force which those in positions of political authority could not wish away. In addition, the church played a significantly positive role in the lives of the members. It gave them a refuge,

---

69. Courage suggests that in *Go Tell It on the Mountain*, this technique enables Baldwin not only to embrace many characters, "old and young, male and female, rough and refined, secular and religious"—but also finds a parallel in the whole black experience within which Baldwin's own life is situated. See Courage, "Baldwin's *Go Tell It on the Mountain*," 218–428.

70. See Macebuh, *James Baldwin*, 24.

71. Baldwin, "Harlem Ghetto," in *Notes of a Native Son*, 67.

72. Cone, *Black Theology*, 93.

a rallying point around which they sought to lessen their pain by sharing one another's suffering. It offered them a "brotherhood of the dispossessed" which they could not find elsewhere.[73]

What Baldwin has done with his stories is to demonstrate that fear of death and overemphasis on eternal life, as the African-American form of Christianity seem to have woven into the consciousness of the members, can overwhelm as result of the inclination to make sin and death the center of religion rather than God and Christ.[74] This line of thought is echoed in the theological analysis of Jacques Pohier who, in the book *God: In Fragments* (1985), argues quite persuasively that an inordinate desire for eternal life can be humiliating and totalitarian especially because, from a biological point of view, death is not a bad thing. As Pohier sees it, life needs death both for the sake of the living and for future generations.[75] As we shall have cause to examine below, all the three works are, one way or another, connected to the personal struggle of James Baldwin himself "to break away from his ties to his step father's God [and] from the bondage of theological terror."[76]

AUTOBIOGRAPHICAL MEMORY

Viewed through the lens of the autobiographical situation, "The Rockpile" and "The Outing" echo a variety of discourses, personal and communal, especially because: "the fictional protagonist, John Grimes like Baldwin himself, is a first-generation Harlemite, a child of the great black migration to the Northern cities. Grimes and Baldwin are both sons of prideful, stiff-necked Pentecostal preachers who have little affection for their off-spring."[77]

---

73. Macebuh, *James Baldwin*, 32.

74. See Pohier, *God: In Fragments*. Pohier had in an earlier book, *When I Say God*, expressed the view that if death does not have the same type of effect on Jesus Christ as it has on us, "his resurrection tips him over into the transcendence of God." Thus, the resurrection inaugurates the absence Jesus from our empirical world and opens up a great distance between what Jesus truly is and what one can say about him. In other words, the fact of resurrection creates a situation whereby Jesus becomes more distant to humans than before the event. See Pohier, *God: In Fragments*, 51–54.

75. Ibid., 84–90.

76. Macebuh, *James Baldwin*, 52, 77.

77. Courage, "Baldwin's *Go Tell It on the Mountain*," 410.

Ethics, Selfhood, and Textuality

This, on the one hand, is a testimony that "there is always a place from which the autobiographer adumbrates his or her perspective on the self,"[78] but on the other hand, suggests that selfhood has no meaning outside the shared notions of a community.[79] It is a contention of this study that the stories reflect Baldwin's attempt to find meaning in his own life history. Inevitably, this raises the question as to whether or not the specific "facts" of the stories are "true" or "false" given that the self, in the context of autobiographical memory, is made up of the experiencing ego, a self-schema associated with sets of personal memories and biographical facts. According to William F. Brewer, some of the information that goes into making up such a self-schema is private and available only to the self. Other information is public and available to any observer.[80] This follows the traditional autobiographical framework characterized by the understanding that the real self is hidden, changeless and too profound to be understood. This line of approach downplays the fact that a person's view of him or herself means little without an awareness of the existential other. For Janet V. Gunn, in fact, being known by others is prior to self-knowledge.[81] Hence, the authorship of autobiography is always multiple: it both discovers and creates the relations of self with the world from which the writer comes. Consequently, it is a self which has its limits given that it forgets as well as remembers.[82]

It is within this context that one should appreciate Baldwin's habit of seeing his private difficulties as being analogous to or synonymous with the sufferings of African Americans.[83] This, in a very significant way, imposes a number of difficulties regarding the difference between the "I-then" and the "I-now."[84] Thus, the autobiographical memory which Baldwin tends to rely

---

78. Gunn, *Autobiography*, 125.

79. Arendt, *Human Condition*, 58.

80. See Brewer, "What Is Autobiographical Memory?" 26–27.

81. "The self must be interpreted or read by others—not as a text complete in itself with a single, unchanging, and transparent meaning, but as a text that requires continuing interpretation." Gunn, *Autobiography*, 140.

82. Ibid., 141.

83. Cf. Eckman, *Furious Passage*, 22. See also Kinnamon, *James Baldwin*, 2. One explanation for Baldwin's success as a spokesperson for the downtrodden is that he is able to blend personal problem with that of the collective. This is very much in keeping with the view that modern autobiography occupies a "place between losing and finding, a liminal space where what has been lost can only be recalled, and what might be possible, only anticipated." Gunn, *Autobiography*, 137.

84. See Courage, "Baldwin's *Go Tell It on the Mountain*," 411.

on is prone to certain fundamental errors, especially because the memories are necessarily selective. They are not easy to verify as they are merely "time capsules, records of an unrepeatable past . . . used to recount past and teach lessons for the future."[85] These difficulties associated with autobiographical memories are compounded by the fact that there are individual differences in mental images such that what can elicit the recollection of events from one person may not succeed in doing the same in another.[86] There is, therefore, a sense in which autobiography can be said to be no more than an interpretative activity[87] which is not often exact even though it is "true" in the sense that it maintains the integrity of the gist of the past.[88]

The foregoing throws light on why some researchers exercise caution when discussing the childhood deprivations and the mutual hatred between himself and his father that feature in Baldwin's works. There is, in fact, the suggestion that the difficulties were far from being personal considering that Baldwin was an "intellectual, who read Dickens, Stowe and Stevens as a boy, made his literary debut in Greenwich Village as a reviewer praising art and enouncing propaganda and spent his middle and late twenties as an expatriate in Paris struggling with the problems of racial and sexual identity."[89]

---

85. Robinson, "Autobiographical Memory," 19. Robinson adds that while historians and biographers are specifically concerned with judicious accounts, remembering *per se*, is dealt with in psychology. In this sense, autobiography can be perceived as a response to finitude and vulnerability that characterize the human condition. It represents an effort to take hold of something in the process of vanishing or disintegrating. Gunn, *Autobiography*, 120.

86. It is for instance, problematic as to how and why a writer decides how to include or exclude aspects of life. The effects of time on memories are no less significant. See Courage, "Baldwin's *Go Tell it on the Mountain*," 411. Brewer points out that events that lead to well-recalled personal memories include uniqueness, consequentiality, unexpectedness and whether or not the events are emotion-provoking. See Brewer, *What Is Autobiography?*, 44.

87. Cf. Gunn, *Autobiography*, 17, who writes: "What is made present is not merely a past that is past. What is presented is a reality, always new, to which the past has contributed but which stands, as it were, in front of the autobiographer."

88. Barclay, "Schematisation of Autobiographical Memory," 83.

89. Kinnamon, *James Baldwin*, 2.

APPRAISAL

What emerges from this introductory chapter is that the short story genre thrives on the art of ellipsis thereby creating opportunities for readers to draw inferences that function as gap-fillers. In "The Rockpile" and "The Outing," stories which, as we have seen, strongly hint at their author's own life history, Baldwin, through a careful manipulation of time with its implications to the past, present and the future, uses family life and religion to connect the characters to their sociopolitical environment. The figure of John Grimes, burdened with childish fear of God and fear of his father, is a classic example of a character who develops a scrupulous conscience due to no fault of his. Such frame of mind is not uncommon in Christian circles where religion is misused to the point where it becomes an instrument for "manufacturing" sin and guilt.

John Grimes, like his creator, imbibed such guilt in childhood, and although it is far from being wholesome, it helped Baldwin himself, and his fictional protagonist, to cope with respective loveless situations at home and the social tensions which motivate popular religiosity in the shopfront churches. This setting, which proved to be a fertile ground for Baldwin's creativity, draws out some hidden truths of his life which enrich the imagination while giving coherence to issues of personal identity. Thus, transformed by his faith, the Harlem Pentecostal Church becomes a shelter where existing realities, through reinterpretation, take on new meanings.[90] But while one can agree with Jacques Pohier's analysis regarding the need for God to be "liberated" from the poor image some fundamentalist Christians have of him, it is still arguable whether true religion should degenerate into a kind of freedom that is independent of God, given that the craving for autonomy should not do away with the human need for consolation inherent in religious practices.[91]

In creating the character of John Grimes, Baldwin seems to be inviting his readers to sympathize with the conditions, actions, feelings and thoughts of this young man. This seems quite understandable given that the options, constraints, and vicissitudes of fictional characters link up with our own predicaments.[92] It is also to Baldwin's credit that in combining

---

90. Stroup, *Promise of Narrative Theology*, 114.

91. Neither should the necessary sense of guilt for sinfulness be sacrificed on the altar of human dignity. See Metz "Suffering unto God," 617.

92. Amos Wilder stresses that like everything else, fictional characters are real in the sense that they are theoretical entities of criticism with metaphysical implications

selfhood and textuality in the two stories, he is neither nostalgic nor does he aim at finding a utopia freed from the contingencies of historical time and space. Instead, he merges private pains with his community's problems while succeeding in avoiding the dangers of moral certainty.[93]

One can therefore say that a profound appreciation of Baldwin's art demands a recognition that "truth" in an autobiographical context should not be seen as verifiable given the complexity of the self.[94] Nonetheless, the intention to tell the truth, in the broad terms of the autobiographical genre, is a sufficient guarantee of sincerity.[95] This means that despite the inherent weakness, autobiographical truth is important "in its capacity to make sense of experience told, shared, and even made newly possible for both the teller and the hearer of the story. Just as authorship of autobiography is tacitly plural, so the truth of autobiography is to be found, not in the "facts" of the story itself, but in the relational space between the story and the reader."[96]

Hence, if contemporary scholarly attention to narrative as a means of exploring how meaning emerges in social, historical and psychological contexts is a critique of the exclusive focus on a narrowly defined set of "sacred texts," the autobiographical aspects of "The Rockpile" and "The Outing" offer a unique insight into the religious commitments of the African Americans of Baldwin's adolescence. More significantly, they throw light on how the author's critical reflections on his own religious experiences enable him to perceive his feelings, ideas, imaginings and choices in a new light.[97]

LAYOUT AND STRUCTURE OF THIS BOOK

Having established the fact that the autonomy of texts does not imply that literary criticism is a value-free enterprise, Chapter 1 of the study has so

---

for readers. See Wilder, "Story and Story-World," 357; and van Inwagen, "Fiction and Metaphysics," 77.

93. Gunn, *Autobiography*, 119.

94. For instance, while philosophers assume that consciousness is aware of itself, theorists of autobiography tend to emphasize the retrospective and therefore non-immediate nature of autobiographical self-awareness. For further comment, see Marcus, *Auto/biographical Discourses*, 5.

95. Ibid., 3.

96. Gunn, *Autobiography*, 143.

97. Nelson, "Imagining Our Lives," 2–4.

far examined the challenge of formulating critical discourse based on the theological paradigm. This facilitated the due claim that, as *intertexts* of the Baldwin corpus, the short stories in the collection *Going to Meet the Man* are not only autobiographically driven but evoke aspects of the religious, the ethical and the transcendent. An appreciation of the functioning of the short story genre, taking cognisance of the preceding analysis, brings into focus Baldwin's fictionalisation of his childhood in "The Rockpile" and "The Outing." The autobiographical memory embedded in the two stories provides a helpful framework for analyzing the mindset of the narrator underlined by a critique of the uses to which religion is subjected. What emerged by way of conclusion is that the characters in the two stories may be mired in obsession with death, sin and guilt, but that the dysfunctional social and religious environment that feed their scrupulous consciences sometimes succeeds in providing margins for Christian love.

René Girard's hermeneutics provide the starting point, as well as the main source of evidence, for the analysis of the scapegoat motif in "The Man Child" (Chapter 2). The chapter undertakes an inquiry into Girard's account of mimetic desires, rivalry and the inevitable violence that result. An evaluation of these phenomena and their implications for the Christian doctrine of atonement add to an understanding of the place of envy and loss of self-control experience by Jamie, the character around whom the plot of the story is structured.

Chapter 3 investigates the problem of evil that admits of a cause, that is, a situation of severe negativity where human agency plays a role. Directed toward a detailed examination of "Going to Meet the Man," the chapter supplies a conceptual framework with which to examine the notion of tragedy as proposed in recent and not-so-recent literature. While keeping an eye on the tendency in philosophical and theological circles to rationalize and justify the goodness of God, the chapter evaluates the proposal that "man's inhumanity to man" is part of being human (J. Cameron). In addition, using Emmanuel Lévinas as guide, the "eye contact" between a white eight-year-old boy and a nameless black victim of public emasculation provides a platform for drawing attention to the experience of what appears to be godforsakenness at the heart of the tragic story. Admittedly, tragedy does challenge the imagination of believers and non-believers; however, within the scope offered by Baldwin's creative insight, it becomes a method for exploring human resilience and moral situations, grounding our reflection on the three phases of the protagonist's life depicted in the story.

James Baldwin and the Short Story

The understanding that the autobiographical impulse and the "personal voice" of James Baldwin permeate the collection of short stories is reinforced in "This Morning, This Morning, This Evening So Soon," the focal point of Chapter 4. The difficulties of the main character are explored as he tries to determine his identity in circumstances that are, understandably, beyond his control. The task of using the story to draw attention to the universalism in Baldwin will be approached by way of showing that his style of writing captures the emotion, thoughts and speech of the marginal *other*, thanks in part, to the positive impact of the Paris geographical environment on his emotions and lifestyle.[98] It will be demonstrated also that apart from embodying authentic representation of realities rather than the chronicle of an indifferent writer, "This Morning, This Evening, So Soon," infuses ethical sensitivities to social discourse. In the light of the foregoing, it becomes quite rewarding to consider societal contradictions through Baldwin's point of view, a point that has been enriched by contrasting experiences that alter consciousness as well as engender a sense of optimism such that is seen in the narrator on self-imposed exile who returns to his home country, the USA, after a twelve-year stay in Paris.[99]

Although the reader's encounter with "Sonny's Blues" is literary rather than musical, Chapter 5 evaluates the emotional response of the narrator to his brother's musical talents. Background discussions include a demonstration of a link between theology and aesthetics, taking into account the capacity of music to function as a mechanism for reaching the unconscious. Jazz and the blues are, in addition, examined as performance art forms—culture-texts that reverberate beyond their origins in the black American social milieu. The chapter then puts into focus the understanding that the narrator's felt response to his brother's artistic performance, despite the depressing setting of their social environment, sharpens his intuition and facilities a new outlook on life. The foregoing adds to our understanding of the symbiotic relationship between imagination and revelation, as well as

---

98. Coverley, *Psychogeography*, 10. See also Self, *Psychogeography*, 5–11 for further insights into how the point of intersection between geography and psychology, the subject matter of psychogeography, can help in understanding why and how the perspectives of life of pilgrims, hikers, tourists, immigrants, foreigners, exiles (forced or self-imposed) might, for instances, be affected (for better or worse) by contrast experiences in a new geographical location.

99. In my opinion, "Come Out the Wilderness" is the least successful of the eight short stories in the Baldwin collection. References to it are minimal.

draws attention to how both provide platforms for philosophical, ethical theological inquiries.

2

Myth and the Scapegoat Rhetoric

> ...the term scapegoat has been used to describe a relatively powerless innocent who is made to take the blame for something that is not his fault. Unfortunately, he is not allowed into the wilderness [as in the Leviticus account] but is usually subjected to cruelty or even death.
>
> —E. Aronson, *The Social Animal*

INTRODUCTION

In his study of ancient and modern myths, René Girard, a French cultural historian and literary critic, paid particular attention to text dynamics including their semiotic, psychoanalytic and sociological dimensions.[1] These enable him to advance a theory that links mimesis or imitation to scapegoat mechanism. He began by demonstrating that human desire has a triangular structure: the desiring subject, the desired object and finally, that which interposes itself between the subject and the object. As Girard suggested, the object of desire is not intrinsically desirable but only in so far as it is desired by others. In other words, a person only learns what is

---

1. Cf. Girard, *Deceit, Desire and the Novel*; Girard, *Violence and the Sacred*; Girard, "To Double Business Bound"; Girard, *Scapegoat*; Girard, *Things Hidden*; Girard, "Generative Scapegoating," 73–105; and Girard, "Victims, Violence and Christianity," 129–35.

desirable by what others desire. Furthermore, desire often evolves to the point where a person takes action to possess the object of desire. Desire, in this sense, "is not only speech that says 'I Want' but also action to get what I want."[2] Rivalry inevitably results from such a psychodramatic clash of desires. With time, it evolves into envy, and then, hatred and most often degenerating into the emergence of a scapegoat. Girard draws on historical documents, Greek mythology and biblical stories to expose diverse forms of scapegoatism in an attempt to focus attention not only on the plight of the victims embedded in them but also to throw some light on the origin of some cultural practices.[3] James Baldwin's "The Man Child" provides an avenue for recasting Girard's hermeneutics as well as demonstrating that literature is an important means of expanding Christian myths—messages hidden within narratives which Christians take to be crucial in their understanding of their faith experience.[4]

The starting point of this chapter will be a focus on the nature of human desire and the potential for violence beneath such desires. This will be followed by a study of the tendency in humans to escape their own fears and frustrations by projecting them onto something or someone else, the scapegoat. René Girard's reliance on historical accounts, Leviticus 16, and the rereading of the anthropology of James Frazer will be taken into account in this study of the scapegoat phenomenon.[5] How the scapegoat motif provides the dynamics for plot development in "The Man Child" will

---

2. Hamerton-Kelly, *Sacred Violence*, 200. Robert Hamerton-Kelly's juxtaposition of the Girardian hermeneutics with several biblical texts merit special emphasis here. I draw on his encyclopaedic insights in this study of James Baldwin's "The Man Child." Works by Hamerton-Kelly that are of immediate significance include "A Girardian Interpretation of Paul," 65–82; "Sacred Violence and the Curse of the Law," 98–118; "Sacred Violence and 'Works of Law,'" 55–57; and *Gospel and the Sacred*.

3. Implicit in Girard's line of argument is the idea that stories of the gospels are historically accurate reports, and that the incidents in the passion narratives arose from a unanimous mobilisation of a crowd in an unconscious persecution of an innocent victim. For a critique of this view, see Mack, "Innocent Transgressor," 135–65 where the notion of the gospels as history is explicitly rejected. Mack suggests that the gospels are, in fact, myths about the Christological and sociological shifts with which early Christians defined themselves as distinct from contemporary rivals.

4. As will be argued in due course, myths are not false explanations given that they stimulate thought and embody modes of knowledge. Moreover, the thinking that humans have transcended the need for mythical forms of thought, traceable to the enlightenment's glorification of reason, is no longer tenable. For comments, see Coupe, *Myth*, 4–13, with reference to Jewett and Shelton Lawrence, *American Monomyth*, 250.

5. Frazer, *Illustrated Golden Bough*.

constitute the core of this chapter. Keeping an eye on Girard's hypothesis to allow for a reading of the short story in the light of critical theory, an attempt will be made to show that Girard's conclusions throw light on the predicament of Jamie, the protagonist of the Baldwin story, whose personal failures end in the loss of self-control, and the strangling of an innocent child. A systematisation of the creative tensions inherent in the short story, first of all, shows how literature can enrich theology. Second, and more specifically it demonstrates how Baldwin's story provides opportunities for exploring not only the atonement theology, but also the similarities and differences between the face of Christ on the cross and a victim of violence in a contemporary fiction.

MIMETIC DESIRE

"The Man Child" is centered around Jamie who murders Eric, the only child of his nameless friend. Jamie had been forced to sell his landed property to Eric's father because of his inability to manage it. In due course, however, Jamie begins to perceive the transaction as a mistake. To compound his sense of failure, his wife leaves him. It soon dawns on Jamie that he envies his friend of all his *possessions*—wife, child, house and land. In the end, Jamie vents his anger, envy and frustration on little Eric. He lures the blond 8–year-old boy to a nearby bush where he strangles him. I argue that the storyline of "The Man Child" goes straight to the heart of Girard's thought on mimesis, scapegoatism and violence. There is, however, no denying the fact that behind Girard lies the influence of ancient Greek philosophy.

In the classical period, there were different nuances of the concept originally in relation to the imitation of reality and, later with reference to the visual arts, nature, music and dance.[6] This understanding shares some similarities with the rites of Dionysian ceremonies which consisted of cultic acts of priests including music, songs, and dance.[7] There is, on the other hand, the vision of Democritus which points to the imitation of natural processes as in weaving, during which humans seem to imitate the

---

6. Weiner, *Dictionary of the History of Ideas*; see Peters, "Behaviorism"; and Nahm, "Creativity in Art."

7. The social function of early Dionysian ritual was essentially cathartic. It purged the individual of irrational impulses and offered freedom at a time when life was seen as something to be escaped from. Cf. Dillistone, *Christian Understanding of Atonement*, 121.

spider, or in building where they tend to imitate the swallow, and in singing, the swan.[8] But while the Platonic concept of imitation stresses that art is synonymous with duplicating the appearances of things in the sense that "the poet always copies an earlier act of creation which is in itself already a copy,"[9] the Aristotelian understanding leans toward free creation of the work of art based on the elements of nature. Implicit or explicit differences notwithstanding, these theories of mimesis are founded on what may now be perceived as a rather curious premise that "human nature is passive and therefore able to perceive only what exists, and even if it were able to invent anything which does not exist, it will be ill advised to use this ability because the existing world is perfect."[10]

For Girard, mimesis, or what he sees as "an inclination to reproduce the action and gestures of others," covers a broad range of issues and embraces ideas with much wider implications.[11] In his view, once the basic needs for food, sleep or sex have been satisfied, a human being is subject to intense desires, though he or she may not know precisely for what.[12] The reason is that each human desires *being*, something he or she lacks which some other person seems to possess. The subject thus looks to the other person, as a sort of model, to inform him or her of what should be desired in order to acquire *being*. If the model, who might seem to be endowed with superior being, desires some object, that object, in the scheme of things, appears to be capable of conferring an even greater plenitude of being.

As an example, Girard draws attention to the mimetic quality of childhood desires, adding that adult desire is virtually identical, except that the adult is generally less likely to be seen imitating others for fear of revealing *lack of being*. The adult likes to assert his or her independence and to offer himself or herself as a model to others; he or she invariably falls back on the formula, "imitate me!" in order to conceal a lack of originality.[13] It is in this sense that desire is mimetic for it actually boils down to the imitation of the

---

8. Cf. Plutarch, "De Sollertia Animalium," 20, 974A, in *Moralia*.

9. Worton and Still, eds., *Intertextuality*, 3.

10. Peters, "Behaviorism," 227.

11. See Dumouchel, *Violence and Truth*, 7. Hamerton-Kelly locates Girard in the philosophical tradition inspired by the understanding that imitation is the "intermental" social characteristic of human beings; it is a way by which one is influenced by others. Cf. Hamerton-Kelly, *Sacred Violence*, 17.

12. A distinction can be drawn between animal needs and human desires. The former is general while the later is specific. See Hamerton-Kelly, *Sacred Violence*, 19.

13. Girard, *Violence and the Sacred*, 146.

model, a rival who, from the subject's point of view, is potentially the enemy that prevents access to the object of desire.[14]

Ordinarily, this "convergence of desires" should evoke images of harmony but as Girard has found out, this is actually not the case: there is an underlying rivalry. Moreover, neither the model nor the imitator is disposed to acknowledge that rivalry is taking place.[15] Girard suggests that the model, even when he or she has openly encouraged imitation, is surprised to find himself or herself engaged in competition. He or she concludes that the "disciple" has betrayed his confidence by following his or her footsteps. The disciple, on the other hand, feels rejected and humiliated, judged unworthy by his model of participating in the "superior" existence which the model enjoys. The reason for this misunderstanding is that, on the one hand, the model considers himself/herself too far above the disciple while the disciple considers himself/herself too far below the model. The psychological gap thus created means that neither the model nor the imitator is disposed to entertain the notion that their desires are identical or that each one is trying to outdo the other.[16]

Girard contends that the mimetic aspects of desire correspond to the primary impulse of most living creatures, and it is only cultural constraints that channel it in a constructive direction. This is because humans cannot respond to that universal human injunction, "imitate me!" without almost immediately encountering an inexplicable counter order: "don't imitate me." Consequently, this "double bind" turns humans into tyrants who transmit contradictory signals to one another. The predicament of mimetic desire at both the personal and societal levels results in disorder unless it is

---

14. Cf. McKenna, "Introduction," 2; Williams, "Innocent Victim," 320. Girard, *Violence and the Sacred*, 145. Hamerton-Kelly's recast of this scenario shows that this process takes place in three stages: First, desires imitate the desires of the other for the object. Secondly, the self replaces the object in the desire for the other. Thirdly, by replacing the object, the self seeks to possess not only the desire of the other but its own desire as it finds it mimetically in the other because the self and the other have become one. Cf. Hamerton-Kelly, *Sacred Violence*, 22.

15. Girard explores this insight in *Deceit, Desire, and the Novel*. For his part, McKenna distinguishes between the "logic of ideas" and the "logic of desire" adding that if we are all thinking the same thing, we will of course agree and there will be harmony among us. However, if we all desire the same thing, which we are bound to do if our desires imitate each other, there will be competition and conflict among us—not in spite of our resemblance but because of it. Cf. McKenna, "Introduction," 3.

16. The role of the "disciple," the imitator, truly defines the human condition. Cf. Girard, *Violence and the Sacred*, 146–47.

actually regulated through scapegoatism which necessitates the emergence of one or more victims on whom guilt is imputed.[17]

Before a detailed examination of the scapegoat motif in "The Man Child," it will be helpful to trace how the motif functions, first in biblical literature and myths, all of which have had much influence on Girard. The detour to the Bible has a dual purpose, first, to show how, in a time of crisis, sin and guilt are unloaded onto a scapegoat figure. Second, to underline the fact that scapegoatism remains alive in our present society, and that Baldwin's use of the phenomenon in "The Man Child" is emblematic of the vicarious death found in Christian religious thought.

The Scapegoat: Biblical Insight

Any discussion on scapegoatism naturally brings to mind the Mosaic laws of the Hebrew Bible. As a part of the ritual of atonement, goats are brought to the altar, and the high, priest, Aaron

> shall cast lots upon the two goats, one lot for the Lord and the other lot for Aza'zel. And Aaron shall present the goat on which the lot fell for the Lord, and offer it as a sin offering; but the goat which the lot fell for Aza'zel shall be presented alive before the Lord to make atonement over it, that it may be sent away into the wilderness to Aza'zel. (Lev 16:8–10 [RSV])

Before the goat is actually sent away by a man selected for the job, Aaron is to lay his hands upon the head of the live goat, to "transfer" his sins and those of the people on the goat. The thinking is that to eliminate the impurities of sin, the people have to localize it in the goat "that eventually suffers what the entire community would have suffered had the goat not been laden with collective impurity."[18] This tradition functioned against the background of the attempts of biblical writers to make the laws of God as clear as possible (cf. Deut 30:11–16). But the people were not always obedient. As time went by, the theologians of the Old Testament times arrived at the understanding that only God could provide the best solution to the problem of human sin. Moreover, the Old Testament often presents sin as uncleanliness, a disease that needs to be cleansed away before it contami-

---

17. Williams, "Innocent Victim," 321; Girard, *Violence and the Sacred*, 147. See also McKenna, "Introduction," 2. Cf. Girard, "Ancient Trail," 30; and Hamerton-Kelly, *Sacred Violence*, 20–21.

18. Cf. Levine, "René Girard on Job," 127.

nates the Community.[19] The underlying idea, according to Dillistone, was that since disease, misfortunes, ritual faults and misdemeanours tended to accumulate in the life of any community, it seemed necessary to carry through periodically some dramatic acts of purgation through symbolic transference to a goat doomed to destruction.[20]

Paul Fiddes' insight into the Hebrew ritual is especially illuminating. He notes that all the images of the sprinkling of blood and ritual purification, so common in the Hebrew Bible, are part of this view of sin as a destructive power that needs to be swept away. But sometimes sin was perceived to be so deadly that it required the physical removal of the guilty for the community to be restored to fellowship with Yahweh. This meant that the sacrificial death of the sinner or that of a surrogate victim, although unstable in itself, was used to get rid of the contamination of sin (Num 15:27–31 [RSV]).[21]

The reference to Aza'zel in the atonement ritual in Leviticus 16 is worthy of special mention. Of all the various views regarding the meaning of the Aza'zel in the atonement ritual, the view that the term refers to a desert demon is quite popular among scholars. It is an opinion that is anticipated in the Book of Enoch where the demon appears as the ringleader of rebel angels who seduce humanity. This offers a fundamental theological rejoinder for, given that the Bible forbids the worship of idols (Lev 17:7 [RSV]), how does one explain the offering of a goat to a demon as is the case with Leviticus 16? To meet this rejoinder, it might be said that in terms of the outward acts, prayers and praises which are an essential part of the whole Leviticus ritual, the atonement rite serves the useful purpose of easing the conscience of the people of ancient Israel by making them conscious of the availability of divine forgiveness. Moreover, the very fact that sin and impurity are unloaded onto the goat is an indication that the goat is only a vehicle of elimination rather than of propitiation.[22] Early Judaism even

---

19. See Dillistone, *Christian Understanding of the Atonement*, 131–32.

20. Dillistone traces this tradition to the time when the suffering and deprivations of the exiles were thought of as punishment from God. It was, therefore, not surprising that the concern of the religious leaders of this time was centered on how to expiate guilt. See Dillistone, *Christian Understanding of the Atonement*, 128.

21. The inherent instability in sacrificial solution means that it always has to be re-enacted. Cf. Hamerton-Kelly, *Sacred Violence*, 204. See also Fiddes, *Past Event and Present Salvation*, 71–74.

22. An alternative opinion is that the term Aza'zel points to a translation of "the goat that Departs," that is, the scapegoat. Another view is that the word signifies the place to

broadened the atonement theology to include the sacrifices of martyrs whose self-giving was thought meritorious.[23] In the context of this study, the claim here is that Baldwin's "The Man Child" was seeded by the author's acquaintance with the scapegoat motif found in biblical literature. Like the scapegoat in Leviticus 16, Baldwin's short story represents a parable of how humans attempt to dismiss guilt through artificial means.

Sacrifice, a word that carries the meaning of making a "costly gift" for the sake of others, suggests how the early Church understood the vicarious death of Jesus. This meaning of sacrifice can be deducted from the suggestion that associates sacrifice with obedience (Gen 22:1–19; 1 Sam 15:22; Isa 1:11–17; Pss 40:7–9; 51:8ff.; 69:31–32 [RSV]).[24] Thus, one can point out, as Hamerton-Kelly does, that the cross is a symbol of violence done to a victim and that Christian theology has made the interpretation of the cross a central task.[25] Although, it would seem that the early Christians were not unaware of the understanding of sacrifice as a gift offered to God, a nuancing of meaning did occur with the result that sacrifice came to connote not only the literal sacrifice of things but also a spiritual enterprise which, like the gift offerings of the Hebrew Bible, has to be accompanied by repentance. From this perspective, sacrifices become means of dealing with the human problem of estrangement, and to remove guilt and free people from the threats of punishment.[26] New Testament references to the death of Jesus bear witness to this. They cohere not only with the ideas inherent in the Day of Atonement ritual but also with images of the Passover festival.

---

which the goat is sent. Cf. Gaster, "Azazel," 326. Other instances of atonement in the Old Testament include the heifer whose neck is broken in Deut 21:1–9, by the Levites (Num 8:19), and the blood of sacrifices referred to in Exod 29:12–14.

23. Cf. Allen, *Broadman Bible Commentary*, 2:46; and Achtemeier, ed., *Harper's Bible Dictionary*.

24. While admitting that divine justice did not demand the death of Christ as a sacrifice of atonement, Schwager does not see anything wrong in calling the death of Christ a sacrifice. He adds, however, that such an understanding of sacrifice has to include elements of (i) obedience to the Father as a willingness to be persecuted; (ii) the identification with all persons who find themselves in similar situations and who are victims of preventable evil; (iii) the intercession for his brothers and sisters before God. Cf. Schwager, "Christ's Death and the Critique of Sacrifice," 120–21. This goes along with Milbank's understanding that the death of Christ is best seen as God's self-offering. For him, it is neither "a dying that is a loss, nor a dying which institutes a debt to be paid back . . ." Cf. Milbank, "Stories of Sacrifice," 64.

25. See Hamerton-Kelly, *Sacred Violence*, 15.

26. Fiddes, *Past Events*, 62–64.

The later commemorates both the exodus, and the making of the covenant between God and the Israelites. Thus in the statements "Behold the Lamb of God who takes away the sins of the world" (John 1:29), and "Christ our Passover has been sacrificed for us" (2 Cor 5:7), the early Christians were attesting to the fact that a new covenant relationship had now been made with God through a sacrificial death sealed with a blood offering associated with atonement for sin. The unique thing about this, as the Christians claim, is that the death of Jesus, unlike the Leviticus ritual, is a once-for-all event (Heb 10:12).[27]

Paradigms in Myths

Girard is also familiar with myths and ancient belief systems traces of which are quite evident in modern practices and attitudes toward societal victims and victimizers. Given that the symbolism in myths can be extremely powerful yet easy to understand, an examination of how some of them function will be helpful in the understanding of "The Man Child" as well as throwing light on how literature can expand myths. Consequently, this section is treated as continuous with the line of argument set out in the previous section. For the purpose of terminological clarification, myth is here seen as typically a story of anonymous authorship set both within or outside historical time. It may be about heroes or superhuman beings or gods, spirits, ghosts, imagined in anthropomorphic terms. It does not necessarily have to be linked to ritual, and it is not unusual for myths to be extravagant and full of seeming inconsistencies.[28]

Myths do more than entertain and amuse: they function to explain, to reconcile, to guide or to legitimize action or inaction. That is why they are used to account for social realities.[29] Moreover, the store which society sets on myths and the realities they deal with is rooted in a number of factors. One of these is the recognition of human frailty and mortality. There is also the realisation that the social group into which the individual is born pre-

27. Other evidence which support the view that the early Christians saw the death of Jesus as a sacrifice taking the place of the victims associated with the Day of Atonement include Heb 9:13–14; 1 John 1:7; 2:1–2.

28. See Coupe, *Myth*, 6, with reference to Cupitt, *World to Come*, 29. Drawing on Ricoeur's *Symbolism of Evil*, Coupe talks of myth's power of discovering possibilities which transcend the actual world. Cf. Coupe, *Myth*, 8.

29. Cf. Douglas, *Scapegoats*, 17, with reference to Baigent, Leigh, and Lincoln, *Messianic Legacy*, 158.

existed and is sure to remain after one is dead. A third factor has to do with human power of thought and awareness of the spectacle of the universe, and the enigma of one's relation to changing forms.[30]

In both ancient and modern societies, myths tend to have unusual characteristics. For instance, in some of them, day and night might be confused or heaven and earth communicate while gods move among men and men among gods. It can also happen that within the story-world, distinctions are not made between gods and human beings. There may also be stories in which sun and moon are twins or antagonists perhaps, because the sun is moving too close to the earth and drought and heat make life unbearable.[31] Myths are further characterized by the type of social contexts that tend to provoke collective violence on victims as in *Oedipus Rex*, the most well-known example where the protagonist manages to combine: "the marginality of the outsider with the marginality of the insider. Oedipus's infirmity, his past history of exposure as an infant, his situation as a foreigner, newcomer, and king, all make him a veritable conglomerate of victim's signs."[32]

Another remarkable aspect of myth with regard to scapegoatism is that the victim's presence is enough to contaminate everything around him or her infecting men and beasts with plague, ruining crops, poisoning food, causing games to disappear, turning friends against one another or parents against their children. Everything shrivels under his feet and even the slightest changes are blamed on him, just as the very presence of Eric embodies and reminds Jamie of all his failures. However, the offence of the mythical character tends to border on the fantastic and its ontological attributes show marks of the sacred, a phenomenon which Girard claims is present in all religions.[33]

---

30. Cf. Campbell, *Myths to Live By*, 22–23.

31. In the mythological monster, "physical" and the "moral" are inseparable. The confusion of animals, men and gods common in myths provide mythology with its most important and spectacular modality of the monstrous. Moral monstrosity, according to Girard, actualizes the tendency of all persecutors to project the monstrous results of some calamity—public or private—into the scapegoat, whose vulnerability is made evident by virtue of infirmity or foreignness. See Girard, *Scapegoat*, 25, 34, 48, 136.

32. Girard, *Scapegoat*, 26.

33. In this context, the sacred consists of all the forces whose dominance over humanity increases or seems to increase in proportion to efforts to master them. Tempests, forests, fires and plagues, among other phenomena, may be classified as sacred. Far outranking these, however, though in a less obvious manner, stands human violence. Violence is thus perceived as something "exterior" to man and henceforth as part of all

As this study of "The Man Child" will confirm in due course, there are similarities as well as differences between scapegoatism in fiction and myth, on the one hand, and in historical texts, on the other. As in myths, scapegoatism in literature can point to persecution similar to those in historical texts but they are more difficult to decode because they are open to abuses. Hence, at first sight, there may be nothing in myths or fiction that seems to have any connection with reality but in the view of Girard, literature and myths normally have their roots in real acts of violence that could have taken place. Thus, literature as well as myths can be used to deceive and to present cultural practices as expressions of human indifference rather than admissions of the violence that is part of the human condition.[34]

A Social Anthropological Viewpoint

Before the emergence of the Girardian hermeneutics, the anthropological insights of J. G. Frazer had a pride of place in explaining scapegoatism at both interpersonal and communal relationships. Frazer predicated scapegoatism on simplistic confusion of word and thing. It arises, he says, from a juxtaposition of the physical with the mental or the material with the immaterial. In this regard, scapegoatism is informed by the belief that guilt or suffering could be transferred from some community to a designed victim, often an animal but, sometimes, a human being.[35] The reasoning, according to Frazer, is that because it is possible to shift a load of wood from the back of one human being to the back of another, people do not find it difficult to move from the physical realm to the spiritual thus allowing for the thinking that it is possible for the burden of pain and sorrow to be shifted to another who would suffer instead. Scapegoating thus embodies a process of "displacement."[36] It functions as a sort of sacrifice by persecutors who see their victims as the source of problems.[37]

---

outside forces that threaten mankind. See Girard, *Violence and the Sacred*, 31.

34. The idea here is that if misused, both literature and myth can function to provide people with metaphorical shields against moral traps. See Girard, "Ancient Trail," 28–29; and Hamerton-Kelly, "Girardian Interpretation," 66.

35. Cf. Girard, *Violence and the Sacred*, 317, with reference to Frazer, *Golden Bough*, 624.

36. Girard, "Generative Scapegoating," 75.

37. McKenna, "Introduction," 3.

Myth and the Scapegoat Rhetoric

While operating at the margins of religious studies, and literary theory, Girard adds a touch of sophistication to the discussion by demonstrating that scapegoatism is a psychological mechanism that takes place not only at the level of interpersonal relationships but also at the level of the collective. At the level of the collective, scapegoatism becomes evident when, instead of directing their frustrations at the object that divides them, rivals pick on a victim.[38] Victimisers, or the persecutors, may be stimulated by the extremes of public opinions which result in times of crisis, weakening normal institutions and favouring mob formations. The cause may be external, such as epidemic, a severe drought, or a flood followed by a famine. At other times, the cause may be internal political disturbances, such as religious conflicts. Hamerton-Kelly's fictional example of this phenomenon sums up how the socio-anthropological mechanism can work. He writes:

> there was a group of hominids that found itself unable to do anything in concert because of the rivalry among them. Each one found himself inwardly compelled to imitate some other . . . Cooperation was impossible until one day . . . [the rivals] agreed to kill someone else . . . The victim, as the source of the sudden unity and order, was regarded as a saviour; and he was blamed for causing the previous disorder. Thus he acquired the double valency of the sacred: attraction and revulsion. From the victim came the building blocks of social order: prohibition to control the course of rivalry; ritual sacrifice to re-enact and so represent to the group the unifying energy of the founding moment; myth to explain and obscure the violence by covering it up with transformations . . .[39]

No matter what circumstances trigger persecutions, the experience of the scapegoats who live through them, is the same. The experience normally included a loss of social order evidenced by the disappearance of rules and "differences" that define cultural divisions.[40] Institutional collapse obliterates or telescope hierarchical and functional differences, so that everything seems to have the same monotonous and monstrous aspects. Consequently, the "terror inspired in people by the eclipse of culture and universal confusion of popular uprisings are signs of a community that is literally undifferentiated, deprived of all that distinguishes one person from

---

38. Hamerton-Kelly, *Sacred Violence*, 25.

39. Hamerton-Kelly, "Girardian Interpretation," 67. Refer also to Wallace, "Postmodern Biblicism," 131; and also to Girard, *Things Hidden*, 42.

40. Girard, *Scapegoat*, 13.

another in time and place. As a result all are equally disordered in the same place and at the same time."[41]

When a society breaks down, time sequences seem to shorten. Not only, as Girard contends, is there an acceleration of the tempo of "positive exchanges" as in barter for example, but also hostile or "negative exchanges" tend to increase. The reciprocity of negative and positive exchanges makes people feel powerless as they are disoriented by their predicament. Nevertheless, they never look into the natural causes of their problems. In fact, since it is a social crisis, there is a strong tendency to explain it by social and especially moral causes. The unstated argument, according to Girard, is usually that if human relations disintegrate in the process of such confusion, the subject of interpersonal relations cannot be completely innocent of this phenomenon. But rather than blame themselves, people inevitably blame "society" as a whole, which costs them nothing, or other people who seem particularly "dangerous" for easily identifiable reasons and who seem to bear identifiable "signs." The ones most frequently chosen might or might not have transgressed the taboos that are considered the strictest in the society in question.[42]

Whether within interpersonal relationships or at the level of the collective, victimisers normally convince themselves that a small number of people, or even a single individual, despite his or her relative weakness, is rather harmful to the whole society. Where there is a group of persecutors, mob psychology is fully played out and members of the crowd dream of purging the community of the "impure" elements that corrupt it, the traitors who undermine it. Indeed, for Girard, the crowd's act of becoming a crowd is the same as the call to "assemble" or "mobilise" (to become a mob), adding that the word "mobilisation" suggests a military operation against an already identified enemy or one soon to be identified by the mobilisation of the crowd. It is of particular interest that, as in "The Man Child," the search for scapegoats remains evident in present-day society.[43]

ERIC'S VULNERABILITY

Given the tendency in texts to "hide" the fate of victims, the question which the preceding analysis is meant to address is: how does one go beneath the

41. Ibid., 16.
42. Cf. Girard, "Generative Scapegoatism," 74.
43. Cf. Wieser, "Community," 83.

surface of texts to be able to find traces of the victims of violence hidden in them? Girard proposes that an attempt to read the scapegoat mechanism into any text has to be preceded by verification as to whether or not one is dealing with a "scapegoat *of* the text" or a "scapegoat *in* the text." In the former, the scapegoat is merely the hidden "structural principle" but in the latter sense, the theme is evident. It is only in the first case that a text can be defined as one of victimisation in that it is written from the standpoint of the victimizer. In the second case, the text concedes the scapegoat effect while highlighting the trust of the victimization. Moreover, persecution texts tend to give indications that: (i) the acts of violence are real; that (ii) the crisis which led to the persecution is real; (iii) victims are chosen not for the crimes they are accused of but for the victims' signs that they bear; and that (iv) the import of the relationship is to lay the responsibility for the crisis on the victims paving the way for their destruction. The irony in Girard's line of thought is that the order that was either absent or compromised by the scapegoat is established once more by the scapegoat, the entity that disturbed it in the first place.[44]

The point of interest here, therefore, is whether or not "The Man Child" is a text of victimization, that is, a "persecution text" as defined by Girard. It is equally of interest to the discussion to determine if this work of imagination has more to recommend it than myths or historical reports of victimisation.[45] It is contended here that "The Man Child" combines both characteristics. A bird's-eye view of this story shows that the "marks of a victim" are all over Eric. In line with Girard's thesis, the act of violence against Eric is real, and the financial and emotional crises that propelled Jamie to such a crime are equally evident. Moreover, Eric, the victim is chosen not because he is guilty but because of the "signs" he bears. These signs, among other things, expose him as the weakest member of his family. This is evidently in accord with the notion that victimisers always choose the weakest and the least protected.

---

44. In this sense, the effect of the scapegoat is to reverse the relationship between persecutors and their victim such that fear of the scapegoat is supplanted by adoration. Cf. Girard, *Scapegoat*, 49–50.

45. In this instance, imagination is perceived as both an activity and an attitude. Inspired by David Hume, Lamarque and Olsen point out that as an activity, human imagination is able to assemble and reassemble ideas, and as an attitude, "it is reflexive," a form of attention, a way of holding something in the mind. Cf. Lamarque and Olsen, *Truth, Fiction and Literature*, 243–44. Cf. also Hume, *Enquiry Concerning Human Understanding*, 19.

The victimizer's choice of victims may or may not be totally at random. It is even possible that the crimes of which the victim or victims (scapegoats) are accused of are real. Nonetheless, the persecutors choose victims who are particularly susceptible to persecution rather than because of the crimes they have committed. Ethnic or religious minorities, for example, tend to polarize majorities against themselves. Sickness, madness, genetic deformities, accidental injuries also tend to polarize persecutors. Indeed, disabilities belong to a large group of innocuous signs of victims and they can take various forms. Girard notes that in the boarding school, for instance, individuals who have difficulty adapting or someone from another country or state, an orphan, an only son, someone who is penniless, or even the latest arrival, is more or less interchangeable with a cripple. Each and every one of these examples is "disabled," and persecutors tend to attribute to chosen victims disabilities or deformities that reinforce the polarisation against them.[46]

Social abnormality can equally function as a criterion for selecting those to be persecuted. Under such a situation, the "average" defines the norm and the further one is from the "normal" social status of whatever kind, the greater the risk of persecution. Thus, extreme characteristics generally attract persecution. The idea of the extreme refers not just to wealth or poverty, but also to success and failure, beauty and ugliness, vice and virtue, the ability to please and to displease. In this regard, the weakness of women, children and old people, as well as the strength of the most powerful, become weakness in the face of the crowd.[47] This explains why, for instance, ugly old women or the spectacularly beautiful are more often identified as witches. Indeed, anyone with extraordinary quality about him or her awakens atavistic fears.[48]

Girard's reference to a fable set in the animal kingdom is illuminating on how social victims are "selected." He tells the story of how the animals set about trying to ward off a devastating plague thought to be a divine punishment for a guilt not shared by all the animals. To avert this plague,

---

46. Girard, *Scapegoat*, 17–18.

47. For details of how this is worked out in the Book of Job, see Girard, "Ancient Trail," 2–42. It needs to be pointed out however, that Girard's reading of the Book of Job attracts the criticism of scholars such as Baruch Levine who argues that Job was merely a "heroic dissident" rather than a scapegoat. As Levine sees it, "there is not a single indication in the speeches of Job, or in those of his dialoguers, of a connection between this suffering of Job and the well-being of the community." Cf. Levine, "René Girard on Job," 131.

48. Hamerton-Kelly, "Girardian Interpretation," 73.

the guilty among them were to be identified and punished. The first to be interrogated in the fable are the beasts of prey, who are immediately excused. Last came the ass, the least bloodthirsty of them all and therefore the weakest and the least protected. According to the story, it is the ass that is finally designated.[49] This fable takes us back to the helpless figure of Eric in Baldwin's story. Given the above theoretical framework, one can suggest that the seed for Eric's violent death was sown during the dinner marking Jamie's thirty-second birthday. When the tabletalk shifted to the good times he and Eric's father had in the course of their friendship, Jamie is desperate to deny that he was a failure. As Eric's father recalls the bygone carefree moments in the friendship, he tells Jamie:

> '. . . all you did was walk around the woods by yourself in the daytime and sit around The Rafters in the evenings with me.'[50] 'You two were always together then,' said Eric's mother.
> 'Well,' said Jamie, harshly, 'at least that hasn't changed.'
> 'Now, you know,' said Eric's father, gently, 'it's not the same. Now I got a wife and kid—and another one coming . . .'
> 'Yes,' said Jamie, 'you really got it all fixed up, you did. You got it all—the wife, the kid, the house, and all the land.'
> <Eric's father said>'I didn't steal your farm from you. It wasn't my fault you lost it. I gave you a better price for it than anybody else would have done.'
> <Jamie replied>'I am not blaming you . . .'[51]

ATONEMENT: HISTORICAL THEOLOGY

It is also being suggested here that in confronting the phenomenon of scapegoatism that arises from psychological propensities in individuals, "The Man Child" is a commentary, and a reapplication of the biblical text of Leviticus 16 which foreshadows the story of redemption in the New Testament.[52] And if, following Girard, this significance is reinforced by the dynamics of similarities and differences with historical, and mythological

---

49. Ibid.

50. Eric's father had earlier made reference to Jamie's wife, and how much Jamie loved poetry, and could not find time to show any affection toward his wife. He later chanted teasingly: 'Jamie, Jamie, pumpkin-eater, had a wife and couldn't keep her!" See Baldwin, "Man Child," 61.

51. See Baldwin, "Man Child," 64.

52. See Hamerton-Kelly, *Gospel and the Sacred*, 131, for additional comments.

texts noted in previous sections, the principal conclusion anticipated at the end of this chapter is that, read as scripture, "The Man Child" constitutes a revisiting of the Christian theology of atonement.[53]

A brief look at the evolution of the theology of atonement in the history of the Christian Church will be helpful in clarifying the present state of affairs. For a start, there is no gainsaying the fact that Christians, both in ancient and modern times, did and still attempt to find a coherent explanation as to how the death of Jesus effected atonement. The evolution of the explanations from the ancient Church to the present day shows that the New Testament Church pictured sin as a kind of impurity or uncleanness, tainting life.[54] It shut out humans from the sphere of the sacred in which God dwelt. From this perspective, atonement was portrayed as sacrifice, in which the blood of Christ was an agent of cleansing, hence images of washing, sprinkling, bathing and fresh clothing were essential in the idea of salvation.[55]

For the early Church fathers, the human predicament was frequently understood as that of being oppressed by hostile powers. People lived in fear of astral deities or of the demons that inhabited the natural world. They thought of themselves as being sinful because of the inability to overcome their weaknesses and enemies. In a sense, the victory of Christ over the devil in all its manifestations, derivable from forms of New Testament exegesis, became a rather popular way of explaining atonement. In time, this view of salvation was overtaken by the influence of Platonic philosophy which stressed that the human body was certainly not evil in itself but seemed hampered in its forward movement to the spiritual world. This was because sin caused mortality and corruption, thereby holding back the soul destined for eternal life. In this regard, the atoning work of Christ was

---

53. Wilder, "Uses of a Theological Criticism," 51, is persuaded that "from the beginning to end, the language of scripture is wedded to all the dynamics of human experience," whether private or social. Implied in the use of "scripture" in this study is a critique of the exclusive focus on a narrow definition of the term. Cf. also Detweiler, "What Is a Sacred Text?" See Kort, *Take, Read*, 5–6. Kort stresses that whatever form the term "scripture" takes, it always succeeds in enabling a person, group, or institutions to have worlds, and to act meaningfully within them. Kort is aware that Scripture also constrains, inhibits, creates fears and sets limits. However, the relevance, and indeed, the survival of any Scripture lies in its capacity to provide resources for affirmation and self-criticism.

54. See Fiddes, *Past Events*, 1–13.

55. It is of particular interest here to note, as Hamerton-Kelly does, that the Gospels never claim that God required the death of Christ to satisfy some violent needs. Cf. Hamerton-Kelly, "Girardian Interpretation," 68.

perceived in terms of a renewal while salvation was tantamount to divination, since it raised humanity to share in God's life.

As Fiddes' research shows, things took another turn in the Middle Ages. It was a time when the problems of society were seen in terms of a disturbance of order. Consequently, individual and social sins arose when loyalty and honour were no longer paid to the overlord by his vassals, and could only be restored if the debts of honour were paid, either by compensation or by penalty inflicted. In this cultural context the human predicament before God was seen as a failure "to render to God his due." Atonement then became a question of settling a debt which human beings were incapable of repaying.[56]

The early twelfth century saw a new intensity of emotion in the poetry of love, and in religious lyrics, which involved the reader imaginatively in the sufferings of Christ or the sorrows of Mary. Indeed, the secular and the sacred merged in poetry which addresses Christ as a lover pleading for mercy on behalf of humankind as a courtly lover begs mercy of his lady. Then, the human predicament was felt to be a loss of love and the corresponding concept of the cross was that of a mighty demonstration of the love of God. In the romantic movement of the nineteenth century, this image became dominant. The movement placed a new emphasis upon the individual and his emotions. From then on the ability of the cross to evoke feelings came to be equated with the power of salvation.[57]

The period of the Reformation, noted for political turmoil and social upheaval, focused a new attention on law to guard rights and punish offenders. It was a time following the emergence of a world when the rule of monarchs had begun to lose influence. Under such social circumstances, Protestant thinkers were insistent on the fact that even kings and emperors were subject to the laws of God although the "godly ruler" tendered to enjoy some latitude in the framing of the laws that governed sociopolitical affairs. Nevertheless, the situation was such that monarchs were careful never to contradict the laws perceived to be of divine origin. Against this background, Fiddes points out that the estrangement of human beings from God was understood in terms of their being lawbreakers, summoned

---

56. See St. Anselm, *Cur Deus Homo*, Book II. Anselm's approach was based on the optimistic belief that humans are capable of performing all that was needed for salvation and that forgiveness of sins was not unconditional. For more comments, see Aulen, *Christus Victor*, 100–111.

57. This line of thought was echoed in the prediction of Matthew Arnold to the effect that literature, would eventually "replace" religion. See Arnold, "Study of Poetry," 161–62.

to receive condemnation at the divine bar of justice. As a result, atonement was a matter of satisfying the demands of the law with Jesus suffering as a substitute for humanity.

The age of Enlightenment brought a new attitude and seemed to provide answers to social issues. Enlightenment tended to engender a disdain for any idea of divine intervention and reason alone was considered good enough in the quest for truth. Not surprisingly, religious experience was interpreted as experience of the moral life, rather than any direct encounter with God.

Under the influence of the sciences of sociology and psychology, salvation is now understood more in terms of healing and individual well-being than anything else. It is worth noting, as Fiddes makes clear, that the various ideas of atonement cannot be confined within the particular historical moments to which they have been attached nor should they then be seen in terms of watertight compartments. Rather, they represent types of human experiences that draw inspiration from New Testament exegesis. In other words, there are periods when certain images were more prominent than others but all the images tend to "persist, overlap and reform into different combinations, and all express a dimension of human experience that remains valid for us here and now."[58]

Having thus provided a bird's-eye view of atonement theology, it will become clearer in the next section that there is a sense in which one can also say that Baldwin uses "The Man Child" to free the atonement discourse from its confinement to particular religious contexts, and the specific historical theology that seems to bind the doctrine to bygone years. Hence, rather than be understood as an attempt to provide answers, the rhetoric of the story constitutes a search for questions that can capture human predicaments in the here and now.[59] As it is, the human interests in the story which help to determine how the events and causes fit together in the plot, echo complementary scapegoat motifs in American politics as well as Baldwin's own specific experiences at home, the Church, and wider society. Consequently upon these, the tension that circulates within the short story can be expressed in terms that capture a narrative discourse in relation with the self, and society—an attempt to structure a coherent world view.[60]

---

58. Fiddes, *Past Events*, 13.
59. Kort, "Take, Read," 13.
60. See Martin, *Recent Theories of Narrative*, 62.

ALIENATION

Having metamorphosed from a model into an obstacle, the situation of Eric's father as a bosom friend, employer and benefactor obscures the personhood of Jamie triggering off chains of events that detach mimetic desire from its original object. Consequently (and following Girard's thesis), the murder of Eric becomes the inevitable end of the escalation of mimetic desire.[61] Against this background, Jamie's experiences of failure engender a sense of alienation.[62] In the context of Jamie's predicament, alienation implies that he is no longer able to have a meaningful relationship with his friends. Such a state of affairs results in a break with what Girard calls the mysterious inner world of one's personality, "a world which may include conscious as well as unconscious elements."[63]

Jamie's sense of failure not only as a husband, and a potential father, but also a farmer hits him hard as his bosom friend lets it be known that all the failures are entirely due to his own fault. He then tries to cling to the past, as he and Eric's father "had grown up together, gone to the war together, and survived together never apparently, while life ran, were they to be divided."[64] However, this happy reminiscence does not last as Eric's father blurted out that times have changed. The result of this brashness was a sort of emotional rupture that soon led to blind rage and the resultant consequences. What emerges from this reading is that Jamie failed in his attempt to re-establish the order that existed when there was neither wife nor child to come between him and his friend. Moreover, he finds this new structure of his relationship with Eric's father quite threatening. However, instead of getting out of town (as Eric's parents suggested), he decides to take matters literally into his own hand and strangles Eric.

Jamie's situation intertwines with Girard's thought on the nature of sacrifice, a process which furnishes an outlet for the human impulses that cannot be mastered by self-restraint.[65] And just as victimisers do not rec-

---

61. Cf. Mack, "Innocent Transgressor," 139.

62. Cf. Fiddes, *Past Event and Present Salvation*, 6–7. Humans may not only be estranged from fellow creatures, but they could also be estranged from their own essence and end. For further comment, cf. Dillistone, *Christian Understanding of Atonement*, 3.

63. Dillistone, *Christian Understanding of Atonement*, 6. Cf. also Girard, *Deceit, Desire and the Novel*, 100.

64. See Baldwin, "Man Child," 58.

65. In this regard, sacrifice is both an illegal and at the same time a legitimate exercise of violence. Girard, *Violence and the Sacred*, 18–20.

ognize scapegoating for what it is, Jamie is blind to the factors, including jealousy and lack of personal fulfilment, which motivate him to strangle Eric. But there is, in such a violent crime, what Girard terms the victimiser's apparition of a "Monstrous Double." This double emerges wherever one encounters an "I" and an "Other" caught in a simultaneous interchange of difference. This phenomenon would seem to explain why Jamie shed tears as he strangled Eric. But why couldn't he stop himself from committing the crime? In losing control, he watches this monstrosity take shape within him and outside him simultaneously as he unconsciously attributes the origin of his frustrations to causes other than himself, and his rival, Eric's father. In a sense, loss of self-control makes him the victim of an assault to which he could not respond. The condition is like being "possessed" and can be equated with an extreme form of alienation.[66]

At the end of this heinous act, the internal turmoil gives way to calm. What appeared to be a hallucinatory feeling vanishes, and the calmness that follows succeeds only in postponing his predicament.[67] He simply walked casually into a cafe as if nothing had happened. If Paul Fiddes is right, Jamie's problems are symptomatic of rebellion, manifesting unbelief, a lack of trust in the friendship offered to those who are estranged.[68] Thus, in the death of Eric, the surrogate victim, violence becomes a deformation of desire which goes beyond physical coercion to include a metaphysical transgression of the other.[69] Viewed against the background of the doctrine of atonement, Baldwin's storyline creates possibilities that allow for a helpful connection to the theology of Christ's death. In this sense, literature seems to continue where The Judeo-Christian Scripture ends and in another sense, it affirms the creative dimensions of the theological task that allows for the story of redemption to be interpreted through human experience as encapsulated in fiction.

THE CHRIST FIGURE IN LITERATURE

This brings to mind the possible similarities and dissimilarities between the figure of Eric and the innocent victims in biblical literature especially

---

66. Ibid., 164–65.

67. The calming effects of triumphant violence are not dissimilar to the effects of sexual and sport activities. Ibid., 152.

68. Fiddes, *Past Event and Present Salvation*, 6–7.

69. Hamerton-Kelly, *Sacred Violence*, 21.

with reference to Leviticus 16, and the New Testament text of the Letter to the Hebrews. Emphasis on a metaphorical use of language is advisable here especially because, for believers, Christ figures in literature will always fall short of the Christian model, a point John Sykes makes when he stresses that the Jesus Christ of faith has an unsubstitutable personal identity.[70] Nevertheless, there is no gainsaying the fact that if either the Romans or the Jewish establishment are, in one way or another, implicated in the death of Jesus, there is a correspondence between Eric and the figure of Christ. For instance, in both stories, punishment is meted out on an innocent victim, and death results. But while, from the Christian point of view, the vicarious death of Christ wipes away the pollution of sin both personal and universal, as well as re-establishes communion "vertically" with God and "horizontally" with humanity,[71] one can appreciate Eric's death only in terms of the elimination of the pollution of personal guilt. And if, as I have tried to argue, a refusal to confront his failings was at the center of Jamie's problem, getting rid of Eric would, at best, provide a "temporary" relief, just like the ceremony in Leviticus which has to be repeated annually in order to be effective. This is further evidence of the difference between the innocent victims of the Leviticus story and the Baldwin story on the one hand, and the innocent victim identified in the Letter to the Hebrews, on the other. In the former, both Eric and the animal in Leviticus have no option. But the salvific benefit in the latter came about through a willed one-time event that contrasts with the old system. The uniqueness of the Christ event is reinforced by the elements of the divine initiative in harmony with Gen 22:8 (God will provide the Lamb) through Romans 8:32 (God did not spare his Son but gave him) to the priest-victim motif in the theology of the Letter to the Hebrews.[72] Atonement in Christian theology also implies that the divine-human relationship can be repaired only through the specific event of Jesus which expresses and reveals the love of God from which everything

70. Cf. Sykes, "Christian Apologetic," 60–61.

71. Gunton, "Sacrifice and Sacrifices," 224.

72. The basic criticism of Israel's cult by the writer of Hebrews is that it did not achieve its intended goal—the removal of the barrier of sin given that it had to be repeated (Heb 10:4, 11). This, according to Isaacs, *Sacred Space*, 92 gives insight into the author of Hebrew's true purpose: "to move its readers away from understanding of sacrificial system as an essential part of maintaining contact with God, to an acceptance of and the Ascension of Christ as its replacement." See also Young, "Gospel According to Hebrews," 209 where it is pointed out that the concern of the writer of Hebrews is to demonstrate the importance of the old Levitical daily ritual which has now given way to a once-for-all sacrificial death on the cross.

else emanates. This love is the means by which reconciliation is effected, an event which is in consonant with the human quest for repentance.[73] It is a state of being which people hope for not only at the end of times but here and now.[74]

As it is, the Christian understanding of atonement is open to enrichment. In fact, as human predicament takes new shapes, new ways of expressing salvation are sure to emerge although it should not be presumed that newer images of atonement will capture all the facts of the Christian mystery. As evidence from history has shown, each of the diverse notions contributes to a wider understanding of God's act of reconciliation. This is because doctrine is always enriched when juxtaposed within the framework of human experience.[75] In its widest sense, Christian understanding of salvation has a healing dimension that not only includes individuals but the non-human world as well. On a narrower level, atonement and salvation can be restricted to restoring a relationship between human beings and God who are estranged from each other.[76]

Sad and paradoxical as it may seem, the "salvation"[77] sought by Jamie comes about through the murder of an innocent child. His was an attempt to re-establish the order that existed when there was neither wife nor child between him and Eric's father. And, if from a theological perspective, human desires should be directed towards spiritual goals (the transcendent) rather than be aroused by a neighbour's desires, Jamie's lot is tantamount to a "deviated transcendence," a state of affairs which Hamerton-Kelly might have equated with idol worship, the antidote to which lies faith in God.[78]

73. Dinsmore, *Atonement in Literature*, 20.

74. Fiddes, *Past Event and Present Salvation*, 4–5.

75. Dillistone, *Christian Understanding of Atonement*, 25–26.

76. Fiddes, *Past Event and Present Salvation*, 3.

77. Salvation (or more correctly "reconciliation") is here used loosely although, over the years, the term has been used interchangeably with "atonement." However, during the nineteenth century, a great deal of emphasis was placed on the differences rather than the similarities between salvation and atonement. The dissimilarities were accentuated by Aulen's study of three "main" types of atonement, namely: (i) Classical (God is both the reconciler and the reconciled), (ii) The subjective (reconciliation as the result of human action) and, (iii) Objective (that is the legalistic) as marshalled out in St. Anselm's *Cur Deus Homo*. While the classical and the subjective types equated atonement with salvation and vice versa, the objective type saw atonement as prior to salvation. Cf. Aulén, *Christus Victor*, 136.

78. Cf. Hamerton-Kelly, *Sacred Violence*, 21; and Gunton, "Sacrifice and Sacrifices," 214.

In the death of Eric, he projects his own "death" through failure. At another level, the violence on Eric is parallel to the ancient ritual of aversion and evokes an attempt to escape personal responsibilities.[79] Eric is at once the focus of Jamie's attention but he also enables him to *unload* from himself the guilt of failure.

FICTION AS SCRIPTURE

Although it is easy to say that Baldwin does not set out to frame a theology *per se*, yet, one cannot but admit that in "The Man Child" he succeeds in articulating sentiments that have profound implications for the theological task. Literary critics and theologians such as David Jasper[80] and Paul Fiddes recognize how works of literature are able to do this. Fiddes, for his part, observes that poems and works of fiction are quite able to hint at the sort of reality which human reason cannot completely grasp.[81] In this regard, novelists are able to move beyond theological pronouncements that sometimes place exaggerated emphasis on vague words and definitions which do no more than generate controversies.[82] Dinsmore makes a similar point in his observation that great artists, poets or story writers seem to say that we should: "let the theologians wrangle about their definitions . . . I will portray sin in hideous colors so lurid and in figures so heinous that men will see its true nature—see it so vividly that they will turn back their feet from the way of death."[83]

A work of literature can, therefore, not only elaborate dogma but also add vitality to it through its ability to capture various manifestations of human predicaments. Elsewhere, Jasper links this task to the very nature of the hermeneutic process. He argues that for text actualization to be relevant, its technique has to be ready not only to follow the narrative order of the given but has equally to be capable of undertaking a constructive "violation" of the text so as to extend its significance through creative responses.[84] Such responses, he says, might entail "reading against the grain

---

79. Cf. Fiddes, *Past Event and Present Salvation*, 74.
80. Jasper, *Study of Literature and Religion*.
81. Fiddes, *Freedom and Limit*, 12.
82. Dinsmore, *Atonement in Literature*, 23.
83. Ibid., 73.
84. See Jasper, "Violence and Post-Modernism," 802.

of accepted or common interpretations."[85] In a world where the doctrine of atonement (and indeed many other doctrines) seem to appear esoteric, it would seem that fiction, in tune with prevailing systems of thought and without watering down doctrine, is able to "reclothe" Christian teachings in ways that dogma cannot do, especially because the language of narrative art "finds such a ready niche in the discussion of our selves."[86]

Admittedly, theology's approach to the doctrine of the atonement of humanity with the deity through Scripture is understandable, at least from the point of view of the believer, but this is not to deny the fact that biblical texts are open to all sorts of possibilities. In Dinsmore's view, the advantages of interpreting the story of redemption by way of literature and the arts are obvious. Not only do artistic sensibilities offer new points of views, but through them:

> old truths become wondrously impressive, when seen from an unwonted angle; fresh relationships are discerned, and unsuspected means are revealed. And unusual methods promote clearness of thought . . . Moreover, reconciliation takes place between persons, and may well be studied from life [since fictional characters are very much like us]—life in its varied aspects as seen by the most penetrating observers . . . Literature is an interpreter of life and great writers are servants to the forces of nature.[87]

It is in this sense that "secular" texts of contemporary literature compare favourably with the "sacred" texts of various faiths, for in both sacred and secular texts:

> we find sin, defeating humanity, breaking the moral framework of the world; retribution, long delayed, hidden often, yet sure as the movements of the stars; reconciliation, obtained at great cost, but bringing peace with self, with the injured, and with God. Out of these three great realities grew what is noblest in art and profoundest in religion, and by studying them in the light of the world's ripest experiences we cannot fail to obtain valuable spiritual insights.[88]

---

85. Jasper, "Bible in Arts and Literature," 47. This method usually exposes "gaps, breaks, inconsistencies and problems" in the encounter between text and readers. Cf. also Bal, *Death and Dissymmetry*, 34.

86. Novitz, "Art, Narrative, and Human Nature," 57. See also Detweiler, *Breaking the Fall*, 31; and Dinsmore, *Atonement in Literature*, 13.

87. Dinsmore, *Atonement in Literature*, 5–7.

88. Ibid., 11.

Myth and the Scapegoat Rhetoric

ARTISTIC SENSIBILITY

The implication of the foregoing is that the story of redemption should be interpreted quite fruitfully through human experience as encapsulated in fiction, especially because the Scriptures assume that the divine is analogous to the human.[89] This is especially important given that the needs of each age will almost always manifest themselves in such a way that a particular theory or explanation will commend itself as more relevant than others at particular points in time. It therefore means that no absolute status should be accorded to any human formulation. Hence, theologians have to be constantly seeking to relate themselves imaginatively to the particular needs of each age.[90]

In the context of our study, the character of Eric's father, revealed without much elaboration, bears testimony to the humanity of fictional characters and reinforces the understanding that the imagination which creates such characters "forms a new world which has indirect reference to the world in which we live."[91] It is therefore, not surprising that Baldwin is able to use his artistic sensibilities to throw light on his conception of friendship and neighbourly love in such a tragic story.[92] Thus, having succeeded in buying out Jamie because of the latter's inability to manage his own affairs, Eric's father still hires him as a farmhand. Moreover, Eric's mother keeps Jamie's clothes clean and Jamie always shared in family's meals.[93] Jamie's birthday party is held in Eric's father's house where Eric's mother had baked a cake for the occasion and fills the house with flowers for Jamie's sake. In a sense, the moral response of Eric's father to his friend's predicament is that of the Good Samaritan, that is doing what we can to stop the suffering, to help those in need. Yet, Jamie, who was "so poetical in those days," a "creator" in a moment of madness, musters the rage that enables him to strangle Eric. Thus, a creator of a work of art, lacking peace of mind and unable to adjust to the realities of his own conditions, becomes a crusher of human life.

It is worthy of note that although, evil is not explicitly punished, nor is the kindness of Eric's father rewarded in the world of this story. Nonetheless,

---

89. Ibid., 15–16.
90. Cf. Dillistone, *Christian Understanding of Atonement*, 26.
91. This understanding is said to have prompted Coleridge's phrase that authors of fiction are "extenders of consciousness." Cf. Fiddes, *Freedom and the Limit*, 21.
92. Suites, "Fictional Characters are just Like Us," 105–8.
93. Baldwin, "Man Child," 58–59.

Baldwin, like other great writers, succeeds in using the deformation of human desire to confront an existential question.[94] By this, attention is also drawn to how all purveyors of violence who, like Jamie, are blinded by hate and are prone to violence as a means of solving problems.[95] In addition, the strangling of Eric highlights how death can often be employed as denouement in narratives as we see in "The Man Child" where: "passions have clashed and sin has displayed its dreadful hideousness, where guilt and innocence, blindness, folly, malignity, have struggled in feverish intensity, comes at last the repose of unconquerable death ... [Under such a situation], death becomes a symbol of eternal peace, beyond the raving malice of foes, an intimation of final vindication that reconciles the spectator to the fate of the guiltless victim."[96]

A question, which at its face value may seem redundant at this juncture, is whether or not Baldwin intends to resolve anything through the death of Eric. In articulating an answer to this question, the opinion of Etienne Balibar and Pierre Macherey recommends itself. They suggest that literary productions need not be studied from the standpoint of their unity which is illusory and false, but from their material disparity. One must not look for unifying effects but for signs of the contradictions which produced them and which appear as unevenly resolved conflict in the story.[97]

Granted that Eric's death is an isolated event, one would, following Dinsmore's reasoning, consider it an "imperfect" form of atonement because the consequences of evil in the lives of those involved in the tragic situation are never made up for. In fact, more hopes are dashed. The absurdity of the situation is further accentuated by Jamie. He does not even emerge as a prototype of the wicked tenants who kill the heir to their landlord's estate in the hope of inheriting the property (Mark 12:1–2). As he tightens his grip on Eric's throat, the little boy, in a flash of insight, begins to understand the basis of Jamie's anger; he offers Jamie the object of his desires. But the man answers: "The land shall belong to one."[98]

Such a *vicarious* death does shadow the Passion of Christ but it differs from the Christian understanding of the death of Christ which not only manifests God's willingness to forgive but also makes apparent the

---

94. Hamerton-Kelly, *Sacred Violence*, 88.
95. Dinsmore, *Atonement in Literature*, 107.
96. Ibid., 92–93.
97. Balibar and Macherey, "On Literature as an Ideological Form," 87.
98. Baldwin, "Man Child," 76.

divine condemnation of sin.[99] It is instructive that Baldwin does not work out the whole problem of reconciliation, a fact that is not surprising given that there is always a gap between verbal signs and the reality they seek to capture.[100] Nonetheless, "The Man Child" does stimulate the mind into the realisation that the primary forms of language about God are metaphors and stories, and that "only a kind of speech which resists being trapped in a single, fixed meaning can begin to express the mystery of the kingdom of God."[101]

APPRAISAL

Mimesis (imitation) and desire (wanting) are at the center of Girard's theory. Mimetic desire is the source of all human rivalries, misunderstandings, and the source of all disorder.[102] Ancient and modern mythologies, and biblical stories of sacrifice, help Girard to establish that the scapegoat mechanism is at the root of cultural formations or the *Things Hidden since the Foundation of the World*, the title of another work of Girard. This means that the human drive to imitate the other disrupts the fragile hierarchy of the "haves" and the "have-nots" such that the object of desire becomes progressively less important while it becomes easier for violence to be visited on a scapegoat.[103]

The immediate reaction to violent desire is the denial that a problem exists, that is, a playing of the proverbial ostrich. This is typified in Jamie's reaction at his birthday dinner when Eric's father made it clear that the money he paid Jamie for his estate was the best offer that was ever made to him. True to Girard's thesis, instead of going within himself to find out the root cause of his failures, that is undertaking an "examination of conscience," Jamie answers evasively: "I am not blaming you." Subsequent events which eventually led Jamie to pick on Eric, the weakest member of the family, soon prove that Jamie is indeed blaming Eric's father for his predicaments. Ironically, one cannot but infer from this act a yearning for a return to the happy times when his friendship with Eric's father was at its peak—with neither land, wife nor child to come between them. (Jamie does

---

99. Dinsmore, *Atone in Literature*, 207–8.
100. See for instance, Detweiler, *Breaking the Fall*, xii.
101. Fiddes, *Freedom and Limit*, 12.
102. Girard, *Scapegoat*, 165.
103. See Wallace, "Postmodern Biblicism," 312.

not, for instance, mince words when, in answer to Eric's question, "Why do you hate my father?" he answers: "I love your father.")[104]

We have also been able to articulate a connection between the poetics of violence in "The Man Child" and the fate of Christ played out in the violence of his executors. Eric's father did everything he could for his friend, but all he got in return was the strangling of his only child. More importantly Eric died for the sins he did not commit, and he was too weak to attempt any retaliation. In dying for the misdeeds of his father it would be appropriate to describe Eric as an archetype of Abel, the prophets and all societal scapegoats. One would add also that this interpretation is consistent with the biblical suggestion that if Christ identifies with victims, then anyone that injures another turns against him.[105] Eric's death is indeed vicarious, but in a limited way in that the meaningless death pulverizes the gospel stories which promote an "ethic of love" thereby focusing on how people should "rid themselves of the murderous lie that scapegoating is inevitable and necessary."[106] Moreover, in that he acknowledges that he loves Eric's father as he strangles the man's son, Jamie's predicament amounts to a dramatization of a deformed self.[107] Furthermore, like the gospels, "The Man Child" narrates the events of Eric's death from the perspective of the victim, pre-empting a dishonest reading. This is coherent with Girard's reading of Jesus' invitation to humanity "to devote themselves to the project of getting rid of violence . . . Escaping from violence is escaping . . . into another kingdom . . . the Kingdom of love, which is also the domain of the true God . . ."[108] Carried to its logical conclusion, it becomes possible to infer from the above line of thought that if Christians follow the injunction to reject violence and love their own enemies, they are on their way to perfection thereby affirming God as one who rejects violence as well as accommodates his enemies.[109]

---

104. Baldwin, "Man Child," 76.
105. Cf. Schwager, "Christ's Death," 118.
106. Wallace, "Postmodern Biblicism," 315.
107. Hamerton-Kelly, *Sacred Violence*, 197.
108. Girard, *Things Hidden*, 197.
109. Cf. Schwager, "Christ's Death," 111.

3

Tragedy
A Method of Inquiry

Man's inhumanity to man is part of being human.
—James Cameron

What might have been and what has been
Point to one end, which is always present.
—T. S. Eliot

At the core of tragedy lies the problem and mystery of evil.
—J. Cheryl Exum

INTRODUCTION

"Going to Meet the Man," the story that bears the title of James Baldwin's collection of short stories will be examined here as a tragic story, and as a consequence, the concept of tragedy will be used as a method of inquiry. The strategic presuppositions that underline this understanding are that tragedy deals with catastrophe, guilt, suffering and their symbiotic relationships, and that the tragic can exist, independent of the works of art which are thought to exhibit it. While the suffering that tragedy brings cannot be explained simply in terms of human action or inaction, it is relevant to literary and dramatic representations of action that lead to a loss or misfortune.[1] Following fruitful deductions from Aristotle, tragedy can be said to incorporate incidents that arouse pity and fear and embody some forms of catharsis beyond mere sensation or bodily feelings. What moves the audience to pity is the fact that the misfortunes of the characters in question seem to be greater than they deserve.[2] Walter Kaufmann's articulation of the phenomenon reinforces this understanding. He believes that tragedy, as a genre, moves into the center of immense human suffering and brings to mind our own forgotten and repressed sorrows as well as those of others. It has also the capacity to engender the realisation that suffering is universal and that the artistic representation of fates worse than our own can be emotionally and intellectually enriching.[3]

Larry Bouchard understandably cautions against an all-embracing definition of tragedy. He suggests that the genre can accommodate the plurality of thematic and structural possibilities inherent in various literary and philosophical traditions.[4] This fits well with the position articulated by

---

1. My use of the term "tragedy" is largely as a hermeneutical rather than as a "mathematical" tool. It is in keeping with what Richard Sewall would see in terms of tragic vision. Such a vision is "a way of viewing reality, an attitude of negation, uncertainty, and doubt, a feeling of unease in an inhospitable world." Cf. Exum, *Tragedy and Biblical Narrative*, 5, 10, with reference to Sewall, *Vision of Tragedy*.

2. Cf. Aristotle, "Poetics," 1460. For comment see Lloyd, *Aristotle*.

3. Kaufmann, *Tragedy and Philosophy*, 85. Richard Eldridge draws specific attention to the beneficial aspects of tragedy in arts and literature, noting that such benefits are rooted in the vulnerability of tragic figures, which points to human frailty; it generates fear in the reading or listening audience. Thus, "when A pities B, A must believe that B is suffering significantly, that B's suffering is underserved, and that A is herself liable to similar underserved suffering ... And when A fears for B, then A must believe that B is in pain and that future pain for B may be expected. The experience of fear for another involves an apprehensiveness about what is likely or liable to happen to human beings." Cf. Eldridge, "How Can Tragedy Matter for Us?" 287.

4. Bouchard, *Tragic Method*, 22. One has also to note, as Anthony Quinton does, that the classical environment of the Aristotelian tragedy was the extraordinary, the peculiar, the unrepeatable. Moreover, examples were drawn from a single literary tradition. Given that a heuristic application of the tragic vision has much wider implications, the

Ludwig Wittgenstein which sees tragedy as a "family of resemblances" embodying themes and questions that are open to multiple interpretations.[5] Thus, when flexibly managed, the classical understanding epitomized in the Aristotelian elements can apply to many plots all of which can at least, serve as a starting point for discussion of contemporary perspectives.[6]

While the Aristotelian vision does provide a starting point for critical analysis, tragedy has outgrown this dimension, and has acquired a much wider significance.[7] As noted above, there are numerous possibilities open to the genre. However, the tragic can frequently be viewed in terms of how manifestations of evil constitute a challenge to human reason, given that the latter is unable to provide all the answers to questions that life is constantly posing.[8] Hence, Cavell is persuaded that "tragic representations have some claim to being regarded as the most illusion free representations of reality."[9] And once such awareness is formed or renewed, ethical thinking develops a new and broader vision through its encounter with tragic art and literature.

This chapter will also examine strands of the tragic in "Going to Meet the Man" against the background of the understanding that "man's inhumanity to man is part of being human." Attention will be drawn to influential reflections on the genre, in order to show that literature forces one

---

demand that tragic representation in the arts be restricted to drama, is, according to Quinton, critically insufficient. Cf. Quinton, "Tragedy," 101–2. Similarly, Arthur Miller takes issue with narrow definitions of tragedy, pointing out that the genre is too profound to be pigeonholed. Its attraction, he says, is due to the human need to face the fact of death in order to prepare for life, in consequence of which there are too many variations of tragedy that will continue to elude simple definitions. Cf. Miller, *Collected Plays*, 33.

5. Cf. Bouchard, *Tragic Method*, 22 with reference to Wittgenstein, *Philosophical Investigation*.

6. Abrams, *Glossary*, 189–90, and Kaufmann, *Tragedy and Philosophy*, 59–69. The implication here is that a strict identification of the tragic with the dramatic form can be quite limiting. Cf. Frye, *Anatomy of Criticism*, 162.

7. Brereton, *Principles of Tragedy*, 27. In demonstrating how tragedy in general and Greek tragedies, in particular, resist theory, Exum, *Tragedy*, 2 argues that the description has been claimed for works of widely different characters. Moreover, since theories are based on existing tragedies, and then applied to other examples, theories are not absolute.

8. Cf. Cavell, *Disowning Knowledge*, 5.

9. Ibid. Cf. also Schier, "Tragedy and the Community of Sentiment," 84, where he notes that tragedy speaks with a universal voice. It reminds us that as humans, we are not islands and that to be in a community is to be bonded with others. Consequently, tragedy in literature and the arts disposes people to imaginatively share in fates that are not yet theirs.

to recognize and reflect on the realities of preventable evil and American racial politics. Using the problems posed by evil to demarcate the boundaries of the tragic has the advantage of presenting fictional characters as interpreters of experiences, although it cannot be presumed that their functions can answer all the questions related to the problem of evil.

The phenomenology of Emmanuel Lévinas will also be used as a guide with a view to demonstrating how tragedy in literature provides metaphysical comfort or the sort of knowledge that heals ignorance, even when what is learned is negativity, evil and desperate suffering.[10] As we shall also see, literary tragedy forces readers to confront uncomfortable truths and conflicts between values and ideals. Hence, "Going to Meet the Man," is examined here as an ironic rereading of the passion narrative. The story gives an account of negativity in life, an acknowledgement that, as Christ was abandoned on the cross (Mark 15:34), what seems to be godforsakenness can be disclosed as something even positive in human experience.[11]

FORMS OF A SUBJECT MATTER

One characteristic which "Going to Meet the Man" shares with others in the collection is that, although the presentation of action is minimal, flashback is the essential device with which the plot is sketched and the revelation of character effected.[12]

For instance, the story begins and ends with Jesse, a forty-two-year-old police officer, lying in bed fantasizing while trying, but not succeeding, to make love to his wife. His frustration triggers off a series of distractions in the form of recollections; firstly of how he used to get his sexual urges illicitly satisfied with black prostitutes.[13] With his status as a deputy police chief, such things are now beneath him. He remembers the events of his working day among the civil rights activists protesting against the exclusion

---

10. Ricoeur, *Symbolism of Evil*, 41–42.

11. Questioning whether or not the gospel is a tragedy is beside the point. Suffice it to say that whichever way one looks at it, there are moments within the gospel which have "points of contact with experiences of abandonment, estrangement, and oppression that remain dreadful and disturbing to Christians even after the Easter morning." Cf. Bouchard, *Tragic Method*, 233.

12. Cf. Jones, "Style, Form, and Content," 147.

13. Fantasy and dreams have often provided a fertile ground where the sexual attractions between the races in America are played out. See Whitlow, "Baldwin's Going to Meet the Man," 195.

Tragedy

of blacks in the voters' registration taking place at the county courthouse.[14] As a police officer, he had no opinion as to whether or not black Americans of the story were allowed to vote. His duty was simply to keep the peace, but he is finding it increasingly difficult to do so. In his resolve to, at least, force the protesters to stop singing, he decides to apply some force. As his foot catches the ringleader on the jaw, he shouts at him: "You make them stop singing." For the benefit of the other protestors, Jesse adds: "you are [all] going to stop coming down to the court house and disrupting traffic and molesting people and keeping us from our duties and keeping doctors from getting to [the] sick ... to give our town a bad name!"[15] Jesse is familiar with the song the protestors are singing, though "it was also the sound of which he had been least conscious—and it had always contained an obscure comfort. They were singing to God. They were singing for mercy, and they hoped to go to heaven, and he had even sometimes felt, when looking into the eyes of some of the old women, a few of the very old men, that they were singing for mercy for his soul too."[16]

The second phase of his recollection takes him back to when, as a young man in his twenties, his job provided him with opportunities to witness, first-hand, and how the illiterate among the blacks are cheated of their money—but what could he do? It was not his business to interfere in such matters. His mind then goes back in time to the lynching he witnessed at the age of eight. The incident provides his first exposure to sexual mutilation.[17] Jesse recalls how the news of the young black man who pushed down old Miss Standish reached their yard, the preparations of his parents to join the other townspeople, and his ride on his father's shoulders during the lynching. With the excitement in the air, preparation of food, and dressing up, little Jesse thought that he and his parents were going on the annual national day picnic. It eventually turned out to be a "picnic" he would never to forget, as the events "revealed to him a great secret which would be the

---

14. The civil rights demonstration led by blacks in Jesse's home town was a typical phenomenon in the 1960s. For more comments, see Millican, "Fire as the Symbol of Leadening Existence," 175.

15. Baldwin, "Going to Meet the Man," 235.

16. Ibid., 238.

17. See Whittle, "Baldwin's *Going to Meet the Man*," 194–204, 196. Refer also to Millican, "Fire as the Symbol," 172, where she contends that the excitement the lynching generated in Jesse's parents and in the mob are comparable to a form of conjugal bliss. Traces of this line of reasoning are evident in the thought of René Girard. Cf. Chapter 2 of this study.

key to his life forever."¹⁸ Finally, as his recollection of the man left hanging many years before merges with his thought of the protestor whose jaw he smashed earlier in the day, Jesse regains his erection and the capacity to fulfil his conjugal obligation.

Although tragedy is not something to be sought or accepted when it can be avoided, philosophers, theologians and literary critics have come to acknowledge that it is sometimes inevitable.¹⁹ For instances, the legitimate pursuit of a legitimate end or an act which is virtuous may bring about injustice, suffering and evil, or severe loss to others. This may either be due to the intentions of the moral agent, or it may be the result of the consequences of an unintended act or omission as it is the case with the young man who was hung for allegedly pushing down an old lady or the leader of the civil rights protesters whose jaw was smashed by a police officer doing a duty for which he is paid.²⁰ The point of interest in this chapter is the contribution which literature makes to the understanding of evil and suffering that admit of a cause; that is where human agency plays a role. In this regard, God does not have to be directly responsible for the suffering that results from human action. Yet, as theologian Joseph Selling reminds us in a 1990 essay on suffering, this does not remove the insinuation that where suffering prevails, human action and/or inaction "might appear more powerful than God's mercy and love."²¹ Moreover, the challenge posed by incidents of severe negativity, whether private or public, seem to indicate that the ways of God do not always seem to flow in the same direction as those of humans. A refusal to acknowledge this fact creates the impression that religious faith functions merely as an instrument of escape from reality rather than the truthful illumination of the human condition.²²

FUNDAMENTAL ELEMENTS

To facilitate a detailed examination of how "Going to Meet the Man" functions as a tragic story in light of the foregoing description of the

---

18. Baldwin, "Going to Meet the Man," 245.

19. More representative surveys on the subject of evil—preventable or not—can be found in Lambrecht and Collins, *God and Human Suffering*.

20. Barbour, *Tragedy as a Critique of Virtue*, 176–77; and Gustafson, *Ethics from a Theocentric Perspective*, 21.

21. Cf. "Moral Questioning and Human Suffering," 156.

22. Bouchard, *Tragic Method and Tragic Theology*, 228.

phenomenon, we shall draw on the methodological insights of Dorothea Krook. Inspired by her reading of Aristotle's *Poetics*,[23] Krook identifies four elements of tragedy: shame, suffering, knowledge, and catharsis.[24] She admits that the elements are closely related to one another but that it is difficult to understand one without reference to others. Thus they mutually modify one another. For the purpose of this study, the elements are treated as an optimal set of constitutes, and not as mathematical formulae. This is in keeping with the understanding that works can contain some of the elements necessary for a tragic vision yet lack other elements. At other times, works which may be thought of as "tragic" may not embody elements that theoretically disrupt the manifestation of the phenomenon.[25]

"Shame," which is at the top of Dorothea Krook's list, defines the events which precipitate the spectacle of suffering. Such acts may be committed by the tragic hero or heroine, although this is not a necessary precondition. It need not be actually committed; it is enough that it is intended or merely imagined. Aware that there are sometimes difficulties in coming to a precise understanding of what constitutes a specific act of shame, Krook notes that the important issue is to determine the act or situation that directly precipitates the central spectacle of suffering. The foregoing account of shame helps one to appreciate the tension surrounding the lynching of the black man in "Going to Meet the Man." He is, as it were, being punished for the "shameful" act of knocking down an old lady.[26]

Another element of tragedy is suffering. Suffering, in the sense that Krook explains it, must be felt to be intense and real; it must attain, in the given circumstances, the furthest reach of human suffering; it must be real both in the ordinary sense of being genuine or sincere and also in the more important sense of being commensurate with its cause. Moreover, the suffering must be felt to be fatally undermining or destructive, involving absolute loss and deprivation for the suffering human vessel. Generally

---

23. Especially Books 13 and 14.

24. Krook, *Elements of Tragedy*, 9–10. Brereton, *Principles of Tragedy*, 27, adds that far more than Aristotle actually said, the elements of tragedy such as those deducted by Krook from her reading of Poetics constitute Aristotle's legacy.

25. Brereton points out that tragedy can equally be used metaphorically, "or with exaggeration which, if it cannot be properly called humorous, is not wholly serious either." Cf. *Principles of Tragedy*, 7; and Powell, *Metaphysical Quality of the Tragic*, 18.

26. Baldwin, "Going to Meet the Man," 246. This, of course, brings to mind the notion of hamartia, the flaw usually woven into the characters of tragic heroes. Cf. Eldridge, "How Can Tragedy Matter for Us?" 288.

(though not invariably, she says), it may culminate in death, that is, the ultimate form of loss and deprivation in human experience. Suffering here can take tangible forms, or as Krook says, it may be somewhat intuitive, and perhaps, not completely understood.[27]

The fate of the victim in the story under scrutiny seems to fit into Krook's thesis. In the story, Baldwin invites the reader to visualize the victim with his hands bound straight above his head, as his weight is pulled downwards, towards the fire set beneath his naked body, held in an iron chain that is attached to the branch of a tree. As the agony progresses, a man steps forward to fuel the fire. At that instant, the eight-year-old Jesse, riding on his father's shoulders, hears the victim scream. He noted that the victim's head "went back, the mouth wide open, blood bubbling from the mouth; the veins of the neck jumped out . . . The cry of the people rose to answer the dying man's cry. He wanted death to come quickly. They [the crowd] wanted death to wait; and it was they who held death, now, on a leash which they lengthened little by little."[28]

As the fire licked the naked body, little Jesse smelled the odour of burning flesh. In the interval, someone, a friend of Jesse's father, brought out a knife. This made the crowd laugh. But as the man with the knife walked up to the hanging body, silence fell over the field and the hanging head looked up: he seemed to be

> fully conscious now, as though the fire had burned out terror and pain. The man with the knife took the nigger's private parts in his hand, one hand, still smiling, as though he were weighing them . . . Then Jesse screamed, and the crowd screamed as the knife flashed, first up, then down, cutting the dreadful thing away, and the blood came roaring down. Then the crowd rushed, rushed forward, tearing at the body with their hands, with knives, with rocks, with stones, howling and cursing.[29]

The third element in tragedy is "knowledge." This may also involve pleasure derived from the suffering and agony associated with the first element of tragedy discussed earlier. For the knowledge in question to be profound, Krook points out that it has to have the quality of "illuminating some

---

27. Cf. Simon, *Pity and Terror*, 52: "tragedy itself, though it involved disaster and suffering, need not end in death." Cf. also Krook, *Elements of Tragedy*, 12.

28. Baldwin, "Going to Meet the Man," 249.

29. Ibid., 251.

fundamental aspects of human nature and condition."[30] This, however, does not mean that the victim shall gain the knowledge that issues from the suffering; rather that the audience shall gain it. Such knowledge spares the audience the protagonist's struggles and reveals the "limits of meaning and order which is something the protagonist in a tragedy does not know."[31]

In "Going to Meet the Man," for instance, one notices that Jesse, while watching the execution, unconsciously began to transcend his immediate surroundings, thinking and asking, "what did the man do?"[32] Although he does not have the courage to voice this question to his father, he seems satisfied that he has now come to know the extent to which human brutality can go. Eldridge rightly points out that tragedy "illuminates the kinds of things that happen in human life."[33] Hence, looking at his mother in the midst of participant-observers at the execution ground, Jesse realizes that her eyes are very bright, her mouth is open and she seems to be more beautiful and "more strange" than he ever saw her.[34] It follows, as has already been suggested, that the knowledge generated by a tragic situation does not necessarily take the form of self-knowledge neither of the protagonist, nor of the victim. Rather, the tragic, in and through the self of the tragic victim, illuminates for the audience some fundamental aspects of human brutality.[35] That, in a way, seems to explain why, after taking in the lynching spectacle, Jesse comes to the realisation that his father is right to point out that he will never forget the "picnic" the family had just been involved in.[36] The knowledge which people derive from the experience of tragedy is reinforced further if one examines the natural desire to come to grips with reality. In this process, it usually does not matter whether or not the truth of the knowledge gained is pleasure-giving since the insight gained usually makes claim on our response despite conscious or unconscious effort to block it out.[37]

30. It does not matter whether or not such knowledge adds to anybody's happiness. Indeed, as Flint Schier argues, there are instances where humans are prepared to sacrifice some happiness in exchange for knowledge. Cf. "Claim of Tragedy," 21.

31. Reiss, *Tragedy and Truth*, 11.

32. Baldwin, "Going to Meet the Man," 249.

33. Eldridge, "How Can Tragedy Matter?" 288.

34. Baldwin, "Going to Meet the Man," 250.

35. Krook, *Elements of Tragedy*, 13; and Eldridge, "How Can Tragedy Matter?"

36. Baldwin, "Going to Meet the Man," 251.

37. According to Shier, "Tragedy and the Community of Sentiment," 87, knowledge in this context is necessitated neither by complete understanding nor practical reason

Artists, poets and creative writers therefore do their audience the favour of providing, through their creativity, pictures of human nature which the audience ought to know about but are sometimes inclined to ignore.[38] The point is that it is natural to yearn for certain forms of knowledge and for the resulting fulfilment to be for one's own good. And if knowing our predicament is part of our good, Flint Schier contends that the knowledge humans glean in the tragic encounter is also for their own good. Nevertheless, it is not as though humans start with an abstract desire to know and then go collecting information which is valued simply as a means to the end of satisfying abstract desires to obtain knowledge. Rather, there are certain facts which humans simply want to know, such as those facts that pertain to the human predicament; and because we want to know about them, finding out about those facts strikes us as rewarding even when we are not made happier. Hence, Jesse's father is, indeed doing him a favour by letting him witness how a mob can whip up emotion and frenzy. The boy learns what it is like for a victim, and understands his misfortune, the suffering and despair, what life can offer, the gruesomeness notwithstanding. The advantage of this experience for the little boy calls to mind the fact that unless one such as the Nietzschean superman were an emotional cripple, tragedy would have no grip on the imagination. Moreover, there would be no need to know the nature and causes of human suffering.[39] On the contrary, tragedies are instructive not only with regard to the occurrence of particular incidents, as in a chronicle or list of events but further as in all human life and its liabilities.[40]

Krook approaches the fourth element of tragedy by way of the theory of catharsis. This theory emphasizes the paradoxical and the final effect of tragedy as it attempts to explain how a spectacle can elicit aesthetic pleasure and pain simultaneously.[41] Having been exposed to a spectacle of suffer-

---

alone. Rather, it is freely given and demands universal accent, although certain responses to the tragic are more appropriate than others.

38. See Schier, "Claims of Tragedy," 22, where a distinction is made between "lower" and "higher" forms of knowledge. In this regard, the lower forms of knowledge points to those one would not purchase at the price of any great pain. On the other hand, the higher forms of knowledge are those one is ready to risk everything in order to achieve.

39. Cf. Schier, "Claim of Tragedy," 22–23.

40. Eldridge, "How Can Tragedy Matter for Us?" 288.

41. Catharsis can also take a metaphorical connotation although the extent to which this is applicable to Aristotle's usage is open to debate. See Brereton, *Principles of Tragedy*, 28; and Packer, "Dissolving the Paradox of Tragedy," 209.

ing in drama, art or literature, one would expect to feel depressed by the hopelessness of the human condition. Krook contends that what one feels is something quite different. One feels liberated from pain and fear; not depressed or oppressed, but in a curious way exhilarated; not angry and bitter but somewhat reconciled; our faith in humanity and the human condition is not destroyed or undermined, but restored, fortified, reaffirmed. This, she says, is the affirmation or the reaffirmation of the dignity of being human and the worthwhileness of human life which, in great tragedy issues from the spectacle of suffering itself and the knowledge that suffering yields.[42] In Aristotelian terms, the pity and fear generated by the artistic redescription of the tragic effects a "purging" of human emotions. Hence, tragedy or tragic spectacle can have a therapeutic function.[43]

The catharsis theory assumes that an audience values tragedy for its purgative effects and takes pleasure in the arousal of painful emotions. The assumption is that the pain given in a tragic work of art is rewarded when one is restored to the real world. It is an approach that hints at hedonism, implying also that a sort of duplicity is generated in the mind of the audience such that the thought of calamity brings distress as well as *relief*. But if fear and pity induced by a work of art bring relief to the imagination, why can the same thing not be said of the calamities outside the theatre? In other words: if we value tragedy because it awakens "disagreeable" emotions and if the said painful experiences are intrinsically bad, why do people still value the disturbing qualities of tragedy? What is there to gain in reading "Going to Meet the Man"?[44]

MORAL SENSITIVITY

In trying to explore this paradox, it will be helpful to attempt to juxtapose the catharsis argument deduced from Aristotle with the conversion hypothesis of David Hume. Hume's line of thought emerged from an attempt to come to terms with the pleasure humans take in watching or reading about

---

42. Krook, *Elements of Tragedy*, 14.

43. The research of Lloyd, *Aristotle*, 280–81, shows that Aristotle was influenced by the uses of catharsis in diverse contexts of his time. In the area of medicine, for instance, catharsis was thought to be synonymous with getting rid of the causes of diseases in the body. In the religious context, on the other hand, it connotes ritual purification, that is, a return to physical and psychological well-being.

44. Cf. Schier, "Claims of Tragedy," 10–13.

a tragic spectacle, or more broadly, the representation in art of what the average human being would generally avoid in real life. For Hume, when an audience is viewing a well-written work of tragedy, two are created in the mind.[45] The noteworthy features of this principle are first, that there is a "quantitative" difference between the two movements in the mind, one predominant and the other subordinate; second, that there is a "qualitative" difference between the two movements, one, agreeable, and the other disagreeable; finally, aided by the quality of performance or the ingenuity of the artist, the subordinate movement is converted into the predominant one.[46] In the words of Hume, this implies that "the uneasiness of melancholy passion is not only overpowered and effaced by something stronger of an opposite kind, but the whole impulse of those passions is converted into pleasure."[47] Hume further treats the dominant movement of the mind as an "object of experience," while the subordinate movement is linked to the subjective aspects of the audience. What emerges from the Human point of view is that the pleasure one takes in artistic description of tragedy is the dominant emotion, while pity and terror are the subordinate emotions. Hume's solution seems to hint at a denial of the possible simultaneity of contrary effects in the experience of a tragic spectacle.[48]

In the context of our study, the overall import of the hypothesis is that tragedy in the arts increases human sensitivity to suffering.[49] As a consequence, something that would have caused sadness and pain may possibly become an object of enjoyment through artistic presentation.[50] This is not to suggest that readers would, for instance, always feel either pleasure or pain rather than a combination of both after reading "Going to Meet the Man."

---

45. Hume, "Of Tragedy," 242. See also Paton, "Hume on Tragedy," 121–32; and Hill, "Hume and the Delightful Tragedy Problem," 321.

46. Hill, "Hume and the Delightful Tragedy Problem," 323.

47. Hume, "Of Tragedy," 241.

48. Packer, "Dissolving the Paradox of Tragedy," 212. See also Hill, "Hume and the Delightful Tragedy Problem," 322; and Paton, "Hume on Tragedy," 122.

49. This, for Flint Schier, is the main criterion for a realistic work of art: that it succeeds in making its audience feel that the characters as represented deserve the same emotional response as real people in similar situations would deserve. Cf. Shier, "Tragedy and the Community of Sentiment," 89. See also Hill, "Hume and the Delightful Tragedy Problem," 322.

50. Cf. Packer, "Dissolving the Paradox of Tragedy," 212.

One other suggestion as to how to account for the paradox of tragedy can be deducted from the "meta-response" argument articulated by Susan L. Feagin.[51] For Feagin, a tragic story produces in the audience knowledge that only compassionate people would feel pain for others who are in the circumstances depicted in the story.[52] But the viability of this approach, as Packer points out, is dependent on the possibility of ascribing three characteristics to the emotions involved in tragic response: namely, (i) contrariety, which in this case involves pleasure and pain; (ii) simultaneity, as the pleasure and pain of tragic response can be experienced at the same time, and (iii) intentionality, where the pleasure takes the pain as its object.[53] One can add here, as Packer does, that the last point presupposes that "there is a pleasure in the shared sense of humanity which one experiences with those whose suffering causes our tragic pain and with those, like ourselves, who feel pain for them."[54] But this does not address satisfactorily the pleasure humans derive from watching or reading a good work of tragedy.

Can aesthetics be helpful in explaining the paradox? In this approach, we find the tragic occurrences, when experienced aesthetically, are divorced from their usual practical consequences. As it were, the audience is freed from all ethical responsibility while being excited but not sensitized. But this raises the question as to whether the relation between pleasure and pain in tragic literature is casual or intentional.[55] Moreover, there is also the problem that if one reduces tragedy in the arts and literature to the purely aesthetic, one would, for instance, be in a position to sympathize with victims of all kinds but without being fully instructed by events depicted in the works. This, of course, amounts to a failure to express one's sense of the possibilities and liabilities in meaningful human life, that is, to participate imaginatively in other people's emotions.[56]

Aristotle and his readers, have thus far, provided a starting point on tragedy, a phenomenon one can now see as an imaginative representation of a fundamental aspect of human resilience.[57] Adjusted, the four elements

---

51. Cf. Feagin, "Pleasure of Tragedy," 95–104.
52. Packer, "Dissolving the Paradox of Tragedy," 212–14.
53. Ibid., 213.
54. Ibid.
55. Ibid., 214; and Eaton, "Strange Kind of Sadness," 51–64.
56. Schier, "Claims of Tragedy," 20.
57. Cf. Quinton, "Tragedy," 101–2, shares the same view. He adds that tragedy in art, drama and narrative fiction represents a condensed, heightened and telling representation

of the concept deducted from Aristotle exhibit their relevance from their connection with existential questions, all of which are worked out in Baldwin's "Going to Meet the Man." The act of shame ascribed to the victim in the story is thus a violation of a specific moral order as defined by the mob of executioners. But even if the suffering precipitated by the act is, for any reason, not considered arbitrary, the brutal mob negates all moral responsibilities in that the lynching, the punishment for the crime of pushing down old Miss Standish, is obviously out of all proportion.[58] For Jesse the insight that issues from the suffering and pain of the victim illuminates a vindication of the emphasis generally placed on tragedy—it provides knowledge of how things are. Nonetheless, whether or not such knowledge gives happiness is of secondary significance; it reconciles humans to evil, enabling them perhaps not to accept it, but at least to acknowledge it[59] in affirmation of the worthwhileness of life.[60] Tragedy need not result in a calming experience, however. Indeed, the lessons one learns from the tragic spectacle in "Going to Meet the Man" are painful. Nonetheless, whether painful or pleasant, the knowledge gained has the possibility of being beneficial since, as noted earlier, the plot of the story sensitizes; it affirms the idea that there is neither a mortally nor an aesthetically relevant difference between witnessing tragic events as they unfold and the artistic depiction of same.[61] That is why the mimetic theory of tragic pleasure as articulated by Schier is quite instructive; it enables one to understand that the mixture of pain and pleasure elicited by a reading of "Going to Meet the Man" are proof of Baldwin's creative insights.[62]

FICTIONAL QUALITY OF HISTORY

In the light of the foregoing, one is persuaded that "Going to Meet the Man" is a tragic story of public execution. With it Baldwin attempts to articulate, in fictional form, the experiences of African Americans—inventing a

---

of the place of human beings in the universe, their situation and the possibilities of action open to them.

58. Krook, *Elements of Tragedy*, 19.

59. See Schier, "Claims of Tragedy," 21.

60. Krook, *Elements of Tragedy*, 18; and Quinton, "Tragedy," 104 with reference to Nietzsche, *Birth of Tragedy*.

61. Eldridge, "How Can Tragedy Matter for Us?" 292.

62. For further comments, see Schier, "Claims of Tragedy," 10–13.

fresh perspective as he retells a story that, in a sense, feeds into the passion narrative.⁶³ His approach echoes the distinction which critical theorists draw between *literary form* and *subject matter* such as is exemplified by the distinction between the story under study and various historical accounts of actual public executions. An example that readily comes to mind is the account of James Cameron about the lynching of two youths on August 7, 1930, at a police station in Marion, Indiana, USA recorded in his autobiography.⁶⁴

In the context of our study, it can be said that while Baldwin's "Going to Meet the Man" as a work of fiction deals with incidents which readers might never have encountered, Cameron's autobiographical account contains passages that describe historical events, persons and real places.⁶⁵ Despite the fact that they are presented under different logical constraints and emphasize different types of discourse, read as intertext, they are concerned with tragic fallouts resulting from mob frenzy. This clarification paves the way for a discussion on what can be gained when creative writers fictionalize actual events.

A juxtaposition of Baldwin's story and the account of Cameron automatically raises questions about truth value in works of fiction. To put it more bluntly, why does one have to worry about tragedy in fiction when there are enough incidents of severe negativity all over the news? Which of the two genres contributes more to the representation of the reality of the African American experiences in the context of racial politics? Which of the stories has a more imaginative denouement or which has a better explanation of how mob action is triggered off?

One way of approaching this problem is to argue that there is always a fictional quality in history. Hayden White, champion of this view, claims that historical narratives have no claims to superiority over fiction. To him, historical accounts are merely "verbal fictions," whose contents are as much *invented as found* with "characteristics which they share more with literature than with the sciences."⁶⁶ This point of view recognizes further that

63. Cf. Lamarque and Olsen, *Truth, Fiction and Literature*, 263.

64. *A Time of Terror*.

65. From a historical perspective, a documentary came about to fulfil the need to inform people: "It takes real people and real problems from the real world and deals with them. It sets value on intimate observation and assesses its worth according to how well it succeeds in capturing reality." Cf. Trin, *When the Moon Waxes Red*, 33; and also Stott, *Documentary Expression*, 73.

66. Lamarque and Olsen, *Truth, Fiction and Literature*, 304, with reference to White,

an historical account involves suppression, subordination, the highlighting and foregrounding of certain aspects of a story. Consequently, some elements are given special attention, while others are simply not mentioned at all. Hence, a historical account cannot but have a limited scope since the criteria for selection of facts that can be identified within a certain period of time, and within a limited geographical area, are almost always, determined arbitrarily.[67] What emerges from this relativist line of thought is that the criteria relevant to establishing the truth of a historical claim vary radically with the type of claim in question.[68]

Another approach to the problem involves the suggestion that literature provides insights, the resources that enable us to relate more meaningfully with our world. This explains, as Lamarque and Olsen point out, why, since the beginning of the novel tradition, writers of fiction have yearned to be taken quite seriously. They cite Charles Dickens, who, in his preface to *Oliver Twist*, contends that it is useless to discuss whether the characters depicted in the story seem natural or unnatural, probable, right or wrong, since to Dickens, they are a true representation of humanity. Graham D. Martin makes the same point, adding that fictional entities such as characters, places, events or action are collages of "familiar bits and pieces." Hence a fiction will "never be entirely fictitious in the sense of there being nothing anywhere that corresponds to it in any way: there will indeed always be things that correspond to its every detail, somewhere, in some way. In short, all its constituent parts will be drawn from reality. It is their non-occurrence together, in that combination, that constitutes the fiction."[69]

This also calls to mind Jasper's contention that the "imagination is able to play over certain images which are rooted in a 'given' set of historical circumstances, and in so doing obtains a release from a simple adhesion

---

"Historical Text as a Literary Artifact."

67. Lamarque and Olsen, *Truth Fiction and Literature*, 304. Among postmodern historians, there is even the view that the past is unknowable because it is no longer with us, and that the language through which we apprehend it is the historian's language, which is subjective and very open to various interpretations. See Evans, "Trust Lost in Vain Views," 18, with reference to Jenkins, *Re-thinking History*; and Munslow, *Deconstructing History*.

68. To be blunt this point of view, the absolutist theorists of truth argue that a "truth claim is true if and only if it corresponds to facts, independently of the beliefs, and criteria of individual communities." Cf. Editor's "Introduction," the *Bible as Rhetoric*, 6.

69. Cf. Martin, "New Look at Fictional Reference," 229.

to fact, which is rediscovered afresh in an eternity of new circumstances which fiction is constantly unearthing."[70]

Flint Schier's view on the advantages of fiction over history and documentary as far as the acquisition of knowledge is concerned, merits attention. According to him, "close knowledge" associated with real-life experiences can lead to intense sympathy that tends to becloud human judgment. This is unlike what one can, for instance, gain in a theatre or in the reading of tragic literature where one can achieve intimacy but with sufficient distance to allow for intellectual enrichment.[71] Moreover, the instinctive capacity to endure enables people in distress to conduct themselves in such a way as to cover up the fullest extent of the pain to the onlooker. Hence real distress is often much less powerfully expressed than theatrical/fictional distress partly because people rarely want to be confronted with the stark realities of their lives. This is very much in keeping with the tendency to use euphemism or to play down the human situation with clichés and hopes that are founded only in a desire to escape the truth. Schier argues that the great artist escapes this restriction by letting their characters speak and act in a much more revealing way than would an actual victim of disaster.[72]

What emerges so far is that although Baldwin's story of the lynching of a black young man and Cameron's account of his experiences many years ago belong to different genres, it is not difficult to identify how events, situations, characters and relationships in one story feed into those in the other. Imaginative response necessarily merges "what might have been" in Baldwin's fiction with "what has been" in a documentary such as the Cameron story. As it is, each of the authors adds sequence and coherence to the collective experiences of African Americans, and the state of race relations in America.[73] Thus, granted that Baldwin might not have invented public executions, he uses his creativity to articulate new aspects of the phenom-

---

70. Cf. Jasper, *Coleridge as Poet*, 152. See also Walter Benjamin's remark: "Nothing is poorer than a truth expressed as it was thought." *One-Way Street and Other Writings*, 95, which validates the power of fiction to reclothe and evaluate human experiences. Given that human beings exist largely within a world created by language, philosophers of literature believe that the interaction between reading and writing gives a humanly interesting content to works of the imagination. Thus, when the epistemic status of rhetoric is juxtaposed with texts, some kind of link with religion can always be established. See Lamarque and Olsen, *Trust, Fiction and Literature*, 291–92, 289.

71. Schier, "Claims of Tragedy," 24.

72. Ibid.

73. See Carr, *Time, Narrative and History*, 168.

enon in his country. Moreover, if literature is *poesis* in the sense that its functionality does not depend entirely on eyewitness reports, Baldwin does not merely retell the story of a particular lynching; rather, he invents a new world in order to highlight themes in African American experience which, for our purpose, provide grounds for philosophical and theological analysis, and finally for Christian ethics.[74]

EMMANUEL LÉVINAS: ONESELF AS ANOTHER

This section of the study is framed, in part, by an examination of the phenomenology of Emmanuel Lévinas as complemented by his readers. The idea here is to draw some lessons from his understanding of empathy, as well as direct attention to what Bouchard sees as the ambiguity of human responsibility, actions and reactions in the interpretation of tragedy.[75] For instance, one notices that while the victim in "Going to Meet the Man" was being emasculated, the crowd roared in excitement. Jesse, on his father's back, screamed also when he caught the eye of the dying man hanging on a tree.[76]

For Emmanuel Lévinas, the simple and everyday fact of one person looking into another's eye has a profound significance: it is a gesture that has both a metaphysical as well as an ethical dimension, given that it is at the very heart of the difference between the self and the *other*.[77] Reference to the face here goes beyond the human figure that could, for instance, be portrayed by picture or painting. It embraces what one experiences or realizes, feels or knows when one's visage is "touched" by another person's looks. It is like an appeal.[78] Thus, for Lévinas, in the face of the other, one

---

74. Cf. Lamarque and Olsen, *Truth, Fiction and Literature*, 262.

75. Bouchard, *Tragic Method*, 12–15.

76. For the eight-year-old boy, that particular instant was, on one hand, a moment of personal "entanglement," that one might as well describe an encounter with the grotesque. For Millican, "Fire as the Symbol," 173, the scene can, on the other hand, be perceived as being symptomatic of the coalescence of the love and hate which run through the story.

77. Lévinas, *Collected Philosophical Papers*, 21.

78. Lévinas, "Ethics as First Philosophy," 83: "The Other becomes my neighbour precisely through the way the face summons me, calls for me, begs for me, and in so doing recalls my responsibility, and calls me into question." To justify how this phenomenon functions, Peperzak writes that language "evokes the speech addressed to me, some living man or woman, and not the linguistic structures or anonymous meanings that can be

is confronted with an exceptional or extraordinary fact that is at once and necessarily a *command and a norm*. Hence, by seeing another looking at me, or by hearing a voice, I "know" myself to be obliged... His or her visage renders what is communicated and the one who is communicating.[79]

In the ordinary scheme of things, there may, indeed, be a number of reasons why one person looks at another. One can, for instance, see another as a person one needs in order to survive or realize certain goals given that "we all belong to different communities in which we function more or less well on the basis of reciprocal needs."[80] But one can equally observe another human being from an aesthetic point of view, taking note of the color of his or her eyes and other facial characteristics. In the phenomenology of Lévinas, none of these ways of consciousness allows the *otherness* of the other to fully reveal itself because the descriptions that start from these perspectives are immediately integrated by the onlooker's self-centered and dominating consciousness which transform those phenomena into moments of the onlooker's material or spiritual possessions.[81] Hence, there is always the need to make a distinction between the "totality of being" and "being in itself," that is, there has always to be "something other than being" given that consciousness is never so universal as to embrace also the whole of its own being.[82]

---

studied objectively or practised by a style-conscious author. Primordially, it is not what is said that is important:: even if the words are nonsensical, there is still their being addressed. Neither is it relevant who speaks to me; any other is revelation of the Other; and peculiar features deserving special attention would only lead me away from the absolute otherness that is at stake." Cf. Peperzak, "The Only for the Other," 441.

79. Hence one's responsibility to another "does not come from fraternity, but fraternity denotes responsibility for another, antecedent to my freedom." Cf. Lévinas, "God and Philosophy," 167.

80. Cf. Peperzak, "The One for the Other," 440, with reference to Lévinas, *Totality and Infinity*, especially Section III, which Lévinas devotes to "Exteriority and the Face."

81. To capture the views of European continental thinkers such as Soren Kierkegaard (1813–1855), Albert Camus (1913–1980), and Jean-Paul Sartre (1905–1980), on this subject, Christine Pohl cites Martin Buber: "If you observe the individual in himself then you can see of the person as it were only as much as we see a moon; only the person with another person creates a rounded picture." Cf. "Is Grief Self-Regarding," 23.

82. In the thinking of Rene Descartes (1596–1650), this can be equated with God; an entity he claims manifests more reality in the infinite substance than in the finite substance. Although this infinite cannot be fully grasped by consciousness, human awareness of this infinite is prior to the awareness of the finite, or as Descartes puts, "my awareness of God must be prior to my awareness of myself." See Descartes, *Philosophical Writings*, 224–25. For comment, see Cottingham, *Descartes Dictionary*, 90–91.

Echoing Lévinas, one can at this stage argue that if Jesse is touched by the tragic spectacle or conscious of being concerned for the victim of public execution, it is not because of anything special about the victim but purely because of his human *otherness*.[83] As it were, this otherness "transcends the limits of a little boy's [self-]consciousness and its horizon such that the victim's look and voice surpass him!—they are too much for Jesse's capacity of assimilation. One can suggest also that Jesse's shock at the horror echoes the irreducibility and non-relativity or absoluteness by means of which the *other* implores or commands the onlooker:

> You are not allowed to kill me: you must accord me a place under the sun and everything that is necessary to live a truly human life! This demands not only the omission of criminal behaviour, but simultaneously a positive dedication: the other's face facing me makes me responsible for his/her and this responsibility has no limit.[84]

Thus, for Lévinas, a chance encounter with another's face is the ground of ethics; the gesture "reveals my being-for-the-other and the inexhaustible responsibility contained in the structure."[85] There is therefore a connection between the selfhood of an ego and the italicize of the other which, for

---

83. Cf. Michael Purcell who writes in "Ethical Significance of Illeity," 133: "the face of the Other reveals itself as absolutely beyond and above me, it is not because he or she is powerful, but because my power has been brought to an end." One can add that in the eye contact with Jesse, the victim of public execution reveals his humanness: "his defenceless eyes and powerlessness confront little Jesse whose head, as he beheld the brutality, of its own weight, fell forward toward his father's head." Baldwin, "Going to Meet the Man," 251.

84. Cf. Peperzak, "The One for the Other," 442. Traces of this line of argument can be found in the thought of Karl Jaspers (1883–1969) who was very much aware of the distinction between "others" as objects and "others" as beings like myself. Cf. Jaspers, *Way to Wisdom*, 30. Refer also to Martin Buber's distinction between "I-It" and the "I-Thou" types of human responses. In the latter, all things, including people are objects to be experienced but in the former, people are encountered not only as objects but as persons in their own right. Cf. Buber, *I and Thou*, 125. These human-centered approaches are used to make a critique of the tendencies that emphasize cold logic in approaches to ethics. See Crellin, "Anachronism of Morality," 9–12.

85. See Peperzak, *Ethics as First Philosophy*, xi, with reference to two works of Lévinas, namely, *Totality and Infinity*, and *Otherwise than Being*. Elsewhere, Peperzak notes that the other's existence reveals the basis and primary sense of one's obligation to the other. Cf. Peperzak, "One for the Other," 442. All these boil down to the fact that for Lévinas, ethical normatively commences in the encounter with alterity, with the face." Cf. Alphonso Lingis' introduction to Lévinas, *Collected Philosophical Papers*, xxx.

Lévinas, lies in the fact that the other's emergence answers the deepest desire motivating the ego. It is to be noted also that the word "desire" should not be understood as merely the synonym of "need" for while need can be satisfied, radical human desire is too "deep" or "great" to be fulfilled; it wants the absolute and the infinite, which do not fit into the "comprehensions" and the capacity of the desiring subject. For Lévinas, the answer given by the absolute is a task: the task of my responsibility toward everybody I shall meet. To "endure" this responsibility, one has to be an independent being with an initiative and a concrete existence. This describes what Lévinas means by "being in the world" in *Totality and Infinity*. Thus for Lévinas, a search for happiness is not bad at all for "only a subject that eats can be-for-the-other."[86] Nevertheless, the claims implied in Other's existence puts limits on one's right to satisfy the self; the limits are so exorbitant that they even threaten to reduce one's claims to zero.[87] But to realize one's responsibility for the Other, one must be an independent being, a selfhood that is meaningful if it implies being for the other.[88]

What is most striking about this excursus is that it typifies how a small area in a short story can become a complex symbol of a larger world. On its surface the incident that inspired this analysis is nothing but a chance eye contact between an eight-year-old boy and a victim of execution, as recollected by a police officer lying in his martial bed. However, its significance goes straight to the heart of the fundamental issues of ethics and the concern for one's neighbour.[89] In this regard, the human face is no longer the color of the eyes or of the skin but embodies, for Lévinas, the sense of responsibility which one bears toward the other. On the one hand, such a responsibility prompted Jesse to question the lynching as he asks himself: what did he do? But, being too scared to raise this question in his father's hearing, his silence can, at best, be explained in terms of fear, of speaking in the face of evil and at worst, an approval of the violence on the victim. One is led to suggest that Jesse's responsibility for the victim, the "Other," goes beyond that which he might or might not have done to help him; it might even be termed a "guiltless responsibility" since in the thinking of Lévinas,

---

86. In this Lévinas seems to be suggesting that personal autonomy is but a necessary condition through which the "I" acquires its substantiality. Cf. Peperzak, "One for the Other," 444.

87. Lévinas, *Otherwise than Being*, 73.

88. Cf. Peperzak, "One for the Other," 443. Cf. also with reference to Lévinas, *Totality and Infinity*, especially section III.

89. Kostelanetz, "Notes on the American Short Story Today," 215.

responsibility for the other pre-exists any self-consciousness; it dates from before one's "freedom in an immaterial past, an unrepresentable past that ... is more ancient than any consciousness..."[90]

It is quite important to appreciate the radical nature of Lévinas' critique of how tragedy is analysed and/or brushed aside in public discourse. One way in which this trivialisation can happen in philosophical and theological discussions, for instance, is to lay the blame on the individual—the victim or the victimizer. At other times, analysts simply fall back on a "divine plan" argument in order to explain how "eschatology" points to the hope that the human predicament is but a moment in experience and that all will be well at the end of time. This approach is not remarkably different from the rationalists who see tragedy as belonging outside the boundaries of moral reflection or inaccessible to ethical evaluation. Useful as they seem, these approaches become inadequate as they move too quickly from historical time to "other worldly" final judgment.

This sort of reasoning was popularised by Gottfried Wilhelm Leibniz (1646-1716), who argued that since God is bound by the rational law of non-contradiction, he cannot, for instance, create a square circle. Neither can he attach too much importance to the rights of things or individuals because they derive their goodness from their belonging to the overarching, forward-looking universe. Hence, moral events and physical suffering are nothing but a partial deterioration of the best possible worlds, the upward and progressive movement of which is not affected by particularities. Hence, human circumstances sometimes seem "good" or "bad" because humans do not possess God's ahistorical perfection; they are embedded in history and matter. Consequently, what is generally considered moral evil is the price humans pay for freedom, while physical suffering is a justified phenomenon necessary for the sake of higher harmony.[91]

TRAGIC HERO

To come to grips with how the tragic hero is characterized, we may once again, fall back on Dorothea Krook's methodological insights. As noted earlier, the knowledge gained from tragic literature need not necessarily be that of the hero nor is it necessary for the affirmation to be made by

---

90. Lévinas, "Ethics as First Philosophy," 84.

91. Cf. De Schrijver, "From Theodicy to Anthropodicy," 96, with reference to Leibniz, *Essais de Theodicee*, 310.

the hero. What is significant is that such a hero or heroes bear(s) the burden which makes the knowledge and affirmation possible. Krook believes that the character in the story or drama who answers to this description is, indeed, the tragic hero.[92] But given that tragic vision does not necessarily distinguish between guilt and innocence, it is not enough to jump to the conclusion that having had a sleepless night due to guilt and bad conscience, Jesse is simply the tragic hero. In the same vein, it would be hasty to argue that having been tied to the stake and then emasculated for "pushing down" an old woman, the victim of lynching automatically qualifies as the hero of this story. For our purpose, a combination of the figures cut by these characters seems to be more helpful; they capture the paradoxical essence of the tragic vision. Hence, on the one hand, while the victim of lynching is guilty in the sense that the crime of pushing down an old woman was entirely his, there is a sense in which one perceives him as innocent given that his punishment is far greater than his crime. For his part, Jesse the policeman, as will be argued below, is guilty both as a member of a society that metes out disproportionate punishment, and by virtue of living in a world where such injustices happen. Nonetheless, there is no gainsaying the fact that the forces at play were beyond Jesse's control. Paul Ricoeur calls this "guiltiness of being." It is similar to what Karl Jaspers describes as "guilt of existence."[93] Both lines of thinking bring to mind the concept of *hamartia* which connotes "error," "fault" or "sin" all of which point to the fact that tragic flaw has mental, and moral dimensions and that both are equally blameworthy. Hence: "Whereas the hero is guilty, the guilt need not stem from wrongful acts . . . nor necessarily be incurred wilfully . . . Or the disaster that befalls the tragic protagonist may result from some sin or wrongdoing; a transgression deliberately pursued or innocently performed, a simple misjudgement, but in any case with the consequences out of proportion to the deed."[94]

Another question which is of interest is whether or not it is necessary for the tragic hero in a work of fiction to be able to elicit sympathy from the reading audience. The notion of sympathy hints at the idea that the tragic hero should be noble in the sense of bearing the stamp of a high distinction

---

92. Krook, *Elements of Tragedy*, 44.

93. See Exum, *Tragedy*, 10, with reference to Jaspers, *Tragedy is not Enough*, 52–55; and Ricoeur, *Symbolism of Evil*, 220–22.

94. See Exum, *Tragedy*, 10, with reference to Jaspers, *Tragedy is not Enough*, 52–55; and Ricoeur, *Symbolism of Evil*, 220–22.

or that his actions and motivations have to be worthy.[95] But this approach is of limited validity and seems to have its origin in the biblical projection that "pride goes before a fall."[96] The approach does not account for the fact that the predicament of the hero should never have happened in the first place. Hence, being of high distinction in the context of tragedy need not be confined to worldly rank but can simply refer to the character whose traits help to project more clearly the significance of the tragic vision.[97]

What is generally understood as the fighting spirit of the hero is another significant criterion in the understanding of tragedy. The argument is that if tragedy does not leave the audience depressed, it is thanks to the fighting spirit of the tragic hero whose resistance and/or defiance in the face of evil illuminates and discloses aspects of the human condition. Krook insists, however, that it is not the moments in which the hero is resisting or defying the evil forces of destruction that is of significance but great moments of insight into the human condition in general.[98] It is a courageous moment which transcends the mere fact of resistance and defiance to embrace another element: reconciliation.[99] Reconciliation here is neither the same thing as resignation nor does it place any limit on the fighting spirit. Nonetheless, the fighting spirit is not incompatible with reconciliation; it is incorporated by it in its relation to the element of reaffirmation in the analysis of tragedy.[100]

It is in the light of the foregoing that one can appreciate John Barbour's provocative categorization of the values of tragedy. He groups these values into two—the one "pessimistic" in outlook and the other having possibilities for "optimistic" interpretations. The former suggests that tragedy depicts human response to suffering evil, and alienation, which so often frustrates human aspirations. Nietzschean in outlook, it perceives tragedy as an expression of nihilism and despair at humanity's subjection to the chaotic dissonance of the universe. Hence, all moral activity is futile and tragedy expresses humankind's despair over a world that at times, seems

---

95. The logic seems to be that if a tragic figure fails to command sympathy in spite of his or her anguish, it is because the suffering is in an important sense insufficient. Cf. Krook, *Elements of Tragedy*, 236.

96. Kaufmann, *Tragedy and Philosophy*, 63.

97. Krook, *Elements of Tragedy*, 237. See also Brereton, *Principles of Tragedy*, 37.

98. Krook, *Elements of Tragedy*, 240.

99. Ibid., 243–44.

100. Ibid., 244–45.

without a purpose.[101] From this perspective, any attempt to "explain away" tragedy leaves much to be desired.[102]

At the opposite pole is the optimistic view of tragedy which stems from an understanding that the genre elicits a mysterious but deeply felt sense of the meaning and coherence within the universe.[103] This understanding reverberates in Richard Sewall's suggestion that tragedy gives suffering a structure, "which shows progression toward value, rather than denial of it, and a relationship between the inner life of the sufferer and the world of values about him."[104] None of the above interpretations in any way suggests that tragedy provides all answers to human dilemmas. In fact, it is not a question of choosing the optimistic rather than the pessimistic outlook. Indeed, rather than declare that one "tragic text" is pessimistic and the other optimistic, a more realistic approach would be to come to an understanding of how much and what aspects of a particular vision a specific texts encompasses and interprets. In addition, understanding the nature of an author's interpretation and assessment of his characters' ways of viewing the world can be helpful in coming to grips with tragedy. In doing so "it may be discovered that an author's work implies a broad statement of hope or despair about human condition. An author may [also] show that the failure of virtues is not only a possibility for one type of moral excellence, but an inevitable fact of human life, and this realisation may provide grounds for radical pessimism or for renewed confidence about moral action."[105]

As things stand, trying to locate the responsibility for evil exclusively in any of the characters or the society in which they operate can lead to an oversimplification of the nature of tragedy. This is not to underestimate the significance of the tragic hero who personifies the understanding that if this can happen to him, it can happen to me.[106] Such a hero is exposed to and receives the impact of pain, terror and humiliation—"the victim of

---

101. Barbour, *Tragedy as a Critique of Virtue*, 44. David Jasper sees this outlook in the contemporary apocalypse of postmodernism typified by a nihilist world view. "Violence and Post-Modernism," 801–6.

102. Murray Krieger, a champion of this view, admits that the approach could be quite subjective. Cf. *Tragic Vision*, 2.

103. Barbour, *Tragedy as a Critique of Virtue*, 42.

104. Sewall, *Vision of Tragedy*, 48, cited in Barbour, *Tragedy as a Critique of Virtue*, 43.

105. Barbour, *Tragedy as a Critique of Virtue*, 45.

106. Krook, *Elements of Tragedy*, 45.

forces he or she cannot control, and cannot comprehend, encountering on all sides unresolved questions, doubts, and ambiguities."[107]

COLLECTIVE RESPONSIBILITY

As has already been hinted at, classical notions of the tragic evaluate the fate of the hero in social rather than in moral terms. The origin of this approach is traceable to a demystification of the guilt and downfall of the victims of tragedy. It places blame on a hypocritical society rather than on the victim on whom the society's guilt is supposedly projected. In this regard, the lynch mob of "Going to Meet the Man" is simply indulging in the process of scapegoating. The scapegoat figure, for his part, is a symbol of certain unwanted evils in society.[108] In addition, the life of the victim can be said to embody conflicting historical forces all of which provide the necessary raw materials which the creative writer uses for his or her art and to address social injustice and oppression. Evident also in this line of thinking are the ethical considerations underlying social relationships which enable one to equate *tragic flaws* with the Christian notion of sin, be it communal or individual in nature.[109]

The issue of virtue also comes to mind at this point especially because of the need to determine what constitutes a violation of a community's moral norms which, for instance, provides the setting one finds in Baldwin's "Going to Meet the Man." Using Barbour as a guide, virtue can be thought of either as a quality of goodness inherent in an isolated character or as a form of a particular culture's idea of moral excellence, expressed in concrete actions in a social context. Whichever way one wishes to understand it, the context of its use is always essential in any understanding of tragic action. Moreover, interpreting virtue in terms of broader cultural values facilitates an understanding of tragedy as both an exploration of

---

107. Exum, *Tragedy*, 5.

108. Barbour, *Tragedy as a Critique of Virtue*, 35. This coheres with what we saw earlier in René Girard who thinks that tragedy exemplifies the universal social process by which a community's origin is stabilized and preserved by unanimous collective violence directed at an arbitrary victim. Cf. Girard, *Violence and the Sacred*, 214.

109. See Henn, *Harvest of Tragedy*, 289–90, which draws on the doctrine of original sin in his explanation of the tragic flaw. Cf. Barbour, *Tragedy as a Critique of Virtue*, 36; and Frye, *Anatomy of Criticism*, 210, cited in Barbour, *Tragedy as a Critique of Virtue*, 37; and Daly, "Interpreting Original Sin," 87–91. For a critique of the notion of tragic flaw as sin, cf. Brereton, *Principles of Tragedy*, 41.

human moral development and a society's beliefs about what is normative. Such an approach overcomes the dichotomy between individualistic and collective-oriented perspectives on tragedy.[110]

This brings to mind the questions about what Baldwin's attitude is to the world of the story and the added challenge of determining how his art constitutes a critique of the system of justice in the world of the story if, as Barbour suggests, literature does not just mirror the morality and experiences of an age but subjects them to critical examination. In other words, what is the point of a tragic text like "Going to Meet the Man"? To approach these questions, let us once again look at the character traits that emerge from the three phases of Jesse's life from whose point of view the entire narrative is structured.

Jesse thinks of himself as a good man, a God-fearing deputy police chief. He tries to be a good person and treat everybody right: it wasn't his fault that by protesting their exclusion from the voters' registration exercise, "niggers" had taken it into their heads to fight against God and go against the rule laid down in the Bible for everyone to read.[111] On the night he recalled the childhood experience of the lynching while trying to make love to his wife, he had the urge to hold his wife and be buried in her like a child, to love and be loved and never have to get up the morning again and go downtown to face the civil rights marchers. He wished he did not have to enter the jailhouse again to be confronted with their bad odour and their singing. He wishes he would never gain feel their filthy, kinky, greasy hair under his hand. "They were animals," he thought. Or rather, "they were no better than animals, what could be done with people like that?"[112]

While fantasizing about himself in his twenties, he remembers his contact with black people in the course of his job as a mail-order salesman. This period, according to Millican, marks the state of his life when he is all-knowing about race relations. Thinking himself an authority on blacks, he saw them as a group of people who enjoyed laughing and playing music; he was sure of their love and respect since their kids used to smile when he came to the door. He gave them candy, sometimes, or chewing gum, and rubbed their heads. Nevertheless, he hated them. Maybe, he reasoned, the candies he gave to their children should have been poisoned.[113]

---

110. Barbour, *Tragedy as a Critique of Virtue*, 38.
111. Baldwin, "Going to Meet the Man," 232.
112. Ibid., 234.
113. Baldwin, "Going to Meet the Man," 234.

It is easy to distinguish these two phases of Jesse's character and to argue that as an eight-year-old child riding on his father's shoulders as he witnesses a public executive, he bears no moral responsibility over the brutalisation of the victim in "Going to Meet the Man." Ethical reasoning seems to justify this stance. As Barbour points out, when evaluating moral responsibility one assumes that the subject must have had the capacity to alter events. But as an eight-year-old, Jesse is innocent since he is unable to alter anything. In the ordinary scheme of things, he can neither be accused of any form of negligence, nor can he be said to have wilfully chosen to do (or not to do) anything regarding the lynching he witnessed. Ironically, tragedy tends to undermine our sense of moral accountability because it shows that agents can become culpable for things for which they are not, strictly speaking, at fault.[114] Gabriel Daly articulates this view against the background of the Christian theology of "original sin" on the grounds that to be human is to be a tainted creature. Hence, "we need to be saved also from unattributable sins—the ones we never had the opportunity, the inclination, or perhaps even the courage to commit."[115] As it were, one can become guilty due to any of several things that are partly beyond one's control, including the kind of person one is, improbable coincidences and circumstances. External factors also influence the way one's actions turn out as can be seen in the juxtaposition of conflicting demands brought about by the society in which one lives.[116]

In the light of the foregoing, it would not be enough to blame the incidents of brutalisation in "Going to Meet the Man" on particular individuals but on the structure of the society in question. Hence, the origins of such incidents are not in a specific moral agent, but remote, yet rooted in the human condition. This brings out one crucial element in tragic literature: its capability of showing "how individuals can suddenly find themselves in a situation in which it is impossible not to do wrong."[117]

With regard to the question of determining what a tragic text aims at achieving, it is quite possible that an author may not necessarily be defending nor rejecting established values but might simply be testing their

114. Barbour, *Tragedy as a Critique of Virtue*, 167.
115. Cf. Daly, "Interpreting Original Sin," 87.
116. Barbour, *Tragedy as Critique of Virtue*, 168.
117. See Barbour, *Tragedy as a Critique of Virtue*, 174–75. See also cf. Scheler, "On the Tragic," 7–8: "in every genuine tragedy we see more than just the tragic event... The remote subject of the tragic is always the world itself, the world taken as a whole makes such things possible."

implication in a crisis: exploring how much human experience in his society's belief systems makes sense in difficult moral situations. Writers do this by showing how particular values a society fosters can bring about moral evil and suffering, or can conflict with other essential virtues. Consequently, whether tragedy has an optimistic or a pessimistic vision becomes a redundant question because a work of the imagination that uses tragedy as a method of inquiry can embody both statements of hope or despair about what it means to be human.[118]

APPRAISAL

Having determined that the classical environment of tragedy is the extraordinary, the peculiar and the unrepeatable, and that the Aristotelian examples are derived mainly from one language and from a single literary tradition, we have attempted to expand our understanding of the genre.[119] This has enabled us to draw attention to how literature sensitizes one to the fact of human suffering, often obscured by cultural, philosophical and theological concepts that would rather rationalize suffering, guilt and the brutalisation of one by another than challenge the factors that make them possible. In the context of Baldwin's "Going to Meet the Man," we see that it would be ethically irresponsible to abandon the project of searching for its meaning, although the difficulties in distinguishing between collective or individual guilt are quite formidable.

Nonetheless, in using his art to address social issues, Baldwin provides a perspective for criticizing accepted wisdom with regard to preventable evils. Although he does not necessarily provide answers nor does he simply set out to contextualize the African American experience. Rather, he uses his story to alert his readers to dimensions of human suffering that are easily ignored because people think they know what suffering is all about. In addition, "Going to Meet the Man" provides theological ethics with the tools to participate in the process of discerning and interpreting the nature of tragedy in affirmation of a constant need for clarification.[120]

---

118. The supposition here is that there are belief systems regarding the nature of moral goodness which an author shares with an audience. Cf. Steiner, *The Death of Tragedy*, 193, 318. Cf. Barbour, *Tragedy as a Critique of Virtue*, 39–45.

119. Cf. Bouchard, *Tragic Method and Tragic Theology*, 22; and Quinton, "Tragedy," 101–2.

120. Selling, "Moral Questions," 179–82.

This reading of the story has shown that powerful ethical elements are at work. As the story echoes the godforsakeness of Mark 15:34, it brings to mind the meaning of the relationship Jesse has (or does not have) with the black people of the story.[121] As a young man in his twenties, he is fairly tolerant of them as he thought he knew what they wanted or did not want; it was not his fault that everybody else hated and exploited them. As a law officer, there is a complete break in communication, a scenario which the story links with the loss of his manhood. Ironically, to regain this same manhood he makes peace with blacks as he tells his wife: "Come on, sugar, I'm going to do you like a nigger, just like a nigger, come on, sugar, and love me like a nigger."[122]

One is therefore led to view his outburst to his wife not only as a yearning to love and be loved, but also an echo of his childlike innocence when he was about eight years old, a point in his life when racial differences meant little as his relationship with Otis, his black childhood playmate, attests. It was also during this period of innocence that he witnessed a public execution, an experience which he recalled as an adult and which provided him with a chance to imagine being in someone else's shoes. The experience which, in the language of Lévinas, amounts to an encounter with the "Face of the Other" led to "a discovery of the I in the thou" and a recognition that each of the individuals he would encounter throughout his life shares his experiences of having a first-person perspective and not just an "IT."[123] Seen against the background of historical reports of actual incidents of lynching as Cameron's autobiographical narrative suggests, one thinks not only of how life imitates art but how Baldwin uses his creativity to highlight the fact that social ills are due not to human being by nature inadequate, but to the world being imperfect.[124] In addition the story draws attention to the

---

121. Bouchard, *Tragic Method and Tragic Theology*, 249.

122. Baldwin, "Going to Meet the Man," 252. In a sense, Jesse cannot be indifferent to the blacks of this story, for as Lévinas points out, the non-indifference to the other as *other* and as a neighbour with whom one exists is something beyond any commitment in the voluntary sense of the term; it extends into one's very bearing as an entity. Cf. Lévinas, *Otherwise than Being*, 138. Cf. also Pohl, "Is Grief Self-Regarding?" 21.

123. This reflects of the metaphysical notion that all consciousnesses are in some sense, one. Cf. Lloyd, "Danger of Moral Certainty," 23.

124. Following Kosher, "Hitler," 172, one is persuaded that Cameron's real-life experience runs the risk of reducing the analysis of racism to binary oppositions (between, for instance, good and evil, black and white, rational and irrational), that homogenize evil. The technique, according to Kosher, faces the difficult task of trying to reconstruct horror, a project that is best left to imagination since a documentary account can neither

functioning of human freewill raising questions as to how one is to perceive the workings of God in circumstances, albeit, fictive, that should never have been allowed to occur.[125] It brings to mind also the age-old question: where is God when humans suffer? And how could one love a God who is apathetic toward the particular destiny of people in their daily circumstances? Is he different from Moloch who feeds on the blood of his children?[126]

This study has nevertheless suggested that the Leibnizian argument that pain and misery bring variety into an otherwise monotonous harmony of life has been overtaken by Nietzschean insight.[127] The approach may not have offered a solution to meaningless suffering as portrayed in "Going to Meet the Man," yet Nietzsche is persuasive in his contention that "happiness and pain are inseparable twin brothers: they go together and remain small together; it is impossible to have one without the other."[128] Thus, having been through a mind-boggling experience of brutality, Jesse nevertheless, asks after Otis. One might say that this show of concern for Otis makes the hatred he witnessed bearable and affirms the fact that, like all victims of unnecessary violence, what befell the victim in "Going to Meet the Man" is not, in the end, part of divine plan but offends the Godhead, who then seems to await human co-operation to initiate changes.[129]

---

identify fully with all historical actors nor with the victims of all evils.

125. Gruner, *Philosophies of* History, 31–32.

126. Cf. De Schrijver, "From Theodicy to Anthropodicy," 101; and Van Bavel, "Where is God When Human Beings Suffer?" in Lambrecht & Collins, *God and Human Suffering*, 139–53.

127. Cf. De Schrijver, "From Theodicy to Anthropodicy," 108.

128. Ibid.

129. Cf. Gudorf, *Victimization*, 6.

4

Contrast Experience
Threshold to Creativity

> My pilgrimage [to Mecca] broadened my scope. It blessed me with a new insight.
> —Malcolm X, *The Autobiography of Malcolm*

INTRODUCTION

Travel has always had an inestimable social and personal benefit whether or not it is invested with religious sentiments. This is because there is always a psychogeographical dimension to the "relocation" of human beings from one place to another. Broadly understood, psychogeography is the study of the specific effects of the geographical environment, consciously organized or not, on the emotions, feelings and behaviour of the individual.[1] This consideration is central to the plot of "This Morning,

---

1. See Merlin Coverley, *Psychogeography*, 10, with reference to Debord, "Introduction to a Critique of Urban Geography," 5. Psychogeography is thus the point of intersection between geography and psychology brought about by "contrast experience" at the heart of research in travel and tourism or as found in the phenomena of migration, exile (self-imposed or forced), secular and religious retreats, and pilgrimage. Refer also to Self, *Psychogeography*, 11–13, for deeper insight into the relationship between psyche and place and how modern psychogeographers approach the subject.

Contrast Experience

This Evening, So Soon."[2] Set in the Paris of the 1950s, the short story tells of an expatriate black American artist on a self-imposed exile in Europe. Appalled by the socio-economic situations of blacks in America, the narrator decides to migrate to Europe without any hope of ever going back to the United States. His exile, he says, is necessitated not just by the things he has seen destroyed in America but also the things he lost there as well as all the threats the country holds for him. Not surprisingly, this dissatisfaction with the social tensions in his country engenders crises—personal, racial and national, culminating in a deeply felt hatred of anything or anybody perceived to be anti-black. Moreover, because he carries this bitterness wherever he goes, he finds that he cannot stop himself from having a fatalistic outlook on life. Fed by this pessimism he assesses everything and everybody he meets in Paris in terms of "black" or "white," "rich" or "poor" where he simply distrusts the world and everything in it.

Soon enough, he begins to learn that life is not as simple as he had constructed it. Interactions with people of diverse racial backgrounds—white and black including "whores, pimps and street boys" as well as a broad spectrum of the social milieu in Europe give him new perspectives such that at some point, he falls in love and marries a white woman, a matrimonial union he could never have thought possible if he were still living in his own country, the United States. Vidal, a French film-maker and a man familiar with pain and anguish, also plays a very significant role in the narrator's reorientation. Vidal uses the film he made with the narrator to teach him a few lessons about how to deal with personal frustrations and the ethics of role-playing, as well as solidarity with the underprivileged.

As will be established in this chapter, what makes the film particularly enriching is that the experiences of "Chico," the character portrayed by the narrator, bears a striking resemblance to the narrator's own life situation. Hence, the film provides avenues that enable the narrator to release his pent-up anger through art and subsequently to re-establish his emotional attachment to America, a land as fascinating as it is fear inspiring.

"This Morning, This Evening, So Soon" will be examined against the background of its author's own experiences as an expatriate in Europe. For Baldwin as for the narrator, life in Europe where Baldwin's career began to see the light of day was refreshingly different as he did not have to prove himself to anybody. To Baldwin, such a situation contrasts most vividly with what he perceives to be the case in the United States both for himself

---

2. Baldwin, "This Morning," in *Going to Meet the Man*, 145–95.

and for fellow blacks struggling against discrimination.³ It will be argued also that the sojourn of the protagonist in Europe is akin to a religious pilgrimage, and that like all pilgrimages—secular and sacred—it has a therapeutic effect, broadening his scope and giving him new perspectives.

Drawing on available literature, we shall examine how the pilgrimage phenomenon involves a certain mapping out of human experience in which one can find what Paul Post calls a "hypothetical diagnosis of time or culture" enabling the pilgrim to engage in a sort of historicization that culminates in the seeing of ordinary cultural elements as expressions of extraordinary things. How such aestheticization transforms almost everything into "the pretty and the beautiful"⁴ will form the backdrop to an investigation into why the narrator gains a healthy frame of mind such that at the end of his twelve-year stay, he is able not only to have a new sense of the self despite the cage of racial stereotyping but also to sing about the march of history towards "Canaan shore"—a metaphor that suggests the eschatological time as well as economic and political empowerment in the here and now.

FEAR OF FAILURE

In *Role Playing and Identity,* Bruce Wilshire articulates very concisely the paradox that is at the heart of the concept of personal identity.⁵ While the concept may be important, Wilshire argues quite persuasively, that it is very difficult to demonstrate how it functions. The identity question, manifested in a love-hate relationship between Baldwin and his home country which runs through several of his works, is given concise treatment in "This Morning, This Evening, So Soon." It constitutes a problem which Baldwin sums up in an interview that at a point in his life, "I could not be certain whether I was really rich or really poor, really black or really white, really male or really female, really talented or a fraud, really strong or merely stubborn."⁶ From various biographical sketches of Baldwin it is common

---

3. Eckman, *Furious Passage of James Baldwin,* 119.
4. Cf. Post, "Modern Pilgrim," 4–5.
5. Wilshire, *Role Playing and Identity,* 196.
6. Eckman, *Furious,* 115. These images capture the schizophrenia and the mixture of hope and rebellion which Baldwin had to deal with at this point in his life. They did help to show him off as a courageous person but the images had also the possibilities of degenerating into dishonest posturing that shield away from other social realities. See

knowledge that this self-doubt extends to his attitude to America as his place of birth, Africa as an ancestral homeland, as well as Europe as a place of refuge.[7]

"This Morning, This Evening, So Soon" tells of a nameless black American artist who has lived as an expatriate in Paris. Having made good his singing and acting talents, the narrator prepares to return to his homeland after twelve years of living abroad. He, Harriet—his Swedish wife—his sister, and his son, Paul are presented as a closely knit family—protective of one another and full of love and goodwill in the face of a future that is, on the one hand, threatening and on the other hand, full of promise.[8] Although millions of people are awaiting his return, the artist is obsessed by fear of failure—that his American fans would not like his songs. His more optimistic wife who thinks that his fans are actually looking forward to his coming, teases him on his pessimism pointing out: "Nothing ever turns out as badly as you think it will—in fact, I am happy to say that this would hardly be possible."[9] This however, does not stop the couple from wondering how Paul, who had never been to America, would fit into American life. There is genuine fear that being of mixed race, he would be called names. Moreover, the narrator could not stop thinking of all the things that racism has destroyed in America. He always feels that he does not exist there, except in someone else's mind, wondering whether his Swedish wife will

---

Bigsby, "Divided Mind of James Baldwin," 95.

7. Available literature shows that Baldwin's identity problem manifested itself in subtle ways. For instance, at the end of his own self-imposed exile in Paris, he did not find it particularly exciting to return to the United States. Coincidentally, he did not get along very well with a number of fellow Americans in Paris especially those who were too critical of America. And so while it cannot be contested that the Paris experience made some differences in his life and career, Baldwin is averse to the idea of anybody, French or American, complaining about how America treats its own racial minorities since, all things considered, the way the French treat theirs is no better. In the midst of all the contradictions, one still notices that Baldwin's African heritage is not accessible to him. *The Furious Passage*, 136. Cf. also Cleaver, "Notes on Native Son," 66–76. Beneath these ambiguities lie what C. W. E. Bigsby sees as Baldwin's rejection of rigid definitions whether in terms of one's nation, race, or sexual orientation. The definitions may be real, but for Baldwin they are merely a symbolic heritage that has to be transcended in order that humans may be free for higher possibilities. There is no gainsaying the fact that Baldwin's own sexual ambiguity adds to the confusion. Cf. Bigsby, "Divided Mind of James Baldwin," 96–104.

8. Hagopian, "James Baldwin," 157.

9. Baldwin, "This Morning," 148.

handle the intolerance in America.[10] But again, Harriet, thinking more positively, declares: "please try not to worry. Whatever is coming, we will manage it all very well, you will see. We have each other and we have our son and we know what we want."[11]

Harriet and Louisa (the narrator's sister on holiday from the US), get on very well. Each seems to find the other full of delightful surprises. Harriet has been teaching Louisa French and Swedish expressions, and Louisa has been teaching Harriet American slang. They engage in speculations as to how a language reveals the history and attitudes of a people. Behind all this is Harriet's desire to learn from Louisa how best to protect her husband and her son. This is why they are going out tonight. For her part, Louisa hopes that the narrator's own night out with Vidal, his friend, would be good for him who has of late, been as "cheerful as a cemetery."[12]

POETICS OF THE SELF

It is of special significance to this study that the narrator's life's experiences have striking parallels with those of James Baldwin, the creator of the character. This is in keeping with what scholars see as Baldwin's habit of taking events from his own life and using them as a platform for exploring issues of a much wider significance.[13] Like the character in "This Morning, This Evening, So Soon," Baldwin left America because, as he says, he doubted his own ability to survive the fury of the race problems in America. On the one hand, the civil rights movement of the time was a fertile platform for his writing career, but on the other hand, he hated the idea of being stranded in the midst of "tribal fights."[14] Hence, he sought and found sense of the self

---

10. Ibid., 176.
11. Ibid., 150.
12. Ibid., 153.
13. Leeming, *James Baldwin*, 73.
14. Cf. Baldwin, "Everybody's Protest Novel," in *Notes of a Native Son*, 19–28. In this essay, Baldwin takes a swipe at what he terms "American social protest fiction." He sees the genre as quite limiting despite the moral demand of the black civil rights movement and especially because, to him, it seems to be the only literary art the majority of the American white critics expected of every black writer. More significantly, he is of the view that protest literature has a tendency for self-destructive violence especially if the root of the violence is not adequately *examined*. This theme is at the core of another Baldwin essay: "Alas, Poor Richard," in *Nobody Knows My Name*, 149–76. For comments, see Bigsby, "Divided Mind," 95.

that went beyond the image of a "Negro writer."[15] He wanted to find out in what ways the peculiarity of his experience as a black American could be made to connect him with people instead of separating him from them.[16]

While considering his trip to Europe, Baldwin had anticipated a "contrast experience" such that he might find people treating each other with more respect outside the United States.[17] In this quest, he found that this vision was shared by the expatiate Americans he knew in Paris who also felt that relocation would have positive effects on their psyche. Like him, they have been alienated from their native land, and it turned out to make very little difference that the origins of white Americans were European and his was African. To Baldwin this seems to imply that white Americans were no more at home in Europe than he was. Hence, no matter their ethnic origins or what their experiences might have been, the fact, as he sees it, is that Europe had formed America (white and black). It is part of the American heritage.[18]

For Baldwin, moving to a new environment in anticipation of unexpected insights had the twin motifs of an imaginary voyage and isolation. From the point of view of psychogeography, the "strangeness" of the Paris surroundings brought about a sense of freedom and detachment of the wanderer, and the resourcefulness of the adventurer all of which had positive impact and enhanced Baldwin's creative insights.[19]

As might also be gleaned from his essays, Baldwin's "Europe" borders on the mythical[20] given his predilection for thinking about the continent

---

15. One of the difficulties of being a "Negro writer," as Baldwin recognized at this time, is that the "Negro problem" is a topic about which everyone claims to be an expert. As he says, it is a situation which "operates usually (generally, popularly) to reinforce traditional attitudes. Of traditional attitudes there are only two—for or against—and I personally find it difficult to say which attitude has caused me the most pain." Cf. Baldwin, "Autobiographical Notes," in *Notes of a Native Son*, 13.

16. Bigsby, "Divided Mind," 99: "the escape to Europe is simply an attempt to create geographically that space for manoeuvre which in America has to be won through exertion of the imagination and the will."

17. Cf. Gates, "An Interview with Joseph Baker and James Baldwin (1973)," 165; and also Eckman, *Furious Passage*, 26.

18. The tendency in Baldwin to regard white Americans, too, as implicated in the struggle for identity is often mentioned with disapproval by critics. Cf. Moller, *Theme of Identity*, 26.

19. Coverly, *Psychogeography*, 36.

20. Cf. Coupe, *Myth*, 6.

in terms of a unified social whole.[21] It is a place where he thinks an artist is released, first of all, from the necessity of apologizing for himself.[22] He adds: "It *is* not until he is released from the habit of flexing his muscles and proving that he is just a 'regular guy' that he realizes how crippling this habit has been. It is not necessary for him, there, to pretend to be something he is not, for the artist does not encounter in Europe the same suspicion he encounters here [in America]."[23]

Baldwin argues that the reason for Europe's comparative clarity concerning the different functions of men in society is that European society has always been divided into classes in a way that American society never has been; a European's choice for a vocation does not cause him any uneasy wonder as to whether or not it will cost him all his friends.[24]

One other aspect of European life and culture which Baldwin considers paradoxical is that though American society is more mobile than Europe's, it is easier to cut across social and occupational lines in Europe than America. Summing up his impression of Europe, Baldwin writes: "A man can be as proud of being a good waiter as of being a good actor, and in neither case, feel threatened. And this means that the actor and waiter can have a freer and more genuinely friendly relationship in Europe than they are likely to have here [in America]. The waiter does not feel, with obscure resentment, that the actor has 'made it', and the actor is not tormented by the fear that he may find himself, tomorrow, once again a waiter."[25]

Baldwin claims that this lack of social paranoia causes the American in Europe to feel almost that he can reach out to everyone, that he is accessible to everyone and open to everything. Being in Europe made him feel as if he came out of a dark tunnel. It was a liberating experience such that he found himself beneath the open sky and feeling that it was up to himself as an individual to make of his own opportunity the most that could be made.[26] As he puts it in the introduction to *Nobody Knows My Name*:

---

21. The narrator has, for instance, always thought of Sweden as being populated entirely by blondes. Reality faced him when he visited there and found the country to be a great racial salad. Baldwin, "This Morning, This Evening," 147.

22. Baldwin, *Nobody Knows My Name*, 19.

23. Ibid.

24. Ibid.

25. Ibid., 20.

26. This is not to say that he renounced his citizenship for as he says, "I love America more than any other country in the world, and exactly for this reason, I insist on the right to criticise her perpetually." Cf. Baldwin, "Autobiographical Notes," in *Notes of a*

CONTRAST EXPERIENCE

> In America, the color of my skin had stood between myself and me; in Europe, the barrier was down. Nothing is more desirable than to be released from an affliction, but nothing more frightening than to be divested of a crutch. It turned out that the question of who I was was not solved because I had removed myself from the social forces which menaced me—anyway, these forces had become interior, and I had dragged them across the ocean with me. The question of who I was had at last become a personal one, and the answer was to be found in me.[27]

For the fictional narrator in "This Morning, This Evening, So Soon," the love-hate relationship with his place of birth constantly hovers around the back of the mind. The narrator, for instance, recalls his visit to New York for his mother's funeral. As he left Europe, all the passengers in the ship looked forward to America in anticipation. For his part, the narrator's fears began to make way for a "secret joy." He becomes nostalgic recalling all the luxuries that were rare in post-war Paris and the friends that might be waiting for him in New York.[28] Nonetheless, as he also recalls, when the ship landed at the New York harbour, one man held his daughter on his shoulders to show her the Statue of Liberty. But the narrator could not but think that the statue had always been an ugly joke for him.[29] Neither does the American flag flying from the top of the ship mean much. Yet, when someone announces, "there is no place like home," the narrator thought: "There dammed sure isn't."[30]

ROLE-PLAYING

Back in Paris after his mother's funeral and burdened with bitterness over the racial tensions in the US, the narrator could identify neither with being completely American nor African. But this state of affairs does not stop him from appreciating his vocation as an artist, an actor, a role-player—a

---

Native, 16. On this, Karen Möller comments: Although Baldwin does not believe that racial identity is of inferior value to national identity, the latter provides a less restricted frame of reference as against the background of the specifically American situation. See Baldwin, *Nobody Knows*, 20–22; and Gates, "An Interview with Joseph Baker and James Baldwin," 165.

27. Baldwin, "Introduction," in *Nobody Knows My Name*, 11.
28. Baldwin, "This Morning," 160.
29. Ibid., 163.
30. Ibid., 164.

universal man. One must note, however, that there is something curious about this for as things are, acting *per se* seems to come more easily if one has identity problems although it might also be said that being an actor is like attempting to run away from oneself.[31] Bruce Wilshire captures the paradox—"detachment within involvement"—that is typical of art. He adds that theatre may be considered "aesthetic detachment from daily living" but that it actually functions to reveal our empathetic and imitative involvements.[32]

It is within this context that one begins to appreciate how the narrator's response to his own role as Chico in the film he made with Vidal, a French director, helps him not only to think but also to feel more deeply as well as show solidarity with the downtrodden.[33] According to the film's storyline, Chico, the son of a Martinique woman and a French *colon*, hates his parents. He runs away from the island to the capital, carrying his hatred with him. With time, the hatred grows to include everyone and eventually leads to his death in the underworld of Paris.[34]

What is the narrator trying to achieve by taking on the part of the marginalized in Paris? The answer to this question underlines the view that theatre, the enactment of events that might have occurred, can function as thought experiments as well as a metaphor for life.[35] Given that role-playing

---

31. What results from this paradox is to be both the "self" and the "other" simultaneously. In doing so, the actors enlarge themselves through engagement with the roles. Jenkyns, *Play's the Thing*, 13.

32. Cf. Wilshire, *Role Playing and Identity*, ix, 21. As Wilshire has found out also, theatre has two temporal dimensions—it must be repeatable and must occur for a given stretch of time. These dimensions allow actors to fully "identify" with the characters they are portraying.

33. Cf. Pattyn, "Emotional Boundaries of Our Solidarity," 101: "Solidarity implies both a feeling and a rational decision. In line with any other emotions, the feeling of solidarity is rooted in motivating factors of which we are not always conscious."

34. Baldwin, "This Morning," 169. From the point of view of technique, the section of the story under study that dwells on the acting career of the fictional narrator functions as metanarrative, that is, a story "within" the story-world of "This Morning, This Evening, So Soon." As we shall see in due course, the enactment of Chico helps the narrator to mediate interpersonal experiences, and then disengage from the destructive dimension of his identity. His role on stage thus echoes as well as critiques the kind of life he might have lived off stage. Cf. Chatman, *Story and Discourse*, 146–47, and Wilshire, *Role Playing*, 201.

35. According to Wilshire, *Role Playing*, 238, theatre involves physiognomic or symbolic metaphors: the displacement of appearances that belong literally to one thing so that they belong to something else that is made to resemble the first . . . The result of this

Contrast Experience

is at the heart of acting and has its roots in the process of imitation, an individual is capable of taking on both psychodramatic and projected roles.[36] The former is natural to one's life situation while the latter involves taking on someone else's character. As researchers in film studies have found out, in portraying another person's character, the actor indulges in a process of identification that opens possible ways of being and at the same time raises questions about the actor's own sense of the Self.[37] Thus, acting is a process which draws attention to the explicit difference between the self, the role one plays and the "Other." It establishes the Self as one's uniqueness, distinguishing a person from all other persons. Paradoxically, the self, as an entity, is only meaningful in relation to others. And as the actor takes on the role of the other, the role is transformed according to one's unique way of forming mental images. Hence, the Self determines both the quality of the role and is determined by the roles one takes in and plays out.[38] Moreover, the more one is able to take in and play out roles of others, the more one develops the talent to undertake further acts of role playing.[39] Yet the self is more than the sum total of roles. Consequent upon this, the portrayal of Chico's character provides the narrator with the context, situation and language, as well as the platform on which to function as a mediator between the self, as well as the social world. Acting can therefore be an effective and necessary form of therapy as it entails both an external as well as an inner shift of feeling of actor and audience.[40]

More importantly, in his role as Chico, the narrator indulges in a mental process of pretending that he understands how the character feels. As it is, acting is lifelike, it is the imitative art *per excellence*, and the actor is "by-for-with-and-in others experimentally."[41] In the context of our analysis, the

---

substitution is a compression in which a whole network of correspondences is displayable on the spot and within a limited duration of time. See also Jenkyns, *Play's the Thing*, 4.

36. Cf. also Wilshire, *Role Playing*, 23: theatre as art gives "release to our prime mimetic absorption in types of doing and being . . ."

37. Landy, *Drama Therapy*, 94; and Wilshire, *Role Playing*, 5.

38. Landy, *Drama Therapy*, 92.

39. Ibid., 92.

40. Cf. Jenkyns, *Play's the Thing*, 4; and Landy, *Drama Therapy*, 93–108.

41. Wilshire, *Role Playing*, 26. Against this background, Bruce Wilshire goes on to articulate a thesis that "actors standing in for characters in the theatre . . . Can discover actual and non-deliberate mimetic enactments and standings in between persons offstage." Cf. ibid., xiv, 16.

gesture echoes the Christian notion of solidarity.[42] Such role-playing can be enhanced by religious sensitivity, apart from the fact that it is a demonstration of a power to transfer past to present, actuality to symbol.[43] From the perspective of the actor, role-playing has the positive function of allowing the actor to perceive himself from the *outside* in order to enter the body, the mind and spirit of another.[44] It is a process that is akin to testing reality from a distance and allows the actor to see himself and others as representations. Acting means also that in this process of transference, external objects and the audience become charged with one's experience of the past.[45]

Mimetic Sympathy

It is of great significance to our analysis whether or not the narrator played the part of Chico successfully. In the normal dramatic process, the self (of the actor) and the role strive toward a harmony, but when any part of the relationship is inhibited an imbalance occurs. A common problem in the dramatic portrayal of fictional characters according to Robert J. Landy, can be explained in terms of "distancing." Distancing can take either of two forms: "under-distancing" and "over-distancing." Under-distanced interaction between actor and the character being portrayed is marked by emotional closeness, a lack of boundaries, as well as a high degree of

---

42. True Christian solidarity has a wide dimension. Unlike what Bart Pattyn terms "spontaneous/emotional solidarity" which reveals the tendency in humans to restrict their compassion to those familiar to them, Christian solidarity embraces everyone, including one's enemies: "it entails a call to all people and presupposes a more well-reasoned sense of responsibility." See Ries, "Introduction," *Ethical Perspectives*, 74; and Pattyn, "Emotional Boundaries," 107, with reference to Matt 5:43–44; Luke 6:27–28.

43. It is, in fact, arguable whether or not any form of communication, or indeed, social intercourse in general is meaningful without some form of acting, role playing or the need to make present what is absent through imitation, or the enactment of the comic or the tragic. As Wilshire points out, "If we could somehow lose common, mimetically inducted behaviours, we would cease to be socialised, cease to be human." Cf. Wilshire, *Role Playing*, 199, 209.

44. Landy, *Drama Therapy*, 96. Refer also to Wilshire, *Role Playing*, 6, 200: theatre and theatre-like activities disclose those general characteristics and potentialities of humans which one should be able to imagine. Such activities, whether formal or informal, enable humans to maximize the realisation of their identity. In role playing an actor attempts, sometimes, quite successfully, to reproduce its "Others" in fiction.

45. This experience of transference is especially important for "it gives form to unresolved feelings situated in the past and sets the stage for their representation through spontaneous enactment." Cf. Landy, *Drama Therapy*, 96.

empathy, and a merging of oneself and the role. On the opposite pole is "over-distancing." This is distinguished by an analytical rigid boundary between himself and the character he is supposed to be portraying.[46] At the center of the distancing paradigm is a middle ground where the actor finds a comfortable physical and emotional balance. Under such a situation, there are clear boundaries between the self and the *other* although the boundaries are flexible to accommodate changes.[47]

Drawing attention to the imbalance in the narrator's portrayal of Chico, during the rehearsal of a scene, Vidal, the film director tells him: "You are playing this boy as though you thought of him as the noble savage . . . all these ghastly mannerisms you are using all the time? . . . You are doing it all wrong . . ."[48]

Given that the life of Chico shares close resemblances to what the narrator himself has experienced in life, it is not surprising that he appears "over-distanced" during the rehearsal. Like Chico, the narrator hated his father, a trait they share with James Baldwin, their creator.[49] The narrator remembers his own past, but he deliberately detaches himself from it; it was too close to reality, a fact which made him uncomfortable. Acting thus forces the nameless narrator to "objectify" and accept elements of himself which he had previously been unable to deal with. This explains why critics contend that theatre can function as an avenue of discovery through which the actor reaches the self—a human being with possibilities of human concern and identification.[50]

Nonetheless, the film did turn out to be a success. What made it so was that after the confrontation with the film director, the narrator begins to put more feeling into his act. That is, rather than be rigid, and over-controlled and without flexibility, he begins to be more sympathetic with the character he was portraying. The significance of this success to our analysis is that in his empathy with a downtrodden character, the actor

---

46. Cf. Landy, *Drama Therapy*, 99.

47. Ibid., 99, and Wilshire, *Role Playing*, 200.

48. Baldwin, "This Morning," 169–70.

49. The autobiographical elements in this story are quite instructive. In *Notes of a Native Son* Baldwin writes: "I had inclined to be contemptuous of my father for the condition of his life, for the conditions of our lives . . . I had not known my father very well. We had got on badly . . ." Baldwin, *Notes of a Native Son*, 84–85.

50. As Wilshire has made clear, theatre as a fictive variation on existence "is a disciplined use of fictionalised imagination which can discover . . . aspects of actuality." Cf. Wilshire, *Role Playing*, 10.

(and narrator) challenges the audience to learn how to feel for others. In so doing, actor and audience experiment on the nature and extent of mimetic involvement, identification and sympathy—and on how these relate to the individual's identity.[51]

In achieving that goal of empathizing with the downtrodden, the narrator's role-playing merges with the personal experiences which he brings to his acting career thereby submerging his own self with the other in sympathetic reproduction. It is a gesture that is quite moral in its objective, scope and motivation. One can also add that the story highlights how acting can function as therapy if it enables the individual to move into a new life where more choice is possible.[52]

Good Ends versus Evil Means

When the narrator agreed to act the character of Chico in the film he made with the Frenchman, he had at the back of his mind the plight of the Arab immigrants he had come across in Paris. Most of them, refugees fleeing a civil war, were very poor and were living: "Three and four together in rooms with single skylight, a single hard cot, or in buildings that seemed abandoned, with cardboard in the windows, with erratic plumbing in a wet cobble-stoned yard, in dark, dead-end alleys, or on the outer chilling heights of Paris."[53]

The character that epitomizes the refugees of this story is Boona, an ex-prize fighter whom the narrator encountered in a café during his last night out in Paris before his final return to America. The narrator used to know Boona quite well but is no longer sure what he now does for a living. Feeling that Boona had probably seen him where he sat in the company of Vidal and three visiting American students and not wishing to risk a rebuff, the narrator invites him to join the group.

Living from hand to mouth, unsure of himself—socially and emotionally—Boona appears to be ill-adjusted to the seemingly sophisticated company of the narrator and his companions. The narrator does his best

---

51. Wilshire, *Role Playing and Identity*, 24.

52. Jenkyns, *Play's the Thing*, 14; and Wilshire, *Role Playing*, 198.

53. Baldwin, "This Morning," 157. One can perceive in this an echo of Baldwin's attempt to make some sense out of his African heritage through sympathy for poor immigrants in Paris, but as events will show, this African identity is largely mythical. Cf. Moller, *Theme of Identity*, 65.

to make him feel comfortable in such a mixed company. He does unwind. But soon enough, and to the narrator's horror, comes the bad news. In the course of their drinking and dancing, he is informed that Boona has allegedly stolen money from the handbag of one of the students. The narrator knows that Boona steals but finds himself in a paradoxical situation where he could neither believe nor doubt the allegation. He was quite shocked and as he tries to keep the situation under control, he finds himself rationalizing that not everyone who steals is a thief.[54]

The distinction the narrator makes between "stealing" and being a "thief" touches on the meaning of moral action. Using Joseph Selling's insight as guide, one might suggest that a moral action often involves three elements: agent, an act of commission or omission, and consequence. Ethics seeks to determine whether it is possible to judge a human act independent of the agent and the consequences that may flow from such action. Against the background of Thomas Aquinas, Selling explains that although one person's freedom fighter may be another person's terrorist, judgment about what is good is necessary if ethical discussion is to take place. Nonetheless, such judgment will not necessarily be moral in nature. This is because to speak of morality requires that the moral agent is free and knows what he or she is doing. Hence, if what is thought of as an "evil" act takes place by accident or is unintended, mistaken, or in some way, forced upon an individual or community, then both freedom and knowledge of the moral agent have been impeded. Under such circumstance, it is inappropriate to speak of morality.[55]

From the point of view of the story under study, it does appear that the narrator's solidarity with the downtrodden is running the risk of going down a "slippery moral slope" to the point where he excuses, or at least, tolerates theft on the grounds of extenuating circumstances. This calls to mind the tradition of morality characterized by the existence of an act which is "evil in itself" no matter the motivation. From a Christian moral standpoint such acts are forbidden without exception on the ground that a good end does not justify an evil means.[56] The position that supports this

---

54. Baldwin, "This Morning," 189.

55. Selling, "Veritatis Splendor," 3–17.

56. Cf. Knauer, "Good End Does not Justify an Evil Means," 71–85. Cf. also Janssens, "Norms and Priorities in Love Ethics," 207–38. Drawing on the double-barrelled commandment of Jesus with regard to love of God and neighbor (cf. Matt 22: 37–40; Mark 12: 29–34 and Luke 10:27), Janssens reflects on what fundamental Christian attitudes ought to be. Love of neighbour, for instance, requires the mediation of the attitudes

line of thought is usually designated as "deontological." Deontology comes from a combination of two Greek words *deon* (duty) and *logos* (discourse). It sums up shades of moral approaches that there may be acts whose ethical qualifications are, *ab inito*, evil/good in themselves no matter what their consequences might be.[57] The idea here is that: "crimes committed for laudable motives are still crimes, i. e. bad acts done for good ends. [Robin Hood is said to have stolen from the rich to give alms to the poor, for instance, but his acts of robbery remain no less wrong.] Conversely, good acts can be done for bad ends; giving alms to the poor, a good act considered in itself, may be done for the evil end of humiliating the recipient."[58]

This system of thought differs from the teleological approach to ethics. Teleology, from the Greek words, *telos* (goal or end) and *logos* (discourse) is the ethical position which posits that "the rightness or wrongness of an action is always determined by its tendency to produce certain consequences . . ."[59] The overall import of teleology is that an action is right because it tends to have good consequences, or wrong because it tends to have bad consequences. Teleological approaches are easily linked to utilitarianism.[60] That is, the ethical theory that the best actions are those which produce the greatest good while those that produce the least good are the worst.[61]

---

which have traditionally been termed virtues.

57. Deontologists give the impression that moral principles are ascertained through a "logical test of consistency" or by intuition. Cf. Salzman, *Deontology and Teleology*, 46, with reference to Broad, *Five Types of Ethical Theory*, 357–58.

58. Cf. Macdonald and Beck-Dudley, "Are Deontology and Teleology Mutually Exclusive?" 616.

59. Broad, *Five Types*, 142. For comment, see Salzman, *Deontology and Teleology*, 47.

60. One might as well add that there is something essentially hedonistic about this line of thought. Two classes of hedonism are relevant here, namely "egoistic hedonism" and "universal hedonism." Both attempt to arrive at a fair way of determining what is good on the basis of consequences although there are irreconcilable differences between one and the other. Universal hedonism holds that only actions which contribute to the general good should be done and hence it may be the case that individuals will have to sacrifice their own personal good for the total good. For egoistic hedonism, on the other hand, humans tend to do what will promote their greatest good. Hence "there is only 'my' own good and 'your' own good and 'my' responsibility is to increase 'my' good and to consider 'my' action in relation to others in so far as it will indirectly affect 'my' good." Cf. Salzman, *Deontology and Teleology*, 44–45. See also Ugorji, *Principle of Double Effect*, 20.

61. One significant fact which the supporters of utilitarianism as well as their opponents do recognize is the difficulty in calculating consequences. Cf. Curran, "Utilitarianism and Contemporary Moral Theology," 240.

Proportionality

One of the moral challenges which Baldwin poses in "This Morning, This Evening, So Soon," is: does the fact that Boona cannot get a job, lives rough and is discriminated against justify his depriving others of their property? In essence, if the fundamental ethical framework is that "good is to be done and pursued and evil is to avoided,"[62] how can we deal with a situation which may lead to the causation of evil (in the context of our analysis, stealing a young lady's money), if the intention of the agent is good (in the case of Boona, buying food, paying his rent)? Given, as Louis Janssens reminds us, that the world is continuously marked by a fundamental ambiguity, by the *simultaneous and inseparable* combination of good and evil, values and disvalues,[63] the Baldwin short story goes to the heart of the moral principle which states: "To be good, every element of an activity must be good, while the presence of only one bad element will result in the entire activity being bad."[64]

At this juncture, the distinction between what is "directly" voluntary and "indirectly" voluntary demands to be made. The distinction is especially significant in a conflict situation where a necessary good can only be achieved only when an evil is caused.[65] A tentative conclusion that emerges from the foregoing is that an act which produces evil as well as good results can be allowed if and only if it is justified by a proportionate reason.[66] Apart

---

62. Cf. Janssens, "Ontic Good and Evil," 76: "Mortality involves that which has its origin in our free self-determination, namely, our inner disposition (virtue and vices) and our acts. On this level we stand before absolute or unconditional demands. It is our strict duty to promote virtue and to resist vice."

63. Janssens, "Ontic Good and Evil," 67.

64. Cf. Salzman, *Deontology and Teleology*, 190ff, and McCormick, "Ambiguity in Moral Choice," 38, where it is noted that in the conflict situations where only two courses of action are available, the basic analytic structure is the lesser evil.

65. Cf. McCormick "Ambiguity in Moral Choice," 7. The discussion that is traditionally made between moral evil and physical evil, though quite ambiguous, can be helpful in this discussion. According to the distinction, moral evil is never permitted although, what constitutes such evil cannot be determined prior to the determination of the underlying intention and circumstances of the action. On the other hand, the principle of double effect is not absolute with regard to physical evil, because "there are some physical evils that we have a right to cause in order to obtain a good effect." A frequently cited example is mutilation, a physical evil, but which one can allow in medicine. Cf. Kelly, *Medico-Moral Problems*, 4, as cited by McCormick, "Ambiguity in Moral Choice," 11. See also Salzman, *Deontology and Teleology*, 213.

66. It needs to be noted here that proportionalism assumes that the agent foresees

from the fact that proportionate reason implies that the value at stake (at least equal to or even) outweighs that which is sacrificed, it has also to be clear that there is no other way of salvaging the situation. In addition, it demands that its protection in the short run will not undermine it in the long run.[67] Peter Knauer, in fact, argues that "proportionate reason" goes beyond saying that what motivated the human agent must outweigh the reason he or she has for causing the harm. It is basically a relationship of "appropriateness" between the act and its reasons both in the long-run and in the context of the whole reality of human relationship in community. Hence, what makes an act morally evil consists in the fact that the sum total of the act is negative and that the gain contradicts the universal value to which it aspires.[68]

The question therefore is, all things considered, whether or not Boona's habit of stealing is evil in itself,[69] exploitative, and as such counterproductive.[70] If it is evil in itself, there is no proportionate reason to justify it.[71] It also implies that if one should not be moved by personal desire to

---

all of its aspects. The agent directly intends the good and only tolerates the evil as an indirect aspect of the good which is intended. Cf. Salzman, *Deontology and Teleology*, 191, and Ugorji, *Principle of Double Effect*, 31.

67. McCormick "Ambiguity in Moral Choice," 35.

68. Knauer, "Good End Does Not Justify an Evil Means," 84, and McCormick, "Ambiguity in Moral Choice," 12. Rules for proportionality are summed up thus: 1. In whatever we do, we should always aim toward the/a good. 2. There should be no contradiction between the good aimed at and the means chosen to achieve the good. 3. We should minimize the presence of ontic evil in our activity as much as possible. We need to pay attention to the whole of human activity. See Salzman, *Deontology and Teleology*, 190; and McCormick, "Ambiguity in Moral Choice," 35.

69. A word of caution is in order here for as Todd Salzman says, "The human act is a complex of intertwined moments and must be recognised as such. It takes place within the human subject, in a particular historical and cultural milieu." Cf. Salzman, *Deontology and Teleology*, 323. This is similar to the "relationality-responsibility" ethics of Charles Curran which "views moral life primarily in terms of the person's multiple relationships with God, neighbour, world and self and the subject's action in this context." See Rigali, "Reimaging Morality," 8, with reference to Curran, *Directions in Fundamental Moral Theology*, 11–14.

70. Cf. Knauer, "A Good End Does not Justify an Evil Means," 80.

71. The "direct" and "indirect" distinction is fundamental to the doctrine. The voluntariness of an action is direct if the agent wills the end and means of an act. The side effects of act, is on the other hand, willed indirectly. Cf. McInerny, *Aquinas on Human Action*, 14–24. As Louis Janssens explains in "Ontic Good and Evil," 76, "an act is morally right when it is objectively, in truth, suitable for realising, our morally good intention . . . Morally wrong acts cause disadvantages for oneself, one's neighbour, or the community."

achieve a goal by freely choosing to destroy, or damage, or impede another instance of some good, Boona's thieving habit cannot be justified. It is not even enough to justify the habit along the line of Kant's categorical imperative which commands one to do as one would be done by. Doing so will amount to saying that a sadomasochist, for instance, should not hesitate to inflict pain upon others since he would not mind the infliction of such pain upon himself.[72] Nonetheless if it can be determined that Boona has exhausted all options, and that those from whom he steals are the cause of his predicament, then it becomes easy to equate his habit with self-defence.

Movie and Morality

James Baldwin's technique of memorializing his experiences constituted the "reality" behind his success as an artist.[73] As noted earlier, this is not unlike the "reality" behind the performance of the narrator in "This Morning, This Evening, So Soon." The realities are examined on a number of levels—ranging from family relationships through interactions with friends to encounters with strangers—all of which parallel Baldwin's own life experiences.[74]

At the family level Baldwin fictionalizes his unhappy relationship with his own father. He dealt with the issue in *Notes of a Native Son* where he recalls that in his youth none of his father's children was ever glad to see him come home. Pointing out that his father's inability to establish contact with other people was one of the reasons why he relocated from New Orleans to New York. Baldwin writes:

> There was something in him, therefore, groping and tentative, which was never expressed and which was buried with him. One saw it most clearly when he was facing new people and hoping to impress them. But he never did, not for long. We went from church to smaller and more improbable church, he found himself in less demand as a minister, and by the time he died none of his friends had come to see him for a long time. He had lived and died in an intolerable bitterness of spirit and it frightened me, as we drove to the graveyard through those unquiet, ruined streets, to

---

72. Cf. Macdonald and Beck-Dudley, "Deontology and Teleology," 617, with reference to Hospers, *Human Conduct*, and Grisez, *Way of the Lord Jesus*, vol. 1, *Christian Moral Principles*, 168.

73. Cf. Eckman, *Furious Passage*, 107.

74. Cf. Hagopian, "James Baldwin," 157.

see how powerful and overflowing this bitterness could be and to realise that this bitterness now was mine.[75]

In the story under study, the narrator and his late father did not get on well. Ironically, this state of affairs made it easier for him to play the part of Chico, a film character who hated his own parents. In one of the scenes of the movie, Chico goes into a dance hall to beg the French owner for a job. And the Frenchman reminds him of his father. This incident in the life of Chico parallels the experience the narrator had when he went home for his mother's funeral. He needed a job and did get one as an elevator boy in one of the town's big department stores. It was a favour from one of his father's friends. However, the narrator was the proud type. He did not seem to show how grateful he was to those on whose goodwill he depended nor could he hide the fact that he detested having to go through life counting solely on other people's kindness. Such patronizing charity always reminded him of the humiliation his late father had to bear. On the one hand, he pitied him but, on the other, he had contempt for him because he could not prepare him fully for the hard realities of society. Yet the narrator found himself eventually exonerating his late father, for how, he asked himself: "can one be prepared for the spittle in the face, all the tireless ingenuity which goes into the spite and fear of small, unutterably miserable people, whose greatest terror is the singular identity, whose joy, whose safety, is entirely dependent on the humiliation and anguish of others?"[76]

This sort of humiliation is behind the reason the narrator's sister, Louisa, never married. Years ago, Louisa, her boyfriend and some friends were going out in a car when some uniformed white police officers stopped them. In the world of the story, it was thought improper for a white girl to be found in the company of black males. The officers pretended not to believe the mixed-race girl inside the car in the company of blacks when

75. Baldwin, "Autobiographical Notes," in *Notes of A Native Son*, 86. Reflection on the father-son relationship is well developed in Baldwin, *Go Tell It on the Mountain*. The novel, according to Fabre, plays with a constellation of fathers—unknown and mythical father, real and legitimate father, putative father, possible father, adulterous husbands and father of bastard. Fabre contends that part of the explanation for the mutual hatred between John Grimes, the protagonist (of *Go Tell It on the Mountain*) and his father, Gabriel, can be seen in the context of John's desire to leave the ghetto as well as the fact that from the son's point of view, the force and the power to love is inseparable from the capacity to resist and to hate. As it is, John's individual survival necessitates this hatred, which unfortunately prevents him from being a true convert. Cf. Fabre, "Fathers and Sons in James Baldwin's *Go Tell It on the Mountain*," 122–25.

76. Baldwin, "This Morning," 173.

she said she wasn't white. The officers claimed that the only way they could be sure of her race was for her to get out of the car. They forced her to do exactly that, pulling down her pants and raising her dress before the car's headlights. To the dismay of Louisa, the narrator's sister, none of the black men inside the car could do or say anything to the police officers.[77]

Against this background, it is not surprising that the narrator's life experiences coupled with the ordeal of the film character he was playing added up into a genuine fear that his son, Paul, would grow up to hate him. Was he doing enough to prepare the eight-year-old for the ups and downs in the wider society? At that moment, the narrator swore that such a day would never come for his son. He would throw his life and his work between Paul and the nightmare of the world. He would do his best to make it impossible for the world to treat his son as it had treated his father and himself.[78] As things stand, while the narrator is unsure of what will happen if he returns to the USA with his family, he could not resist the attraction the country now holds for him especially because he is now in a better frame of mind to deal with life in the USA after his twelve-year stay in Europe.

GEOGRAPHICAL AND SOCIAL SEPARATION

Psychogeography, that is, the study of the geographical environment consciously organized or not, on the emotions and lifestyle of individuals is central to the thesis of this chapter. This is because the narrator's relocation from America to Europe, like that of Baldwin himself, had such a positive outcome as might be associated with a successful religious pilgrimage. How this is effected is the subject of the following section. The human need for such a pilgrimage comes about when one begins to look beyond the local environment and to feel the call of some distant lands especially those that culture and religious traditions have endowed with some measure of myth and sacrality.[79] From an anthropological point of view, this call is quite natural. As Victor Turner suggests: "if one is tied by blood or edict to a given

---

77. Ibid., 175–76.
78. Ibid., 173.
79. Cf. Post, "Modern Pilgrim," 1–9. The journey (of the pilgrim) which is undertaken is in important ways seen as a journey into the "past" whether real or mythical. Paul Post contends that through such a detour to the past, pilgrims seek identity and quality of life by means of a series of contrasts in experiences, a tradition that offers hope and meaning. Cf. "The Modern Pilgrim," 5.

set of people in daily intercourse over the whole gamut of human activities—domestic, economic, jural, ritual, recreational, filial, neighbourly—small grievances over trivial issues tend to accumulate through the years, until they become major disputes over property, office, or prestige which factionalise the group."[80]

Driven by fatigue, hope, or countless other motives, ordinary tourists and people who undertake a pilgrimage decide to separate themselves from the social and spiritual status quo. Studies show that at times, this geographical and social separation is symbolized by the taking of a vow, the making of a promise, or the affirmation of an obligation to leave home and travel to a holy place. It might even lead to the taking of a new name, the discarding of the usual wardrobe, the writing of one's last will or testament, the cutting of one's hair, or the speaking of new language. The crucial point is that the pilgrimage begins by one being set apart.[81] Whether the separation from home, social status and daily routine is voluntary or obligatory as in the case of the Moslem pilgrimage to Mecca, a break with the social and spiritual status quo can have therapeutic effects.

The foregoing helps one to have an inkling into Baldwin's state of mind by the fall of 1948 when a friend warned him: "Get out—you'll die if you stay here." He took this advice especially because, two years earlier, a friend of his had committed suicide. The fear that Baldwin might end up like his late friend was therefore genuine. As he tells a researcher:

> What happened is that I was born in Harlem, which is not New York. And at a tender age, I left Harlem, which seemed, you know, like a prison, to come downtown which is New York. And uptown, you know, I have been beaten up half to death—and got almost slaughtered downtown, y'know . . . So by the time I was twenty-four since I was not stupid, I realised that there was no point in my staying in the country at all. If I'd been born in New York, there is

---

80. Turner and Turner, *Image and Pilgrimage in Christian Culture*, 10–11.

81. Pilgrimage sites are normally separated from the political and social center of culture. David Carrasco's examples from South America are instructive. As his research indicates, there are in Mexico pilgrimage centers of the Virgin of Guadalupe at the Tepeyac, which attracts pilgrims from all over the world, Our Lady of Zapopan near Guadalajara, which attracts pilgrims from many areas of Mexico, and Our Lady of Ocotlan in Tlaxcala. All located (or were originally located) on the outskirts of the populated areas of cities and towns. It is also worthy of note that "many pilgrimage traditions lead people to shrines and temples in mountains and other landscapes covering hundreds of miles through and beyond urban settings." Cf. Carrasco, "Those Who Go on a Sacred Journey," 15. See also Malcolm X, *Autobiography of Malcolm X*, 317.

no place that you can go. You have to go out. Out of the country. And I went out of the country and I never intended to come back here. Ever.[82]

The question that arises here is: how does "change of environment" affect the narrator's (and indeed, James Baldwin's) vision of life? The answer to this question emerges if one examines the quest for temporal and emotional release that characterizes the pilgrim's journey. A pilgrimage as hinted above, is an attempt to establish ties with entities that one holds dear in order to "gain physical and spiritual healing, and receive new knowledge so that life can be renewed . . ."[83] Alienated from their society, some pilgrims find a place on the periphery of society as they seek and with the hope of finding what the place where they live and/or work has not been able to offer them. This "mystery" of pilgrimage, according to Elizondo, is consistent throughout the history of humanity, regardless of the changes and advances civilisations make. The very nature of the pilgrimage allows ordinary social divisions to fade out as the great diversity of pilgrims experience a common bond based on a unifying experience. The peaceful and harmonious mixture of peoples from all classes, ethnicities and races which gather together at the pilgrimage site (and resorts) can certainly be an image of the ideal humanity of the future; multiracial and multicultural. For the fictional narrator in "This Morning, This Evening, So Soon," Paris was like a "sacred site" symptomatic of a place that enables one to undergo a spiritual as well as an emotional renewal.

Phases of Emotional Renewal

Consistent patterns are evident in religious pilgrimages which might be said to conform to the experiences of the narrator. Socio-anthropological studies demonstrate that many pilgrimages exhibit in some way to some basic phases. Firstly, there is separation from spatial, social and psychological status quo. This leads, as Carrasco explains, to a marginal or luminal space and set of social relations within which a new vision takes place and which results in a profound sense of community among the pilgrims. A distinctive form of social community which Victor Turner calls *communitas* emerges at this stage of a pilgrimage. *Communitas* means relationships

---

82. Cf. Eckman, *Furious Passage*, 115; and Bigsby, "Divided Mind," 101.
83. Carrasco, "Those Who Go on a Sacred Journey," 13.

among people "jointly undergoing ritual transition." Through oneness of purpose they experience an intense sense of intimacy and equality, an 'I-Thou' awareness. *Communitas* can be spontaneous, immediate, concrete, undifferentiated, egalitarian, direct, non-rational . . .[84] It is a total clash of identity and personalities of the pilgrims and results in a momentary sense of profound freedom from social norms and biases and a new sense of collective identity.

The idea here is that pilgrims encountering the music or the silences of pilgrimage sites, the experiences of equal status, the fatigues and perhaps, the dangers of the journey, may undergo this kind of *communitas*. There is also what has been identified as "normative communitas" or the mapping out of the pilgrimage where, according to tradition, participants must follow the requirements of preparation that ensures proper education (Baldwin, for instances, had to spend time learning the French language). Another kind of *communitas* is ideological. It is rather utopian as might, for instance, be deduced from scriptural exegesis. Examples include the many images of the Virgin Mary which are said to offer healing, forgiveness and love to the faithful. All these, according to Carrasco, "allow the pilgrim eventually to return home and face the routines of life with a new sense of purpose and hope."[85]

One sees this sort of transformation in the protagonist of "This Morning, This Evening, So Soon." More often than not, he had, as a musician and singer, an audience made up of students in the weird Paris bistros where he worked. But he made a success of it and subsequently became popular enough to attract critical reviews in a local newspaper. Given that his reputation took a turn for the better, it is not surprising that he soon acquired a legal work permit which enabled him to make extra money.[86]

From the perspective of Baldwin's personal experience, this sort of metamorphosis from a penniless expatriate to a successful writer did not happen overnight. As Eckman observes, even outside the ghetto, away from his place of birth, Baldwin was still its victim physically and emotionally sapped by the ordeal instigated by his stepfather and extended by his nation. Moreover, the process of fighting off the carefully cultivated defences that concealed Baldwin from himself was gradual, and only partial, as he

---

84. See Carrasco, "Those Who Go," 14–15, with reference to Turner, *Dramas, Fields and Metaphors*, 196–97.

85. Carrasco, "Those Who Go," 17. See Coverley, *Psychogeography*, 39.

86. Baldwin, "This Morning," 161.

could not shed what he once decried as "the profound, almost ineradicable self-hatred" with which the United States endows its Negro citizens."[87]

There is, therefore, no gainsaying the fact that the narrator's geographical separation from the USA facilitated exposure to a new vision of life. Of his own experiences, Baldwin tells a biographer: "You know, I saw some—I saw tremendous things. And some of those people [including whores, pimps and street boys] were very nice to me and—in a way, I owe them my life. D'you know? These were people that everyone else despises and spits on. And it was—it humbled me, in a way. It did something—very strange for me. It opened me up—to whole areas of life."[88]

In the light of the foregoing, one can conclude that in pilgrimages and tourism, people come from diverse cultures, backgrounds, ages and personal situations searching for something beyond the ordinary. The sense of pilgrimage seems to respond to a need that is beyond the limits of ordinary experience. Pilgrimage sites (Paris in the case of Baldwin and the fictional narrator) seem to have the force of a geographical biological-spiritual magnet attracting visitors into their life-giving mystery. Yet pilgrim sites, as anthropologists maintain, are not ends in themselves; they often serve as thresholds into new stages of life. One does not, for instance, go as a pilgrim to stay, but to pass through a privileged experience that will change one in unsuspected and uncontrolled ways so that one returns to ordinary life in a completely new way.[89] Thus, there is an initiatory quality in pilgrimage which allows the pilgrim to enter into a new, deeper level of existence than was previously the case.[90]

APPRAISAL

What we have here is a first person narrator telling the story of the struggles of African Americans, descendants of former slaves in the United States of the nineteen forties and fifties. Intelligent and overburdened with his own prejudices, the nameless narrator cuts the image of a supersensitive character reacting to every "gesture by a white man that might conceivably be interpreted as anti-Negro."[91] Coming from the imagination of James

---

87. Eckman, *The Furious Passage*, 120.
88. Ibid., 122.
89. Elizondo, "Pilgrimage," viii.
90. Turner and Turner, *Image and Pilgrimage*, 8.
91. Hagopian, "Black and the Red," 57.

Baldwin, such a character is not difficult to create since he himself had, on a number of occasions, been a victim of racially motivated provocations. His own life story was such that at some points he began to blend his contempt for white law enforcements agents with disdain for his own stepfather, and all incidents of personal misadventure. It is a situation which commentators now see, with hindsight, as a gesture symptomatic of an unsatisfied thirst for love and tenderness in a hostile social environment.[92]

As the story unfolds, it becomes clear that putting life in simple categories of "white" and "black" or dividing humanity between the "oppressed self and the hostile world" is very unhelpful. We have attributed the origin of this realisation to the therapeutic effect of the narrator's stay in Europe, a stay that is no less significant than a pilgrimage to sacred shrines and holy places as understood in orthodox religious exercises. It was this that enabled the narrator to learn about life through daily experiences and role-playing. These contrast experiences broadened his mind such that he is able to put his own experiences and those of the Arab refugees he came across in their proper perspectives. Hence, while acknowledging the bitterness of refugees in Paris the narrator could not bring himself to be angry with their French hosts who did not seem to have done enough to ameliorate the plight of the refugees. The narrator is rather grateful that the French have allowed him the psychological space to sort out his identity as well as learn to love and be loved. Having now come to grips with himself, he feels excited to return to his native land after twelve years as an expatriate.

But where can one anchor his enthusiasm to return to the USA, a country where, as he says, he had seen many things destroyed? For him, America is full of dangers but remains attractive. This is not to say that he and his family would not miss the life and friends in Paris. Bolstered by the sense of well-being engendered by the refreshing Paris life, the narrator is ready to sing with Pete during what turns out to be an impromptu farewell party:

> *Preach the word, preach the word, preach the word!*
> *If I never, never see you any more*
> *Preach the word, preach the word*
> *And I'll meet you on Canaan's shore*

The tension in this song can be understood in terms of the contexts of the Spirituals with their echoes of hope, despair, joy, sorrow, death and life.

---

92. Fabre, "Fathers and Sons," 135.

Contrast Experience

Against the background of the hermeneutics of the Spirituals, one would argue, as James Cone does, that the song is both a longing for a new world and a criticism of the present one.[93] Implicit also in the song is the understanding that death is inevitable but that a new life is sure to begin at "Canaan's shore." It is reality that cannot be denied, and as a consequence, the next verse of the song goes on:

> *Testify!Testify!*
> *If I never, never, see you any more!*
> *Testify!Testify!*
> *I'll meet you on Canaan's shore.*[94]

As it is, Pete's song might have been composed under different circumstances, but Baldwin adroitly weaves its language into the plot of his story allowing the song to function on a number of levels: first, as a farewell song marking the narrator's departure from the city of Paris. It functions, in the second place, as a pointer to eschatological times where the singer can find peace, freedom and self-fulfilment.[95] This analysis is consistent with the understanding of Frederick Douglas who writes of the significance of songs and dance in Black American Christian worship:

> We were at times remarkably buoyant, singing hymns, and making joyous exclamations, almost as triumphant in their tone as we had reached a land of freedom and safety. A keen observer might have detected in our repeated singing of "O Canaan, sweet Canaan, I am bound for the land of Canaan," something more than a hope for reaching heaven. We meant to reach the North [i. e. the liberal

---

93. Cone remarks that the Spirituals are the people's response to the societal contradictions. It is the black community in rhythm, swinging to the movement of life, and that to evaluate it, one has to feel one's way into the cultural and historical milieu of the people's mind. Cone, *Spirituals and the Blues*, 31.

94. Baldwin, "This Morning," 184–85.

95. Cone, *The Spirituals and the Blues*, 80, with reference to Frederick Douglas, *Life and Times of Frederick Douglas*, 159. Cone adds that the notion of heaven as other reality only became significant when black slaves realized that the part of the United States that were supposedly anti-slavery were not remarkably different from those that approved of slavery. Moreover, considering the Fugitive Slave Act of 1850 which made escape to freedom very risky for the slaves, the blacks found it necessary to develop an idea of freedom that included but did not depend entirely on historical possibilities. For what could freedom mean for those who could never expect to participate in the determination of their own destiny? Cf. *The Spirituals*, 82.

Northern Parts of States that had abolished slavery] and the North was our Canaan.[96]

Pete's song with its biblical overtone, invites listeners to "Preach the word" (and the word was God?) and to "testify" in acknowledging of both existential and transcendent realities. The first reality that is echoed here is that history is in motion and that singers and listeners may not meet again. Another reality is that death is inevitable, yet it is not the ultimate reality. Hence, it might be said that history is moving toward divine fulfilment on "Canaan's shore" with its earthly and eschatological dimensions. Like all Spirituals, the songs used by slaves to respond to societal contradictions, Baldwin's effort is not only a criticism of the present order of things but also a longing for a new world—"here and now" as well as in the time to come.[97] Originators of the Spirituals did not see the gospel as an "apocalyptic myth" but a divine message "about the future . . . breaking into the reality of the present."[98]

It is instructive that "This Morning, This Evening, So Soon," does not end in an earth-shaking reversal of fortune. What is significant is that at the end, everything is deconstructed, and there is a deep-rooted "altered consciousness of the individual."[99] The protagonist's role as an artist puts this fact in sharper focus given that he has a highly developed imagination and is able to conceive of a "New World" that can escape its own myths and break its own taboos. Moreover, the communicative act inherent in art "becomes a model for a coherence which is generated by the sensibility and not imposed by social fiat."[100]

To appreciate the story is to recognize how successfully Baldwin has been able to infuse highly theological language into the social issue of being an expatriate or what has emerged here as "secular pilgrim." This exercise in Psychogeography was an honest attempt to win a "psychic territory" that allows for self-criticism while providing room for hope. Beyond this, by using the narrator to function within various ethical positions, especially in

---

96. Cone, *Spirituals*, 80, citing Douglas, *Life and Times*, 159.

97. Singers of the spiritual find no difficulty in investing scriptural language with meaning that is consistent with their struggle to affirm themselves as a people. Cf. Cone, *Spirituals*, 61.

98. Ibid., 85–86.

99. Artists, no matter the nature of their calling, have in one way or another, been in the position to project alternative worlds. Bigsby, "Divided Mind of James Baldwin," 96.

100. See ibid.

the use of "meetings"—potential, actual, eschatological—the story exhibits a possibility that points to the transcendent where it no longer makes sense for people to be hampered by artificial categories.[101] This is not to say that the individual should be without identity but such an attitude presupposes the acceptance of the contradictions of life. It is within this context that one can appreciate Baldwin's confession in *Notes of a Native Son*: "I love America more than any other country in the world, and exactly for this reason, I insist on the right to criticise her perpetually." Nonetheless, Baldwin is not in a hurry to forget his debt to Europe for it was the city of Paris which, in his own words, "saved my life by allowing me to find who I am."[102]

---

101. Cf. Hagopian, "James Baldwin," 160.
102. Moller, *Theme of Identity*, 158.

5

Music and Revelation

> I am music.
> Servant and Master am I.
> Servant of those dead, and master of those living.
> Through me spirits immortal speak the message that
> make the world weep, and laugh, and wonder and worship.
>
> —Anonymous

> Revelation . . . is a function of the discursive power of poetic language, language that has the disturbing ability to rupture our everyday perceptions of reality by rendering transparent features of experience that were previously opaque . . .
>
> —Mark Wallace, *Postmodern Biblicism*

INTRODUCTION

In *Notes of a Native Son*, Baldwin outlines his frustration at being perceived by some critics as merely an ethnic writer perpetually neck-deep in racial questions. He knew that being thought of as an ethnic writer could

Music and Revelation

be limiting given the tendency in such an approach to art to reinforce traditional stereotypical attitudes. This is not to say that Baldwin was unaware of the significance of life experiences on an artist's work since, as he says: "One writes out of one thing only—one's experience."[1] "Sonny's Blues" symbolizes how Baldwin draws on his African cultural heritage without being circumscribed by his ethnicity.[2] His achievement in the story lies in being able to use available tools to grapple with issues of universal concern.[3]

"Sonny's Blues" is structured around two brothers who are alienated from each other, that is until the last scene of the story when jazz music, examined here as "culturetext" with its own language and vocabulary, functions as a means for articulating sentiments which provide meaningful connections to human hopes, fears and aspirations. To be able to study how this is worked out, we will begin by providing the context of the communication problems between the brothers. Attention will then be shifted to a number of philosophical and musicological arguments on which the symbiotic relationship between music and emotion are normally anchored. This is meant to anticipate the conclusion that the emotional impact of Sonny's music on his brother affected reconciliation because music, by its nature, has a sacramental quality about it. Indeed, one proposal that underlines this chapter is that in "Sonny's Blues" the sacramental quality of music is manifested through the combination of grace and human creative skills. Moreover, in as much as the secular can be redeemed by the sacred, the study will throw light on the power of music to solemnise.[4] It is within this framework that we would appreciate how Sonny's music becomes, for the narrator, a vehicle of revelation in the sense of facilitating the unveiling of that which has always been there but which has hitherto been hidden from view by the narrator's narrow-mindedness.

---

1. Cf. Baldwin, *Notes of a Native Son*, 12.

2. Baldwin, "Sonny's Blues," in *Going to Meet the Man*, 103–42.

3. Against the background of Lionel Trilling's observation that there are certain individuals who contain the "yes" and "no" of their culture, C. W. E. Bigsby draws attention to the fact that Baldwin's artistic sensibilities are sometimes drawn in opposing directions. Hence, while it is true that Baldwin fled from the role of a writer and individual who is circumscribed by his ethnicity, he recognizes that his African American root is a key to his art. Cf. "The Divided Mind of James Baldwin," 113–39. Similarly, Michael F. Lynch argues that Baldwin's artistic method is essentially dialectical and rich in irony. The result is that Baldwin always succeeds in using opposing ideas to reinforce rather than contradict each other. Cf. Lynch "Just Above my Head," 285.

4. Lancelot, "Music as Sacrament," 183.

Considering the large amount of secondary literature on the story, it is no exaggeration to suggest that "Sonny's Blues" stands out as one of the most widely studied stories in the collection. Apart from the fact that it is recognized to be much less polemical than the other stories in the collection, there is the obvious fact that it offers other literary themes such as individualism and alienation, as well as grappling with the question: "Am I my brother's keeper?"[5] Although our examination of this story will reinforce the relevance of these themes, we will go further to study how Baldwin deals with the narrator's selfish desire to live a respectable life in face of his younger brother's multiplicity of problems, including lack of interest in school, troubles with the law, bohemian lifestyle, and the general low morale engendered by limited life opportunities.

COMMUNICATION PROBLEMS

The story opens with the shock of the elder brother at the news of his brother's arrest for peddling and using heroin. By the time of Sonny's arrest, the brothers hadn't seen each other for one year, and although the communication between the brothers was rather poor, the elder man was taken aback by the arrest. He did remember that Sonny's face had been bright and open with a touch of gentleness. He had suspected that something was not right with Sonny but kept putting the thought away. He tried to persuade himself that "Sonny was wild but wasn't crazy."[6] He thought that he had always been a good boy; he had not turned evil or disrespectful as had the young people around him. But there he was, trying to imagine what would become of his brother who had now turned into a drug addict and was literally on his way to jail. To the narrator, Sonny's predicament had a touch of a self-inflicted injury.

On his way home from the school where he was an algebra teacher, the narrator made up his mind to keep in touch with his brother who has now been incarcerated. However, it took him quite a while to keep his promise, in fact, only after one of his children died. It so happened that on the day

---

5. Albert, "Jazz-Blues Motif in James Baldwin's 'Sonny's Blues,'" 179. Echoes of these themes are obvious in Baldwin's *Just above My Head*, the story of Arthur Montana, a gospel/blues singer, as told by his older brother, Hall Montana. As in *Just above My Head*, the music of a younger brother enables the narrator of "Sonny's Blues" to make connections with his cultural and spiritual roots. For comment, see Traylor, "I Hear Music in the Air," 95–106.

6. Baldwin, "Sonny's Blues," 104.

the child was buried, the narrator was by himself in his livingroom when his thoughts shifted to Sonny. At that instant, he decided to write to him. In his reply, Sonny confessed that he didn't know the full implications of what he was doing, adding that if he did, he would never have behaved so badly. He expressed remorse, and asked the narrator for forgiveness. Not only did this make the narrator feel guilty but also angry that he had not lived up to the promise he made to his mother. Their late mother had specifically pleaded with him to look after Sonny, noting: "You got to hold on to your brother ... and don't let him fall, no matter what it looks like is happening to him and no matter how evil you gets with him. You may not be able to stop nothing from happening. But you got to let him know you's *there*."[7]

When Sonny was released from jail, the narrator was on hand to receive him. But it soon became evident that there was really a chasm between the brothers, traceable in part, to the young man's choice of music as a profession. The elder man didn't see why Sonny would "want to spend his time hanging around nightclubs, clowning around on bandstands, while people pushed each other around on dance floors."[8] As he saw it, being a musician might be good for other people but not for his brother. To make matters worse, Sonny wanted to be a jazz musician, and had Charlie Parker as a role model. The communication gap between the two brothers became more apparent when the narrator realized that he did not know anything about Charlie Parker and his kind of jazz music. To humour Sonny, he spoke of going out to buy all Parker's records as he wonders whether or not Sonny could make a living out of playing jazz. He would rather Sonny finished school but the younger man would not hear of such a suggestion. Sonny thought that he was not learning anything at school. In short the two brothers did not see eye to eye on a number of things especially because the elder brother never really paid attention to Sonny's ideas. It is not surprising therefore that they simply did not understand each other.

When the story is picked up after a time lapse of several years, Sonny, now living with his brother and his family, has dropped out of the school but the distrust between the brothers remains unabated. One Saturday afternoon, while his wife was out to visit her parents, the narrator, now an ex-soldier, was relaxing in his own living room as he tries to resist the temptation to search Sonny's room. Sonny was usually out whenever the narrator was at home. But the narrator was soon distracted by the sound

---

7. Ibid., 119–20.
8. Ibid., 121.

of music from a nearby avenue where a religious revival meeting was in progress. All that the organisers, three women and a man, had were their voices and a tambourine. People of all sorts, including some tough-looking women, paused to watch.

As the songs of the revivalists filled the air, the narrator saw his brother Sonny standing on the edge of the crowd. When the singing stopped, and the tambourine of the revivalists turned into a collection plate, the narrator observed Sonny drop some change in the plate, while looking at the women as he started across the avenue toward home. He entered the house, and soon realized that his elder brother had also been watching the religious revival. The two brothers talked about how they liked the voices of the singers and how the lady who beat the tambourine was such a good drummer. Sonny, who meanwhile had become a musician, informs his brother that he would be playing at a music show that night and invites the elder man. In the course of the chit-chat that follows, the narrator, for the first time, catches himself feeling like curbing his tongue to give his brother a chance to talk. The narrator actually does listen as Sonny tried, albeit not quite successfully, to unburden his mind. Sonny sums up the problem thus: "You walk these streets, black and funky and cold, and there's not really a living ass to talk to, and there's nothing shaking, and there's no way of getting it out—that storm inside. You can't talk to it and you can't make love to it, and when you finally try to get with it and play it, you realise *nobody's* listening . . ."[9]

It is significant, as Patricia Robertson notes, that the two brothers should begin to communicate after they had both witnessed a street religious revival. (They both watched how the meeting broke up across the way from where they were sitting in their living room.) Sonny's loneliness and travails had been private and having witnessed how people ruin themselves on drugs and lived rough on the streets, he was not in a hurry to forget what he had been through in and out of prison. Even before he went to prison and knowing how vulnerable he was to the influences around him, he had tried to run away from Harlem. Unfortunately, he was, hitherto, unable to articulate the issue to his brother. The prison experiences provided an opportunity for him to attempt putting the problems across through letterwriting, but he was too inarticulate to say what he meant. It was not until he had heard what seemed to him to be a "painful rendition" of the

9. Ibid., 135.

revivalists' songs that he realized that other people also face private battles, perhaps, worse than his own.[10]

MUSICAL EXPERIENCES

The jazz concert performance to which Sonny invited his brother provided a unique opportunity for Sonny to unburden his soul in a way that was as shocking as it was inspiring and revealing to his brother, the narrator. The atmosphere at the nightclub was a world alien to this narrator and people were glad to welcome him simply for his younger brother's sake. As it were, his identity in such a setting depended on his younger brother's reputation. When the musicians came on stage, Sonny was on the keyboard and it struck the narrator that Sonny hadn't been near a piano for over a year. Watching his face, he noticed how hard he worked to be able to hit the right key. Summing up Sonny's initial difficulty, the narrator thought that "the piano stammered, started one way, got scared, stopped; started another way, panicked, marked time, started again; then seemed to have found a direction, panicked again, got stuck."[11]

The concert took a different turn during the second set as the drummer literally "spoke" with his instrument and Creole, the bandleader, responded with his bass fiddle. The bandleader made it a point of duty to step forward and tell the audience that what they were playing was the blues, a jazz art form usually associated with a capacity to elicit extreme emotions—be it sadness or joy. According to the bandleader, it was not something new, but:

> ... it always must be heard. There isn't any other tale to tell, it's the only light we've got in all this darkness ...
>
> And this tale, according to that face, that body, those strong hands on those strings, has another aspect in every country, and a new depth in every generation.[12]

At last, having apparently found his rhythm, Sonny began to play well, to the delight of his audience. He seemed to have found something which touched everybody, including his fellow musicians, and the narrator. Everybody soon gathered around him as he played on the piano with dexterity. In a

---

10. Robertson, "Baldwin's 'Sonny's Blues,'" in *The Scapegoat Metaphor*, 193.

11. Baldwin, "Sonny's Blues," 140. Cf. Albert, "Jazz-Blues Motif," 181, where it is suggested that Sonny's struggle with the piano is indicative of his struggle with life.

12. Baldwin, "Sonny's Blues," 141.

sort of introspection, it occurred to the narrator that not many people listen to music with full attention and that when they occasionally do, what is heard, or corroborated, are personal, private, vanishing evocations. On the other hand, the musician may seem to hear something else as he imposes order on sound though it is not always possible to verbalize the emotions that are evoked.

As it is, the effect of the music triggers off a revealing train of thought, making the narrator recall his late mother's face. He:

> felt, for the first time, how the stones of the road she had walked on must have bruised her feet. I saw the moonlit road where my father's brother died. And it brought something else back to me, and carried me past it, I saw my little girl again and felt Isabel's tears again, and I felt my own tears begin to rise. And I was yet aware that this was only a moment, that the world waited outside, as hungry as a tiger, and that trouble stretched above us, longer than the sky.[13]

As he listened and noted that Sonny's music had become beautiful and unhurried, the narrator experienced a sense of well-being and of freedom enabling him to reflect on the importance of *listening*. Thus, music facilitated, in the final scene, not only Sonny's own reminiscences but that of the narrator as well. This image, according to Michael Clarke, signifies that music taps into the very roots of existence, that it puts the artist in touch with the fluid emotions.[14] But how did it happen that Sonny succeeded in using his artistry on the piano as a bridge to his own and the narrator's own past?[15] Although, the answer to the question pervades this chapter, we will consider its philosophical underpinning, in the next section.

Listener-Response Theories

Philosophers, literary critics and musicologists have expended much energy studying music's ability to stir up the deepest recesses of the human

---

13. Ibid., 142.
14. Clarke, "James Baldwin's Sonny's Blues," 204–5.
15. Ibid. As Albert puts it, Sonny's achievement brought his brother to a realisation of the importance of his roots through a kind of rebirth and acceptance of his heritage. Cf. "Jazz-Blues Motif," 182. This accords with Klaus F. Heimes' remark that "there is something to testify to the human soul, something that needs music rather than language to reveal itself." Cf. Heimes, "Interdisciplinary and Intercultural Aspects of Music," 26.

mind. In the context of our study, it may be asked: how does music generate emotion as is obviously the case with the narrator in this story? Opinions on this matter are legion. The lines of arguments that are often proffered will be approached, in broad strokes, from two perspectives—cognitive and emotivist.

Cognitivist Perspective

From the point of view of cognitive theory, the interpretation humans give to musical sound is a result of a conscious process of inference. Implicit in the line of thought is the idea that music has certain expressive properties that listeners recognise.[16] Cognitivists claim that there is a resemblance of the music in its pitch, volume and rhythm and melody to the natural expression of emotions in the human voice,[17] demeanour and behaviour.[18] This, according to this line of thinking, explains why "sad" music tends to be low, soft and slow. "Angry" music on the other hand, tends to be high-pitched and loud with rapid unpredictable rhythms and sharp breaks in melodic contours. Hence minor keys are associated with sadness or a negative emotional state just as bright colors express certain moods by arousing them. This brings to mind the thought of David Hume expressed in "On the Standard of Taste" (1757), an essay where he noted that some qualities are calculated to please and others to displease, a point of view that assumes a uniformity in human sensibility.[19]

If one stretches this point further, it becomes quite possible to argue that humans are biologically programmed to "react emotively to recognition of human-type states in perceived phenomena."[20] Peter Kivy stands out as representative of the cognitive approach, although he is by no means an extremist.[21] He suggests that when we characterize music as angry, joyous

---

16. Cf. Kivy, *Music Alone*, 141.

17. The presupposition, as Francis Sparshott explains in another context, is that instrumental music is, to a very large extent, an extension of vocal music in affirmation of the fact that what can be sung can be played. Cf. Sparshott, "Music and Feeling," 29.

18. Goldman, "Emotions in Music," 62.

19. Hence, sensibilities may be all of a kind, but this should not necessarily lead to the conclusion that all humans are, to the same degree competent aesthetic judges. Cf. Gardner, "Aesthetics," 233, with reference to Hume, "Of the Standard of Taste."

20. Goldman, "Emotion in Music," 63. Cf. also Gardener, "Aesthetics," 245; and Kivy, *Sound Sentiment*.

21. On his preference for a rather middle ground, Kivy writes: "I take the cognitivist

or melancholy, we are merely identifying the heard qualities of the music—"the extra-musical accoutrements that give the expressive qualities of the music their *raison d'être*."[22] This, however, is not to say that a particular piece of music makes one angry, joyous or melancholic.[23] Musical pieces, he says, do not provide objects to which ordinary emotions can be attached. If a piece of music expresses anger or sadness, we are not angry *at* the pieces nor *about it*. Rather, we are only moved by the way in which certain pieces of music capture certain emotions which play critical roles in the listening experience. Beyond this, "listening attitudes" play an important part in either suppressing or facilitating the tendency of the expressive qualities of music to arouse the corresponding emotion in listeners.[24] This happens because the piece of music is, by virtue of custom or convention, heard as appropriate to the expression of something which contributes, in a particular context, to forming an expressive contour.[25]

Arousal of the Emotions

From the perspective of the emotivist theory, music is both a cause and an effect of sentiment. That is, in perceiving music as a human product we react to it *affectively* in that recognition and the arousal of emotional states interact and reinforce one another.[26] Jenefer Robinson articulates this understanding quite clearly, noting that: "music can induce physiological

---

point of view ... But I reject utterly the notion that I am committed to a coldly analytic response to music." Cf. Kivy, *Music Alone*, 147. Cf. also Kivy, *Corded Shell*.

22. Kivy, *Music Alone*, 171.

23. Kivy, "Auditor's Emotions," 2.

24. Kivy points out that listening attitudes can be manipulated. He adds that the capability of "happy" and "sad" music to change people's mood seems to be too insignificant to turn the sad happy or to deprive the happy of their state of bliss. See Kivy, "Auditor's Emotions," 4, with reference to Aristotle, *Nicomachean Ethics*, 27.

25. Robinson, "Expression and Arousal of Emotion in Music," 18. As Robinson points out, Kivy's argument is quite persuasive if one considers examples of music with texts. As we shall see, this line of thought is different from the theory of "make-believe" in which Walton argues that the arousal of emotion takes place in the listener's imagination. That is, the listener "imagines experiencing and identifying particular stabs of pain, particular feelings of ecstasy, particular sensations of well-being as in viewing painting one imagines seeing particular things." Walton, "What is Abstract about the Art of Music?" 359; and Walton, "Pictures and Make-Believe," 300. Cf. also Robinson, "Expression and Arousal of Emotion," 18.

26. Goldman, "Emotion in Music," 63–64.

changes and a certain quality of inner feeling . . . Music can make me feel tense or relaxed; it can disturb, unsettle me, and startle me; it can calm me down or excite me; it can get me tapping my foot, singing along, or dancing; it can maybe lift my spirits and mellow me out."[27]

Drawing on Leonard Meyer's thought on listener-response theory, Robinson explains that the direct arousal of emotion such as being surprised, disturbed, satisfied, relaxed, etc. is a clue to the structure of emotional expressiveness such that "disturbing passages disturb us; reassuring ones reassure. Passages that meander uncertainly make us feel uneasy . . . Passages that move forward confidently make us feel satisfied: we know what is happening and seem to be able to predict what will happen next. Passages that are full of obstacles make us feel tense and when the obstacles are overcome, we feel relieved."[28]

Kendall Walton shares the view that there is a connection between the presence of an "emotional quality" in music and the arousal of that emotion in the listener although, for him the relationship should neither be seen as "direct" nor as metaphoric but in terms of "make-believe." This means that the way to explain the transition from hearing a specific type of music to a particular kind of emotion, say anguish, is to "imagine that in experiencing music I am undergoing an experience of anguish."[29] This approach facilitates a distinction between the experience at the level of make-believe and the experience of anguish apart from the world of the imagination. Furthermore, the make-believe account easily accommodates any indefiniteness in the musical expression of emotion.[30]

How is this fact to be recognized by the listener? One suggestion is that the composer uses the mastery of the rules of "make-believe" in the construction of the musical piece. The listeners, for their part, understand the work only if they exercise upon it their own internalized mastery of the rules. These rules map audible features of music onto make-believe facts about the occurrence of emotions of various kinds. But if music appreciation here seems to be nothing but an imaginative awareness of auditory sensation, does not this approach seem to make the emotion induced by

27. Robinson, "Expression and Arousal of Emotion," 18.

28. It is important to be aware that the feeling expressed is not always what is felt. For instance, an uncertain, diffident passage may make one uneasy while a confident music piece may make one feel reassured or relaxed. Cf. Robinson, "Expression and Arousal of Emotion," 20, with reference to Meyer, *Emotion and Meaning in Music*.

29. Cf. Budd, "Music and the Communication of Emotion," 134.

30. Ibid., 138.

music rather too abstract?[31] In defending Walton's idea, Budd writes that "music expresses not an imaginary emotion, but a quality of emotion, not a real or imagined instance of emotion, but the property of emotion."[32]

Limit of Rationality

From the foregoing, it has become evident that both the cognitivist and the emotivist arguments proceed on the assumption that it is possible to come up with an all-embracing rule of thumb that explains the symbiotic relationships between music and emotion.[33] Behind the attempt of the emotivists to establish the fact that sad music can make one sad lies the desire to show that listening to music is a sublime and emotional stimulus rather than a heartless, analytic and dispassionate exercise. On the other hand, the cognitivists who think that sadness, for instance, is a property of some kind, are fighting against letting emotion distract one from reading the meaning of music correctly. In his attempt to blend these streams of thought, Francis Sparshott has added important insights that will be particularly helpful in our quest to understand why the narrator of "Sonny's Blues" reacted the way he did to his brother's music.[34]

Sparshott is persuaded that music-making does not arise as a form of mathematics to be worked out in the fabric of life as both the cognitivists and the emotivists have tried to do. Rather, musical practices are integral to social engagements whose structures are connected to diverse phenomena. The emotion or what is termed "the affective side of life" is not something with a simple identify or structure, given that: "the information processing system in the human brain, to which all musical procedures belong, are shown by scientific research and medical experience not to correspond to anything that sound engineering practice would suggest, or common sense, or to Aristotelian functionalism, but are sort of subtle bricolage."[35]

While not denying that there is a link between music and emotion, Sparshott blames the tendency by which cognitivist, and emotivist theorists situate the affective function of music to a particular entity on a sort of

---

31. Cf. Robinson, "Expression and Arousal of Emotion."
32. Cf. Budd, "Music," 137.
33. Robinson, "Expression and the Arousal of Emotion," 20.
34. Sparshott, "Music and Feeling," 23–35; and Heimes, "Interdisciplinary and Intercultural Aspects of Music," 26–27.
35. Sparshott, "Music and Feeling," 29.

physicalism that perceives the world as a mechanical system.[36] For him, it is a simple fact of life that people have moods in ways that affect the things they do. Consequent upon this, they have reactive feelings towards events, things and people for which words such as love, rage, hope, etc., are useful descriptions. Also, humans sometimes identify things, events or persons as annoying or adorable, and the field of action can be effectual, enabling one, for instance, to perceive a landscape as gloomy, sinister, or peaceful without the experienced quality being referred to having any verbal identification.[37] Hence, music is, in itself, effectual, and though it emanates from an external source, it has no meaning without the listener. But composers, performers, and listeners need not always be concerned with the affective aspect of a piece of music nor is it necessary for meaning to be assigned or situated in any particular entity. Yet, it remains a fact that music is a communication system in which performers and hearers are engaged. Thus "the affectual character of music may, on occasion, be assigned, wholly or in part to the subjective states of composers, performers, or listeners, either inferentially or as heard characters in the music itself. This explains why it is sometimes said that the painful character of a particular piece of music is the outcome of the composer's pain."[38]

The foregoing assumptions enhance the mapping out of a number of ways in which music and feelings can relate to each other.[39] In the first place, musical pieces have affective qualities that can be perceived directly and based on musical relationships, as heard by people whose ears are attuned to the musical systems being used. This affective quality of some music may be such that if a competent hearer is asked to apply it to one of two contrasted moods or words, the hearer will easily be able to comply. Yet Sparshott is aware that one need not suppose the mathematical consistency is expected in all cases.[40] Furthermore, musical forms are such that the af-

---

36. Ibid.; and cf. Kivy, *Music Alone*, 146.
37. Sparshott, "Music and Feeling," 25.
38. Ibid., 26.

39. Sparshott is of the view that the problem does require continued investigation. Moreover, he doubts whether any solution that will lead to a final resolution is necessary even if it is ever possible to arrive at such a solution. Cf. ibid., 27.

40. The competence under reference here includes musical accomplishment and familiarity with appropriate vocabularies and associated cultural codes. Cf. ibid. One is reminded also that a distinction between the emotions felt by composer, listener, or critic is in order although it should not be confused with the emotional states denoted by different aspects of musical stimulus. Cf. Meyer, *Emotion and Meaning*, 8; and Kivy

fective quality of a piece of music may be more congruent with some named emotion than others, given that: "The human animal is uniquely the animal that makes culture, that lives by being prepared constantly to reinvent itself and the conditions of its existence. For such an animal, music, like the arts in general, would be a crucial device to maintain the necessary perceptual acuity, world-making flexibility, and range of emotive resource."[41]

This line of thinking is further grounded in the context of the sound to which animals and humans use in response to events around them. In this regard, vocal music is an extension of the natural phenomenon of the voice as a communicative system, with its cognitive function and affective capacities going hand in hand. The sounds which animals make evoke attitudes, feelings, and responses and humans have an added advantage: the capacity to modulate their speech by linguistic schemes and to subject it to reflection and modification. This can be expected to affect virtually all uses of voice, in as much as they form part of the human culture that echo beyond the cognitivist and emotivist arguments.

The implication of this is that if music is accepted as sound-making and felt-response, one can see how such an endeavour can be related to the emotions. Through a culturally accepted form of music, the artist can emit a sound that is open to interpretation. This explains why:

> a musical experience may give rise in some listener to a subjective feeling or emotion. That feeling may or may not be "identical" with, or congruent with, a feeling ascribed to the music. If it is not, the relation may be a matter of psychological causation, dependent on the listener's personal make-up and history... The listener may [correctly or incorrectly] identify a piece of music as having, or as being meant to have a certain conventional affective significance... [or] identify a piece of music as evincing [being caused by, being symptomatic of] a certain feeling or disposition in composer and/or performer.[42]

What becomes evident here is that musical practices have intertextual elements, given, as we have seen, that music is very much related to social structures connected with diverse phenomena which sometimes resist the

---

Music Alone, 155.

41. Sparshott, "Music and Feeling," 28.

42. Sparshott, 32. Kivy shares this view stressing that musical cognition and musical emotion are not incompatible. Cf. Kivy, *Music Alone*, 147.

restrictions of language.⁴³ Against this background, one begins to appreciate how, in the story, the narrator's enjoyment of his brother's music conjures up his mother's face, his uncle's death, his daughter's death, his wife's sorrows, all of which enabled him to come to empathize with his brother.⁴⁴

One is then able to argue, as Bieganowski does, that "Sonny's Blues" chronicles the narrator's growth from self-absorption to authentic self-knowledge gained through listening to Sonny.⁴⁵ It was a shift from narcissism to openness to the *other* which facilitated self-criticism. Within the narrator's experience of the concert there is also a sense of freedom and a realisation that "honest understanding of others depends upon truthful acceptance of one's self . . . The ability to see someone else requires looking selflessly beyond one's own immediate needs."⁴⁶ Though the narrator's preoccupation with himself makes him intolerant of his brother's lifestyle, the younger man's music brings to the fore the pains in the loss of a child, his wife's sorrow and his brother's needs, all of which underline the emotional impact of the jazz blues phenomenon.⁴⁷ It is of particular interest to our study that attention is paid to the place of jazz and the blues musical art forms in the AfricanAmerican mindset. Such an exercise will throw light on how secular music can become invested with sacred resonances.⁴⁸

HISTORY IN CULTURE TEXT

As we have suggested above, the jazz blues heritage in American culture is easily linked to expressions such as depression, misery, low spirits, all of

---

43. Heimes, "Interdisciplinary and Intercultural Aspects of Music," 26. Gadamer was very much aware of this when he wrote that although artistic experience is able to transmit truth, such a mode of knowledge is of a unique kind and "certainly different from that sensory knowledge, which provides science with the data from which it constructs the knowledge of nature." Cf. Gadamer, *Trust and Method*, 87.

44. See Byerman, "Words and Music," 370.

45. Bieganowski, "James Baldwin's Vision of Otherness," 71. Thus music becomes a bridge which the narrator crosses in order to get closer to Sonny. Cf. Savery, "Baldwin, Bebop and Sonny's Blues," 166.

46. Bieganowski, "James Baldwin's Vision of Otherness," 79.

47. See ibid., 71–73, where it is noted that "Pain or suffering or death constitutes the bleak substance of experience from which these people fashion themselves." See also Byerman, "Words and Music," 370.

48. The studies of Terrence Thomas and Elizabeth Manning on the relationship between culture and religion are quite instructive. Cf. "The Iconic Function of Music," 160, where they argue that religion is always clothed in cultural garments.

which are suggested in dictionaries. From a cultural historical perspective, researchers find this useful as they have much to say about the unhappiness of the African Americans who, in the time of slavery and the segregation that followed, had a deep-rooted sense of alienation. Robbed of their identity and denied access to mainstream culture and political institutions, African Americans had to fall back on resources like music and dance in order to structure their own social processes. Indeed, available literature shows that from the earliest times they have used their music to document their history, and to fashion an identity that articulates their past, their present, their dreams and hopes.[49]

In the time of slavery, for instance, scholars have found out that the Spirituals were particularly helpful in serving life-preserving purposes, in that they enabled the slaves to create alternative worlds necessary for survival. The Spirituals were also a means of communication. Their call-and-response structure was a way of celebrating the oral tradition and the interactive process characterizing the individual and the community. Music and dance thus served as means of communication—means by which "meanings are produced, maintained, negotiated and transformed";[50] it was, indeed, a regenerative resource for survival.[51] There is therefore, a sense in which it can be said that a close relationship exists between the music of the Black Americans and their way of life.[52]

It is worth pointing out here that academic interests in other musical genres of the AfricanAmericans took time to develop given that scholars with different personal and often political agendas paid attention to and collected only what they wanted and ignored other forms.[53] An example of

---

49. Cf. Lipsitz, *Time Passages*, 236.

50. Kong, "Popular Music in Geographical Analysis," 192. For emphasis, one can add here that music is not just harmless luxury but a field of knowledge that easily provides avenues for interdisciplinary study. Cf. Heimes, "Interdisciplinary and Intercultural Aspects of Music," 26.

51. Cf. Gerhard Putschogl, "Black Music—Key Force in Afro-American Culture," 264. Cf. also Ostendorf, "Black Poetry, Blues and Folklore."

52. As Kong argues quite convincingly, it is very much in the nature of music to be able to do this. Music can serve as a source material from which a people convey their experiences to the extent that "moments of spectacle or historic import are often captured in song through the filters of music-makers." See "Popular music in Geographical Analysis," 184.

53. Earliest collectors were usually ministers, children of ministers, or workers affiliated with religious organisations. Cf. Jackson, "The Afro-American Toast and Worksong," 246. This is not to say that the religious establishment has always been enthusiastic

a neglected folklore is the "toast," a folk poetry associated with black men. Although this genre is occasionally linked to drinking situations, scholars are not absolutely certain whence the toast entered the black tradition. But it is agreed that most of the poems depict street characters generally treated at a comic distance. Also marginalized are the worksongs. Worksongs, as Bruce Jackson explains, are simply songs used to help people to work. They gave the singers, especially those doing forced labour, a regular outlet for emotions that had no other legitimate outlet. Jackson points out that worksong lyrics are sometimes quite poetic and interesting, but when they are banal and stupid they are legitimized by the musical context.[54] Worksong was particularly common in group activity and need not have any audience. Consisting of brief verses sung by a leader and brief simple choruses sung by the group, worksongs merely kept large groups moving together while at work.[55] Not only did the songs help to ensure the woodcutters, for instance, kept perfect rhythm, they also helped to prevent anyone from being far behind in the task at hand.[56] Jazz music, of which the blues is a form, is thought to be one of the attempts of the blacks to acculturate in America while remaining distinct.[57] Archie Shepp sees its evolution in phases, namely, the formative, the transitional, the romantic and impressionistic. The latter has an aspect known as the "Free Jazz," a random and

---

about music forms that originate from the cultural experience of the African Americans. Studies by Archie Shepp show that, in times past, the Church, including those attended by prosperous African Americans, might have acted as a restraining force on African American music. The authorities tended to emphasize the singing of hymns from standard hymnals, while discouraging the show of emotion during services. Cf. Shepp, "Innovations in Jazz," 257.

54. Jackson, "African-American Toast and Worksong," 253.

55. Leaders were not selected for having a pretty voice or for being particularly creative in their lyrics. What was important was the ability to sing loudly enough and the ability to keep perfect time. Cf. Jackson, "The African-American Toast and Worksong," 254.

56. From this standpoint, music serves as both the medium and the outcome of experience. Cf. Kong, "Popular Music in Geographic Analysis," 184.

57. As Putschogl found out, apart from signifying an attempt to continue the African oral traditions, the blues, in another sense, tries to adapt while resisting assimilation into the mainstream culture. Cf. Putschogl, "Black Music," 265. Thus, the blues, as an art form "is looking both within and without the black community for means of sustenance, identity and survival." Cf. Putschogl, "Black Music," 265, with reference to Levine, *Black Culture and Black Consciousness*, 189.

subjective attempt by musicians trained in various traditions to bring coherence into their art.[58]

In attempting to understand the blues and the role it plays in the story under discussion, it is equally important to note that there is a very profound sense in which the linking of the AfricanAmerican folk music, to misery, low-spiritedness and unhappiness runs the risk of overstatement because "a vast amount of blues music isn't actually all that blue."[59] Unhappiness seems merely to be one of the many possibilities of blues given that it is a flexible medium for humour, satire and topical commentary. According to Savery, the blues is, at times, performed for its recreational values, or in celebration of the joy of sex; at other times their uses are non-serious—even to the point of being boring. Quite often though, the blues is performed as a sign of excitement. Against the background of the role music has played in American life, it cannot but be said that music and dance are able to function as means of articulating social and aesthetic order both of which have therapeutic aspects.[60] It is part of the paradoxical nature of music to add here that the blues has also been quite effective in times of collective sorrowing.[61]

Characterized by a simple musical plan that makes it a fertile area for improvisation, critics find in the blues an appealing balance of familiar and exotic elements.[62] It is also recognized by its embodiment of conversational exchanges between the lead instrument and the human voice. Almost always, this creates a unique rhythmical sound based upon adaption of the

---

58. Shepp, "Innovations in Jazz," 256.

59. Sandall thinks that the notion that the blues emerged unmediated out of the suffering of freed slaves is not only patronizing to early performers but also misrepresents the vitality of the art form. Cf. Sandall, "I Woke Up This Morning . . . Happier," 17; and Russell "Jerry McCain," 43–44.

60. As noted earlier, during the times of slavery the Spiritual enabled the slaves to fashion an alternative world which they used in transcending their situation. Against this background, Lily Kong is right to point out other possible uses of music: it can operate not only within the context of political, social and economic conditions but also as a way of expressing protest and resistance. See Kong, "Popular Music in Geographical Analysis," 188, and Putschogl, "Black Music," 264.

61. This heritage has had a lot of influence on both old and contemporary African American Church. Cf. Savery, "Baldwin, Bebop, and Sonny's Blues," 169.

62. In this context, "innovation" is a quasi-technical term. "It is a process of discovery, synthesis, and refinement, predicated on discipline." Cf. Shepp, "Innovations in Jazz," 258.

call-response patterning traceable to traditional African music.[63] Another recognisable quality of the blues is that it has a capacity to embody experiences of the artist and the audience. Drawing on intuition, taste and athletic prowess, artists use the blues to tell their story.[64] Indeed, it makes sense to suppose that if they are to earn a living, the careers of the performers cannot but depend on an ability not only to display an awareness of the human problems that confront the audience but also in being able to direct "attention away from the dreary circumstances of their everyday life."[65] Both the musicians and their audience can therefore be said to be engaged in dialogues that can be located in space and time.[66]

MORAL DIMENSION OF AESTHETICS

In the light of the foregoing, we propose that, for the narrator, Sonny's performance on stage epitomizes how art can fulfil emotional and/or psychological needs. This is in keeping with Kendall Walton's account of how some works of art, including music, stimulate or soothe while others are just provocative or even upsetting.[67] Some allow for intellectual pleasure, others fulfil emotional needs offering insights or catharsis.[68] It can also happen that some works provide escape from everyday cares while others help humans to deal with them. To be worthy of evaluation, some works require careful study and analysis while the beauty of others is clearly obvi-

---

63. Sandall, "I Woke up this Morning," 17.

64. That this fact is not always recognized may be due to the tendency in people simply to attend concerts, or watch television as a matter of course sparing no thought for the message of the artists themselves. Cf. Lipsitz, *Time Passages*, 3–4.

65. Sandall, "I Woke Up This Morning," 17.

66. As our examination of the emotivist and the cognitivist interpretations of music has shown, it is not out of place to suppose that meaning can be encoded in music such that the resulting text, is "read by the audience, in a manner sometimes concordant, at other times discordant, with the encoded meanings. These meanings are then incorporated into lived cultures and social relations; feedback loops may then provide material for the production of new texts or lead to the modification of existing ones." See Kong, "Popular Music in Geographical Analysis," 188.

67. Walton, "How Marvellous," 499.

68. Catharsis as the value of negative emotions assumes that such emotions exist in humans and needs release. The releases may be enjoyable in themselves or mitigate their harmful effects when they do occur in real life. There is also the controversial suggestion that those who experience them tend to be more sensitive. The evidence of this point of view seems tenuous. Cf. Goldman, "Emotion in Music," 68.

ous. Great works can be exuberant or gloomy, intense or severe, or painful or funny.

From an aesthetic point of view, the narrator's judgment was simply a *felt experience* and although subjective, it was a sort of judgment facilitated by culture texts which provide the relevant vocabularies. One can discern from here an echo of Kendall Walton's proposal on the purpose of the arts.[69] Beyond this, one is also reminded that in appreciating a work of art, no matter the form it takes, one does not merely enjoy it but has also to recognize the creator's accomplishment and how successfully the work provides insight into important truths as well as facilitating the conveyance of ideas.[70] Implicit in this line of thought is the moral dimension of aesthetics, for if the pleasure taken in a work of art is tainted by malice, the pleasure becomes at best, questionable and at worst, unethical.[71]

As it is, the reaction of the narrator to Sonny's music is not only appropriate but a pointer to the inadequacy of rational knowledge in making conscious connections with the realities of human existence. Hence, if issues of beauty sometimes burst rational discourses, and if Paul Fiddes is right in arguing that theology is but a responsible reaction to human experience,[72] it becomes possible to suggest that beauty has a semi-religious and moral significance. This explains why Immanuel Kant calls it "a symbol of the good."[73] It is able to embody a Christian meaning for those who accept the concept of God as the ultimate human concern.[74] Herman-Emiel Mertens

---

69. Lamarque and Olsen, *Truth Fiction and Literature*, 441.

70. Commenting on the significance of such artistic achievement, Kendall Walton notes that its value lies in its "desirable capacity to induce the appreciator's pleasurable admiration although this capacity may not belong to the physical work itself, but to the work understood in a certain way—as the artist's attempt to accomplish certain possibly arbitrary objectives." Cf. Walton, "How Marvellous," 507. The point here is that aesthetic values can be arbitrary yet the pleasures they give can be real.

71. This makes aesthetic pleasure an intentional state, not just a buzz or a rush caused by experiencing a work of art. Cf. Walton, "How Marvellous," 504 and 505. In his comment on the functioning of literature, Lionel Trilling made the same point when he proposed "literary situations as cultural situations, and cultural situations as great elaborate fights about moral issues." As quoted by Samuels, "Don't Delight," iv. See also Lamarque and Olsen, *Truth Fiction and Literature*, 441.

72. Cf. Fiddes, *Freedom and Limit*, 32.

73. Reaching such ideal condition comes through practice, and the ability to make relevant comparisons while being free from prejudice. Where differences occur they can be explained as a result of "differences in delicacies." Cf. Gardner, "Aesthetics," 232–33.

74. Cf. Fiddes, *Freedom and Limit*, 12. One is deeply aware here that God-talk is most fruitful when the use of language is at the level of metaphor. Yet no metaphor is adequate

reminds us, however, that although interaction between faith and aesthetics is always fruitful with one modifying the other, aesthetic experience does not necessarily lead explicitly to religious faith or to conversion.[75] That is why Baldwin's role in this process can be perceived in terms of the relationship between poetry and divine inspiration. Granted that the two processes are different from each other, one requires and supposes the other.[76] This, at another level, affirms the writer's capacity to share in the creative process which the Christian mindset associates with the divine inspiration.[77]

REVELATION

The tentative conclusion that derives from the above discussion is that aesthetic experience can be illuminating, indeed, revelatory.[78] Revelation is here understood in the light of the Latin term *revelare*, which means "to unveil" or "disclose."[79] As Dulles has suggested, even outside a religious context the term *revelation* suggests "a sudden or unexpected receipt of knowledge of a profoundly significant character, especially that which gives the recipient a new outlook or attitude towards life and the world."[80] The experience of the narrator of "Sonny's Blues" brings this out most vividly. Coleridge might have termed his ordeal an "inward experience" that simu-

---

to describe the concept of God completely. Mertens, "His Very Name Is Beauty," 316, with reference to McFague, *Metaphorical Theology*.

75. According to Mertens, the beautiful adds to the good. Moreover, there is no gainsaying the fact that human quest for beauty, like the quest for the divine, is a never-ending endeavour. Consequent upon this, the quest for the beautiful provides grounds for hope. Cf. Mertens, "His Very Name Is Beauty," 322–26.

76. Cf. Jasper, *Coleridge as a Poet and Religious Thinker*, 144–45. Cf. Farrer, "Revelation," 84–107.

77. Shelly, *Defence of Poetry*, 105–6.

78. For Paul Fiddes, this could not have been otherwise, considering that the quest for new world order would be mere escapism if we did not feel that works of art are reaching out beyond themselves to something of "ultimate concern" to humanity. Cf. Fiddes, *Freedom and the Limit*, 8.

79. Dulles, *Revelation Theology*, 9. In a scientific experience, for instance, the "revelatory" aspects of human endeavour is simply a situation with natural phenomena, on the one hand, and human abilities on the other. The idea is then set in propositions in order to be perceived in terms of a scientific or an anthropological finding. Cf. Wimmer, "What Makes Experience Revelatory?," 11.

80. Cf. jasper, *Coleridge as Poet*, 149. Such images are indeed made relevant by human experiences and it is within this context that one can meaningfully talk of revelation.

lates biblical images.[81] But before going into a detailed study of the part which imagination can play in the process of revelation, and how the narrator's experience points directly to the Christian concept of revelation, it will be helpful here to examine how the theology of revelation has evolved in history. This will enable us to guard against identifying revelation and faith with narrow outlooks that may be blind to new perspectives. The discussion will, understandably, begin from the Bible.

The dominant notion of revelation in the Old Testament is that of the word of God addressed to ancient Israel through chosen messengers. From this perspective, God's word is a dynamic force demanding prompt obedience and motivating people to act or not to act. It carries with it a guarantee of protection and prosperity to those who rely on it. In this sense, revelation is primarily for the nation and only secondarily to individuals "who became part of the covenant people."[82] The New Testament concept of revelation takes the form of a covenant in Jesus as Messiah and Lord.[83] But things have never been quite static. For instance, medieval scholasticism presents revelation as a body of Divine doctrine which furnishes answers to important questions about God, humanity and the universe. In this regard faith is an intellectual assent to doctrines on the strength of God's word.

As time went on, there emerged an insistence on the role of the Church as authoritative teacher. Consequent upon this, revelation came to be viewed objectively as the content of the Church's doctrine as derived from the Scripture and tradition. In this regard, faith becomes a matter of submission to the teaching of the magisterium.[84] Between the World Wars, the doctrine of revelation was affected by existentialism such that the concept came to be viewed as the summit of all human concern.[85] Dulles, a Catholic systematic theologian, acknowledges that Protestant thinkers have tended to be more creative, and more heavily influenced by current philosophies because they find difficulty in the idea of supposedly infallible, sacred sources. The Protestant theologians seem to be unwilling to be tied to the body of belief which reached completion in the first century of the Christian era. They equally shy away from giving unconditional reverence

---

81. Dulles, *Revelation*, 171.

82. Dulles, *Revelation*, 172.

83. This theocentric view is still discernible in the theology of Rahner, and Edward Schillebeeckx and in the teaching of Vatican II. Cf. ibid., 175.

84. Ibid., 174.

85. Ibid., 176.

Music and Revelation

to agencies that claim to speak decisively in the name of God; nor do they see any relevance in many doctrines which their forefathers accepted as matters of faith.[86]

The above understanding enabled Dulles to distinguish three distinct types of revelation theology. First, revelation is perceived as concrete event discernible in the events of biblical history, culminating in the death and resurrection of Jesus Christ. The downside of this approach is that it gives rise to a "biblicistic" theology of revelation.[87] The second approach is that of the rationalist-idealists who think of revelation as an experience that is only meaningful through reason. This is rather remarkably different from the third outlook, the intuitive-mystical approach, perceived as an indescribable encounter with the divine. This last approach, in turn, can be broken into two subtypes. On the one hand, there are the immanentists who experience God as one with themselves and with the world. On the other hand, there are those theologians who look upon God as the "wholly other," the "beyond."

What is evident in the third approach to theology is that revelation is a personal matter in which a high value is normally placed on symbolism and liturgy as means of invoking and inducing new experiences.[88] The approach relies on the literal sense to explain revelation in terms of how humans peer into the beyond. It is an approach that is quite meaningful for the intuitive minded and those that have regard for the "numinous."[89] Despite these various components of revelation (the factual, the doctrinal and the mystical), Dulles insists that the concept of revelation:

---

86. Ibid., 177.

87. Ibid., 178. See also Forsman, "Revelation and Understanding," 49–52, where biblical revelation, for instance, is expressed in terms of truth about God directly communicated an subsequently expressed in propositions and then written down by human hands. In time, such propositions become the objects of belief, and theological systemisation. Apart from the fact that the prepositional view depends on the appeal to authority in order to vindicate claim to knowledge, Forsman explains that it always needs to be shored up by theories of inspiration.

88. Dulles, *Revelation*, 179. This is in keeping with David Jasper's observation that it is in the nature of a poet's vocation to touch on the human spiritual constitution and needs. Cf. Jasper, *Coleridge as Poet*, 19, 150. The power of art to achieve this goal has historical examples. For instance, around 1800, it was held that romantic poetry, stage performance and the fine arts, could serve as extensions of the transcendent life of the philosophical contemplation or, indeed, as secular surrogates to Christianity. Cf. Goehr, "Political Music and Politics of Music," 103.

89. Dulles, *Revelation*, 180.

> is never a mere fact, in the sense of a verifiable historical occurrence; it is a fact pregnant with abiding divine significance. Revelation is never a mere doctrine, in the sense of abstract prepositional truth; it is always doctrinal which illuminates a unique event; the events occur not merely in the world outside man, but also within him; it has an objective and subjective pole, neither of which can be suppressed. The most properly revelatory element would seem to be precisely the *inbreaking of the divine* [my italics] in a manner that overcomes the subject-object dichotomy characteristic of our ordinary thought and speech.[90]

In the context of our study, another warning of Dulles' is equally apposite at this juncture. For him, no one definition could possibly do justice to a reality so rich and many-sided. Every definition is necessarily abstract, confronting its subject matter with a particular outlook, concern, and a specific conceptual framework. While this is legitimate, Dulles further warns against forgetting that revelation itself, as a concrete and mysterious self-communication of the divine, cannot be circumscribed by definition. It is apprehended as much through clear distinct ideas.[91] Hence the theologian should not analyse and present some abstract conceptof revelation in isolation from the rest of reality. Rather, revelation should be confronted in the concrete shape and circumstances in which it comes to humanity. Revelation should, therefore, have some affinity with the totality of human experience.[92]

In the light of the foregoing, it seems there is a sense in which one cannot but agree with Bieganowski that Sonny's artistry on the piano has some redemptive qualities in that it becomes "a moment of revelation for his brother and the reader and others through listening."[93] This is because, through the music, the narrator began to appreciate from a fresh perspective, his own life's experiences, his parents' struggles in life, his daughter's death and his wife's grief.[94] In this sense, music functions as a bridge which

---

90. Ibid., 11.

91. Ibid., 10.

92. Cf. Bieganowski, "Baldwin's Vision of Otherness," 79. See also Stroup, *Promise of Narrative Theology*, 65, for insight into how images are echoed in revelatory events. Aided by the imagination, the events, according to Stroup, "take on an illuminating and disclosing power, and it becomes the task of reason to search through memory with the assistance of these revelatory images . . ."

93. Cf. Robertson, "Baldwin's Sonny's Blues," 191.

94. Bieganowski, "Baldwin's Vision of Otherness," 79. Cf. also Nelson, "James Baldwin's Vision of Otherness and Community," 122, where Nelson comments: "self-discovery

allows Sonny and his brother to become united and Sonny to find meaning in his own individuality.

Baldwin uses the relationship between the brothers to make it explicit that the ability to understand oneself is dependent on being able to look selflessly beyond one's own immediate needs. This permits what Bieganowski terms a "reciprocal vision of otherness" between Sonny and his brother.[95] Against this background, Goldman is right in noting that those who appreciate music do not always listen passively and passionlessly, given that music has the capacity to engage human hopes and fears.[96] Hence despite the tendency of the mass media to turn music and art into commodities while obscuring the origins and intentions of artists, both music and art are, nevertheless, able to provide meaningful connection to our own past and the past of others.[97] For the narrator, music has far-reaching vibrations and for the reader, whose experience of the text is literary rather than musical, there is certainly room for a sense of the sublime that is at once real yet beyond the grasp of reason.[98] One can add also that for the reader, the process of coming to grips with the text is symptomatic of an adventure with immense potentiality.

Altered Consciousness

One remarkable aspect of this story is the portrait of the narrator which the reader is forced to deal with. At some point, he appeared disenchanted and distant and doing all he could to avoid getting emotionally entangled with anything or anybody. For instance, "Well, I guess it is not my business," was

---

is never an entirely private battle: it can be achieved only in spiritual communion with others."

95. However, it is worth bearing in mind, as Goldman argues, that composers need not be sad to compose sad music. Moreover, an audience might be moved to sadness or anger by a musical piece purely because of how bad it is. Cf. Goldman, "Emotion in Music," 59–61.

96. Lipsitz, *Time Passages*, 3–4.

97. Needless to add here that apart from being an exercise in theological criticism our point of interest can be appreciated also in terms of literary aesthetics whose objectives, as far as this story is concerned, include identifying those features of "Sonny's Blues" in virtue of which it is judged a work of art. It is within this framework that attention is paid to critical, moral and emotive responses to the story in so far as its themes overlap with those of the other stories in the collection. For more on the dimensions of literary aesthetics, see Lamarque, *Philosophy and Fiction*, 4.

98. Baldwin, "Sonny's Blues," 109.

one of the things he told himself about his younger brother's arrest.[99] At other times, however, the narrator emerges as a rather sensitive personality. His fear is such that on the day he heard the news of the arrest, great blocks of ice that seemed to settle in his belly kept melting as he taught his algebra classes. He had actually sensed that something was not right with his brother but he was afraid of finding out given that he did not want the safe and respective middle-class world he had constructed to be destroyed by his brother's trouble or those of any other person for that matter.[100] Yet the narrator was too sensitive to stop thinking about the unhappy young people around who seemed to be "growing up with a rush and their heads bumped abruptly against the low ceiling of their actual possibilities."[101] He was also able to observe that at play, the children shouted, cursed and that their laughter was devoid of childlike innocence.

The narrator's sensitivity was again manifested, when at the end of a working day, he encountered a friend of Sonny's, a boy he never liked.[102] On this occasion, however, he was forced to walk with him toward the subway station. Not long afterwards, he and the boy were distracted—they found themselves peering into a roadside bar where Sonny's friend did not seem to find whoever he was trying to find. For his part, the narrator, in his disenchantment, noticed a dancing barmaid and saw in her "the doomed, still struggling woman beneath the battered face of a semi-whore."[103] They soon parted company but not before Sonny's friend begged and received some money from the narrator. This young man who still hung around street corners and was always "high and raggy" now seems to personify the hopelessness the narrator saw around him. The young man even admitted that it was he who introduced Sonny to drugs and hinted at the difficulties he had been through, but the narrator blurted out, "don't tell me your sad story . . ."[104] But true to the flipside of his character, he quickly felt guilty for his outburst and regretted not having supposed that the boy might truly have his own personal problems.

99. Cf. Albert, "Jazz-Blues Motif."

100. Baldwin, "Sonny's Blues," 104.

101. This frame of mind, according to Keith B. Byerman, prepares the reader for an example of failed communication. See "Words and Music," 368.

102. Baldwin, "Sonny's Blues," 109. In labelling the woman as he does, the narrator is not only trying to distance himself emotionally but seems also to be inducing a "superiority complex" over the situation. See Byerman, "Words and Music," 368.

103. Baldwin, "Sonny's Blues," 107.

104. Ibid., 111.

Music and Revelation

The narrator's reactions on the day Sonny was released from prison again point to another dimension of his sensitivity. On that particular day, meeting Sonny made him recall a number of things he thought he had forgotten. He worried that prison life seemed to have made Sonny "older and thinner and it had deepened the distant stillness in which he had always moved."[105] He recalled that he had been there when Sonny was born, heard the first few words he spoke and was present when Sonny took his first step and how he caught him before he fell.

While the two brothers drive home, another element of the narrator's character becomes manifest—his hunger for self-knowledge and for answers to many social questions. And as he and Sonny beheld the sights and sounds of Harlem where they grew up, it occurred to the narrator that the:

> streets hadn't changed . . . [and the] houses exactly like the houses of our past yet dominated the landscape, boys exactly like the boys we once had been found themselves smothering in these houses, came down into the streets for light and air and found themselves encircled by disaster. Some escaped the trap, most didn't. Those who got out always left something of themselves behind, as some animals amputate a leg and leave it in the trap.[106]

The narrator was, nonetheless, filled with a sense of grateful thanks to fate—not only for his modest achievement as a school teacher but also that Sonny's problems had not been worse. But such a frame of mind did not make him indifferent to the hidden menace he perceived in the streets of Harlem. And the moment he and Sonny started into the house, the feeling that he was bringing him back into the danger he had tried to escape reared its head. And so while it could, on the one hand, be said that the narrator has been very protective toward his brother, it can, on the other hand, be pointed out that he has certainly not been at ease with himself and the social conditions within the environments he and his brother were forced to deal with.

What seems to accentuate the narrator's concern for his brother as well as provide a backdrop to his own circumstances does have some bearing upon the story his mother told him about an uncle whom he never knew.[107] This uncle used to have a job in a nearby mill and was quite musi-

---

105. Ibid., 112.
106. Clarke, "Baldwin's Sonny's Blues," 201.
107. See Baldwin, "Sonny's Blues," 119. See also Byerman, "Words and Music," 369. "The musically-talented uncle is Sonny's double and the helpless father is the narrator's."

cal as well—he liked to perform on Saturday nights. On the day he died, he and the narrator's father were coming home from somewhere a little drunk, when the late uncle was run over by a car. As the narrator found out from his mother, this incident made his father bitter. It would seem that the narrator was unconsciously haunted by the fear of being like his father who lost a younger brother under circumstances beyond his control.[108]

One other significant message in this story is that being protective toward Sonny, (the "baby brother") was not enough; the two brothers needed to be able to communicate with each other to enable the narrator to accept Sonny's individuality and come to terms with his own lifestyle.[109] The narrator's vision of life became enlarged only when he moved from being overbearing to being a good listener to what Sonny has to say through verbal and non-verbal communication. And when the narrator actually listened, he became "his brother's keeper—in words and in deeds, a growth from "apparent self-reflection, really self-absorption, to authentic self-knowledge gained through" honest listening.[110]

WORDPLAY AND THE SHIP OF ZION

Baldwin's success as a storyteller and a master of poetic language is well demonstrated especially with regard to his adroit use of contrasting images of *light* and *darkness* which form patterns of correspondence with *death* and *life* in the story. For instance, in a flashback, the narrator, in the voice of a child, tells of the usual after-dinner discussions of his elders and how, as dusk approached the child:

> could see *darkness* growing against the widow-panes . . . The *darkness* outside is what the old folks have been talking about. It's what they've come from. It's what they endure. The child knows

---

See Byerman, "Words and Music," 369.

108. It is instructive that Baldwin's choice of profession for Sonny is that of a jazz player given that jazz is a kind of music noted for each musician's ability to improvise while keeping in harmony with other members of the group. Cf. Albert, "Jazz-Blues Motif," 179.

109. Cf. Bieganowski, "James Baldwin's Vision of Otherness," 71.

110. Baldwin, "Sonny's Blues," 115–16. This echoes Wordsworth's "Ode: Intimations of Immortality" where growing up is pictured as an initiation into the troubles of this world. Youth is characterized as a time of "light" while adulthood overwhelms "like the doors of prisons, closing around us, darkening our lives." Cf. Clarke, "Baldwin's Sonny's Blues," 199.

MUSIC AND REVELATION

that they won't talk anymore because if he knows too much about what's happened to *them*, he will know too much too soon, about what is going to happen *to him*.[111]

Such play on contrasting themes is reinforced when the narrator reads the news of his brother's arrest in the swinging *lights* of the subway car, and in the faces and bodies of the people, and in his own face, trapped in the *darkness* outside.[112] As it is, the narrator's fears are concretized and then submerged into opposing images enabling him to recollect Sonny's childhood innocence. With this vision of innocence in mind, he notes that when Sonny was as old as the pupils in his algebra class, his face had been *bright* and open. The same level of meaning was maintained as the narrator hints at how scared he was to contemplate the possibility that all that *light* in Sonny's face might have gone out.[113] Thus, *darkness* came to symbolize failure, despair, and rage, as he sees in the faces of some of the pupils in his algebra class about whom he says:

> All they really knew were two *darknesses*, the *darkness* of their lives which was now closing in on them, and the *darkness* of the movies, which had blinded them to the other *darkness*, and in which they now, vindictively, dreamed, at once and more together than they were at any other time, and more alone.[114]

But the narrator's spirit was soon to be lifted such that the word *bright*, with its embodiment of *light* pops up once again. For instance, as the working day ends he steps out of the class to go home, the narrator hears one of the schoolboys outside "whistling a tune at once complicated and very simple, it seemed to be pouring out of him as though he were a bird and it sounded very cool and moving through all that harsh, *bright* air."[115] This depiction of polar opposites features once more in Sonny's letter to the narrator. Summing up his efforts to overcome his drug addition, Sonny tells his brother how, like a man trapped in a hole, he seems to be looking up from inside the hole and trying to get out because he is attracted to the *sunlight* up there.[116]

---

111. Baldwin, "Sonny's Blues," 103.
112. Ibid.
113. Ibid., 104.
114. Ibid., 105.
115. Ibid., 110.
116. Ibid., 111.

On his release from jail Sonny's smiles made the narrator look hopeful, "like an animal waiting to be coaxed into the *light*."[117]

The theme of contrast features also as the narrator tries to capture the image of the streets he and Sonny were passing as they drove home from the prison gates; each of the brothers was peering through his own side of the cab windows. They beheld a green park, the lifeless elegance of the hotels and apartment buildings. And while recalling the violent deaths he witnessed in childhood, the narrator thought of the boys who had once lived in the house that dominated the landscape. Some who had found themselves smothering in the houses did come down into the streets for *light* and air but ended up being damaged.[118]

The story of the narrator's uncle as told by his mother adds to the eloquent use to which Baldwin puts images of contrasts between light and dark. The *night* the narrator's uncle was killed was preceded by a *bright* day. And after the man had been crushed by the car driven by some drunken youths, the narrator's father, alone with the lifeless body of his brother and the busted guitar "never in his life seen anything as *dark* as that road after the *lights* of the car had gone away."[119]

Baldwin further uses the scene of revival carried on by "three sisters . . . and a brother" to echo the contradictions of life. Apart from the fact that the revivalists were not saying anything new, they seemed to embody all sorts of paradoxes and incongruities. In the first place, their song: "*'Tis the old ship of Zion . . . it has rescued many a thousand . . .*" did not ring true for the listeners who had not seen much in the way of rescue work being done around the Harlem environment.[120] Moreover, the listeners did not particularly believe in the holiness of the sisters and the brother; everyone knew them too well, yet they listened still. Comparing and contrasting two of the women, the narrator notes that the woman with the tambourine, whose voice dominated the air, and whose face was *bright* with joy, was divided by very little from "the woman who stood watching her, a cigarette between her heavy, chapped lips, her hair a cuckoo's nest, her face scarred and swollen from many beatings, and her black eyes glittering like coal."[121] Curiously enough, the revivalists were watched by what might be described

---

117. Ibid., 112.
118. Ibid., 118.
119. Ibid., 130; my italics.
120. Ibid.,130.
121. Robertson, "Baldwin's Sonny's Blues," 192.

Music and Revelation

as a cross-section of humanity—kids, workers, tough-looking women, old men.[122] The audience eventually got emotionally caught up in what was happening as the music, blending sadness with joy: "seemed to soothe a poison out of them [the listeners]; and time seemed, nearly, to fall away from the sullen belligerent battered faces, as though they were fleeing back to their first condition, while dreaming of their last."[123]

The remarkable fact is that in spite of themselves, the music of the revivalists helped the listeners to take a quick look at the mixture of sadness and joy that can be found in the human condition. For Sonny, the insight into the suffering he perceived in the faces of the revivalists made his own pain bearable but that did not stop him from asking: "why do people suffer?"[124] Nonetheless, he came out of the experience feeling like reaching out to his brother whom he invited to his performance that same evening.[125]

Baldwin continues to play on polar opposites up to the final scene which begins with a subtle shift to the first person plural as against the singular that has, hitherto, characterized the story.[126] As he and his younger brother went into the nightclub where the younger man would perform, the narrator noticed that the *light* inside was very dim and that heads turned in the *darkness* as he and his brother arrived. As Sonny began to introduce his brother to his friends, a cheerful-looking man whose teeth gleamed like a *lighthouse* began to confide in the narrator. Not long afterwards, the bandleader installed the narrator in a *dark* corner from where he noticed that the *light* from the bandstand spilled a little short of the band members making it seem as if the musicians were avoiding the center of the circle of the glare.[127] Then the narrator noticed that one of the musicians moved into the *light* which turned indigo, signalling that the session was about to begin. The narrator uses the image of *fire* to capture Sonny's initial failure to blend into the musical performance: everything had been *burned out* of

---

122. Baldwin, "Sonny's Blues," 131.

123. Ibid., 134.

124. Robertson, "Baldwin's Sonny's Blues," 192.

125. Here Sonny's brother functions as both a character in his own story as well as an omniscient narrator who has access to the inner feelings of other characters as well as his own psychology. Such a narrator has two possibilities at his disposal: "He has his own subjective point of view, and he can also, because of the duality of the subject, adopt the point of view of the hero." See Edmiston, "Focalization and the First-Person Narrator," 730, and cf. Bal, "Narratology," 122–23.

126. Baldwin, "Sonny's Blues," 138.

127. Clarke, "James Baldwin's Sonny Blues," 203.

his efforts and paradoxically, some hidden things had been *burned* in by the fire and fury of his experiences. But not for long, because the narrator soon began to hear the *burning* with which Sonny had made the music his. On the whole, what comes across very clearly is that the narrator is trapped in all sorts of contradictions and that events of the story would eventually enable him to break free.[128]

CUP OF TREMBLING

After Sonny's first performance, the service girl came by—in the *dark*—and the narrator asked her to take drinks to the bandstand at the center of the stage where the musicians were awash in indigo *light*. The girl did send a scotch and milk to Sonny from which the latter sipped and, looking up, nodded his thanks towards his brother. As the band began to play once again the unfinished drink, left on top of the piano, glowed and shook above his head "like the very cup of trembling." This phrase has attracted the attention of a number of commentators.[129] Its origin can be traced to such biblical texts as Isa 51:17, 22; Zech 12:2; Ezek 23:33; Jer 25:15; and Rev 14:10. From this point of view, the cup of trembling seems to point to the justice handed by God, master of the heavenly banquet, to the guilty. From the perspective of the New Testament, it can be linked to the cup of Gethsemane which Christ drank, and which, in a sense symbolizes the removal of sin for believers.

The above references point to how Baldwin has deliberately grafted his meaning onto biblical passages and in so doing extended his context.[130] This is not surprising, given as Samuel Ijsseling has noted, a text always and necessarily alludes to and relies upon other texts. Ijsseling insists that "no matter how original a speaker or writer might be, he or she always

---

128. Baldwin, "Sonny's Blues," 142. For comment, see Byerman, "Words and Music," 371–72; Clarke, "James Baldwin's Sonny's Blues," 204–5; Robertson, "Baldwin's Sonny's Blues," 193–96, citing William's, "The Black Musician," in *Give Birth to Brightness*, 145–66.

129. This is very much in keeping with the process of reading, writing, speaking and listening. Moreover, "the boundaries at which one permits a context to begin or end are always arbitrary, and can always be shifted." See Samuel Ijsseling, "Deconstruction and Ethics," 90.

130. Ijsseling adds that if a text appears in one place, it is never completely the same with those on which it depends for its existence elsewhere. Interestingly enough, it is through such continuous transposition that meaning comes into existence. See ibid., 97–100.

follows a prior code, complies with the rules of the genre, takes up existing themes, submits to arguments or text according to prescribed scheme, and complies with language which is always a language of others."[131] However, this is not to say that texts cannot be "original." Originality can come about when earlier texts are absorbed and transformed to create something new, as Baldwin has done.

In the light of the foregoing, Robertson is quite persuasive in arguing that the cocktail of scotch and milk hints at an emblem of simultaneous destruction and nurture or a relief from suffering that YHWH promised those who keep his command.[132] But the circularity of thought inherent here cannot be ignored for one has to bear in mind that it was YHWH who gave a cup of suffering to his chosen in the first place. There is therefore, a dialectic at work here in the acknowledgement of the limits to which language can function as a means of conveying meaning.[133] Hence, "Sonny's acceptance of it (cup of trembling) indicates that his life will continue on the edge between the poison of his addiction and the nourishment of his music."[134]

The point of this interpretation seems to be that while not denying him his individuality, Sonny's problems will be made easier by the narrator's willingness to be involved in his life, a point of view that seems to echo from the double personality of the narrator.[135] For his part, Clarke sees in the glow of scotch and milk a symbol of Sonny's success given that "milk, childhood, and light all suggest that this *man-child* has achieved a reconciliation with reality that is more profound than the narrator's conventional lifestyle."[136] This coheres with the suggestion that the cup of trembling is an assurance that as God took away pain from ancient Israel, and as Christ takes away the sin of the world from the believer, so has Sonny taken the pain and guilt of his brother. Hence, Sonny's music "reveals both his suffering and his understanding of others' pain. His music becomes a mystical,

---

131. Robertson, "Baldwin's Sonny Blue," 197, citing Ps 75:8 and Rev: 14:10.

132. This, according to Byerman, comes about because in describing experiences and explaining them, the narrator is locked in the linguistic pattern that restricts understanding. Cf. Byerman, "Words and Music," 371, with reference to Frederick Jameson, *The Prison-House of Language*.

133. Byerman, "Words and Music," 371.

134. Ibid.

135. Clarke, "Baldwin's Sonny's Blues," 205.

136. Robertson, "Baldwin's 'Sonny's Blues,'" 190.

spiritual medium, an open-ended metaphor simultaneously comforting the player, the listener and releasing their guilt and pain."[137]

APPRAISAL

This chapter has attempted to identify the literary features in "Sonny's Blues" that make it possible for one to come to a value judgment as to the significance of human imagination in the theological inquiry. And although the study is literary rather than musical, it has been possible, thanks to the power of music, to understand how a story that was initially structured around the lack of communication between two brothers ends in a reversal. It is also of particular interest to this study that the brothers began truly to communicate with each other after both have experienced a religious revival, an acknowledgement of a worldview beyond themselves. From such an everyday occurrence in the Harlem environment, Sonny learns from the revivalists that suffering is universal but that one need not wallow in it; self-discipline is required.

For his part, the narrator evolves from being, first, protective, then, empathetic and more profoundly, "his brother's keeper" in line with a promise he made to his late mother. The instructive fact here is that this new frame of mind emerged after the narrator had come to terms with his past. One might therefore suggest that his initial problem with the narrator stemmed from a crisis of identity. Not surprisingly, this crisis is at the core of the hopelessness he saw everywhere—in the schoolyard, the underground train station, the Harlem housing environment and even the depressing memory of his parents' home. This same frame of mind was also at the heart of his fear for Sonny's future in general and his choice of career in particular.[138]

We have equally shown that music is not only an issue of sound-making and felt-response but also a mechanism that speaks to the unconscious. Not only does it help to effect transformation but it sharpens the narrator's intuition, thereby preparing him for the revelatory moment with

---

137. Robertson, "Baldwin's Sonny's Blues," 190

138. Cf. John C. Ries, "Remembrance of Things Past, Remembering of Things Future: The Exile of Indigenous People," *Inter-Sections* No. 3 (1995), p. 9. Drawing on Hannah Arendt, *Between Past and Future: Eight Essays on Political Thought* (New York: Viking, 1968), Ries agrees with the view that when we no longer ascribe significance to the past and the future, for whatever reason, we have lost our identity and our humanity disappears.

its sacramental qualities. Hence, one would argue, as Robinson does, that music functions in the story as "a spiritual medium, an open-ended metaphor, simultaneously comforting the player and listener and releasing their guilt and pain."[139] One can add also that "Sonny's Blues," draws attention to the fact that a full understanding of any piece of music would require interdisciplinary approaches in view of music's capacity to echo paradoxes that criss-cross intellectual and emotional borders. Baldwin is not unaware of these paradoxes for, as he says: "I am using [the blues] as metaphor . . . they contain the toughness that manages to make . . . this experience of life or the state of being . . . out of which the blues come articulate . . . I want to suggest that the acceptance of this anguish one finds in the blues, and the expression of it, creates also, however odd this may sound, a kind of joy."[140]

Baldwin's use of music in stimulating and guiding the reader's imagination functions on both horizontal and vertical dimensions. From the horizontal perspective, the imagination is the arena where the Christian creative writer, and indeed, all artists, realize the vision that provide the ground for theology. The vertical dimension, on the other hand, confirms the understanding that imagination is the faculty, which, according to Schleiermacher, humans use for perceiving the divine.

---

139. Jasper, "From Theology to Theological Thinking," 303.
140. Cited in Taylor, "I Hear Music in the Air," 105.

6

Conclusion
A Spiritual Autobiography

I

The study has attempted to impose order on the short stories of James Baldwin so as to demonstrate that they are autobiographically driven. Moreover, if as Lionel Trilling argues, literary situations are cultural situations and the latter are no more than elaborate fights about moral issues, the Baldwin short stories do provide platforms for theological ethics.[1] Undertaken against the background of the stories' powerful evocations of the transcendent to the extent that they throw light on the author's quest for self-understanding, the study has shed some light on the stream of questions relating to Baldwin's spiritual and emotional growth. In the process of achieving this goal, it has also been possible to address the challenge implied in T. S. Eliot's remark that literary criticism is best completed by criticism from a definite theological/ethical standpoint.[2]

We have also explored how stories can, in the words of Wayne Booth, function as "spiritual transport" with which creative writers struggle as they try to come to grips with what it means to be human. Hence, while it can be argued that art in general, and literature in particular, may not

---

1. Trilling, *Beyond Culture*, 12.
2. Helsa, "Religion and Literature," 182.

Conclusion

always be theologically relevant, it would seem that any critical approach to storytelling which excludes the possibility that literature provides avenue to the transcendent, creates an unnecessary gap.[3]

It has equally emerged from the study that it is limiting to research the works of Baldwin without an understanding of the social climate of the author's own life experiences. Thus, insight into his sociopolitical background has enabled us to come to the understanding that the author's mindset is deeply embedded in his early encounter with the Bible as well as the African American brand of Christianity: they provide him with the language he uses in his writings and artistic self-exploration. Consequent upon this, our finding shows that the stories are best understood against the background of the author's search for self-understanding. Hence, in as much as a sincere quest for the divine is implied in a quest for the self, and that the latter is sterile and academic unless it discloses the former, the Baldwin short stories function as a spiritual autobiography.[4]

We see that in "Previous Condition" Baldwin hints at his own experiences by fictionalizing an incident in the life of an unsuccessful and sensitive black actor. With adroit use of "flashbacks" and "flashforwards" to present isolated pieces of information in the protagonist's life, Baldwin uses the story as a problem-setting mechanism to unearth the "extraordinary" from the "ordinary" enabling the story to display a quasi-revelatory characteristic.[5] At the end, each of the characters, in his or her own way, is portrayed as vulnerable in such a way that the story becomes a metaphor for the human condition. And although the story is rooted in the author's real and immediate experiences, it goes beyond the confines of racial questions with each of the characters recognizing his or her human limitation. It is within this perspective that one can locate the literary success of the story: Peter (the protagonist) receives a free and unsuspected gift (grace) which appears through the commonplace atmosphere of a bar enabling him to initiate an act of reconciliation with another figure whose friendliness he had earlier spurned. It was a gesture in self-knowledge.

Lack of self-knowledge sets the stage for our study of "The Rockpile" and "The Outing" where we encounter the difficulties of John Grimes, the protagonist, as he tries to come to grips with the chaos of his personal life against the background of a dysfunctional social environment. His

---

3. Booth, "Story as Spiritual Quest," 165.
4. Stroup, *Promise of Narrative Theology*, 19.
5. Syreeni, "Metaphorical Appropriation," 324.

vicissitudes are not unfamiliar for not only do they bring our humanness to mind, they also provide new visions and options. Mired in obsession with death, sin and neighbourly love, the setting of the stories provides avenues for a profound sense of guilt, the sort of guilt that is evident also in "The Man Child," another story where Baldwin focuses attention on the way people try to escape their frustrations by (metaphysically) projecting them onto something or someone else in the unconscious belief that the human predicament could be transferred to a substitute bearer. By recasting the logic of vicarious death, "The Man Child" facilitates an expansion of the gospels' critique of violence and scapegoatism. Its success lies in how Baldwin uses it to highlight human capability to juxtapose the physical world view on the metaphysical. In the end, the personal failure of Jamie, the protagonist in "The Man Child" results in the loss of self-control, and the strangling of an innocent Eric. We have been able to show how, and why Eric's tragic death, by its vicarious nature, mirrors Christ's, and that the creative tension woven into human relationships in the short story not only provides opportunities for an exploration of Christian doctrine of atonement but facilitates a hermeneutics of the cross. Moreover, by focusing attention on how people should "rid themselves of this murderous lie that scapegoating is inevitable and necessary," given the human tendency to shift blames, "The Man Child" promotes an ethic of love.[6] One can pick up also an echo of the ultimate purpose of tragedy in literature. Is tragedy merely a reflection of our sense of the disorder of life?[7]

II

In "Going to Meet the Man" Baldwin demonstrates what Jasper might have termed "a movement away from a rationalist attempt to 'prove' the goodness of God, or to structure and delimit the experience of evil, in endless deferment."[8] Evidently, evil and suffering in the story admit of a cause and human agency plays a role. On the one hand, Baldwin is able to force readers to confront uncomfortable truths and conflicts between values and ideals. But on the other hand, this story like a number of biblical texts, gives account of negativity on life, an acknowledgement that like Christ abandoned on the cross (Mark 15:34), godforsakenness can equally be made mani-

---

6. Wallace, "Postmodern Biblicism," 315.
7. Fiddes, *Freedom and Limit*, 82.
8. Jasper, *Study of Literature and Religion*, 135.

CONCLUSION

fest in contemporary human experience. And although Baldwin is able to impose powerful elements of ethics on the reader, one is persuaded that he could never have achieved this if he had been merely judgmental. We see that in the end, tragedy in this short story, like the Christian theology of the cross, challenges the imagination while hinting at the various ways in which theoretical presuppositions are used to pre-empt the seriousness of evil and the tragic.[9]

This understanding brings to mind the meaning of the relationship Jesse, the protagonist, had (or did not have) with the black people of the story. As a young man in his twenties, he is a little tolerant of them. He knew what they wanted or did not want; it was not his fault that everybody else hated and exploited them. As a law officer, there is a complete break between himself and blacks, a scenario which the story associates with the loss of his manhood. But he regains this manhood and literally makes peace with blacks in the world of the story as he tells his wife: "Come on, sugar, I'm going to do you like a nigger, just like a nigger, come on sugar, and love me like a nigger."[10] One is, therefore, led to interpret his outburst as an ironic echo of the childlike innocence at the time when he was about eight years old and did not make any distinction between himself and Otis, his black childhood playmate. It was also during this period of innocence that he witnessed the execution of a black man, an experience which provided him with a chance to imagine being in someone else's shoes. This experience which, in the words of Lévinas, amounts to an encounter with *the face of the other*, might have led to a discovery of the *I in the thou* while facilitating a recognition that each of the blacks he would encounter in his life shared his experiences of having a first-person perspective and not just an *it*. But more relevant to our study is that in the final analysis, Jesse is never indifferent to the blacks as *other*. Read in this way, the story manifests Baldwin's attempt to make sense of the experiences of blacks in American history. Less obvious is the fact that he has been trying to persuade his readers that human beings are not incapable of doing good and that any attempt to do better within history is a step in the redemptive process.[11]

---

9. Ibid., 126; and Bouchard, *Tragic Method*, 249.
10. Baldwin, "Going to Meet the Man," 252; and Lévinas, *Otherwise than Being*, 138.
11. Gruner, *Philosophies of History*, 31–32.

III

The universal dimensions in the Baldwin short stories are further demonstrated in "This Morning, This Evening, So Soon." This narrator's sojourn in Europe leads to new "aestheticization" and fresh perspectives in that the contrast experiences broadened his mind such that he is able to put his own experiences and those of the refugees, expatriates, exiles, and migrants he came across in their proper perspectives. Having fallen in love with the French who left him alone, and who did not judge him on the basis of skin colour, the narrator is in a better frame of mind to return to the USA despite all the things he lost there, and all the threats it holds for him. The optimism is echoed in what can rightly be dubbed Pete's farewell song with its biblical overtone. Pete invites listeners to "Preach the word" (and the word was God?) and to "testify" in acknowledgement of both existential and transcendent realities. Within the context provided by the song, the first reality that is echoed is that history is in motion and that singers (about to return to the US) and listeners (staying behind in France) may not meet again. Another reality is that death is inevitable, yet it is not the ultimate reality. Hence, it might be said that history is moving toward divine fulfilment on "Canaan shore" with its earthly and eschatological dimensions. Like all Spirituals (the songs used by slaves to response to societal contradictions), Baldwin's effort is not only a criticism of the present order of things but also a longing for a new world—"here and now" as well as in the time to come.[12] This is consistent with the understanding of the originators of the Spirituals who saw the gospel not just as "apocalyptic myth" but a divine message "about the future . . . breaking into the reality of the present."[13]

It is instructive that "This Morning, This Evening, So Soon," does not end in an earth-shaking reversal of fortune. What is significant is the altered consciousness of the characters.[14] This is very much in consonance with the protagonist's role as an artist, a sort of individual with a highly developed imagination and who is able to conceive of a "New World" that can escape its own myths and break its own taboos. Moreover, the communicative act inherent in art "becomes a model for a coherence which is generated by the sensibility and not imposed by social fiat."[15] To appreciate the story is

---

12. Cone, *Spirituals*, 61.
13. Ibid., 85–86.
14. Bigsby, "Divided Mind," 96.
15. Ibid.

Conclusion

to recognize how successfully Baldwin has been able to infuse very theological language into the social issue of being an expatriate or what has emerged here as secular pilgrimage. His has been an honest attempt to "win a small psychic territory" that provides room for hope.

In "Sonny's Blues" Baldwin touches on the value of music as a universal medium of non-verbal communication with a power to generate feelings. And although the reader's encounter with this story is literary rather than musical, there is in the process of its exploration, the possibilities for a perception of the sublime deeply connected to the values that humans stand for thus confirming the capacity of stories to be beneficial to the Christian mind. In this instance, music enables the narrator to become his "brother's keeper," a reversal of the position of the hopelessness he saw everywhere in Harlem including the depressing memory of his parents' home. This frame of mind was at the heart of the narrator's fear for Sonny's future in general and his choice of career in particular.[16]

Baldwin shows in this story that music is not only a question of sound-making and felt-response but also a mechanism that speaks to the unconscious; it sharpened the narrator's imagination thereby preparing him for his new outlook on life which comes about as a result of the revelatory moment that arose from the sense of well-being he felt while listening to Sonny's music. David Jasper would agree that from the horizontal perspective, the imagination is the arena where the Christian poet and indeed all artists, realize the vision that provides ground for theology.[17] The vertical dimension, on the other hand, confirms the understanding that the imagination is the faculty which, according to Schleiermacher, humans use for perceiving the divine.

On the whole, it can safely be asserted here that by fusing existing ideas, it has been possible to articulate fresh insights that reinforce the symbiotic relationship between literature, ethics, aesthetics and spiritual autobiography. One is equally persuaded that Baldwin's use of short stories allows him the freedom to adopt various ethical positions (with their theological implications) in affirmation of the fact that the art of storytelling provides us with images that bring meaning to the chaos not only in personal lives and faith communities but within the fabric of the society in general.[18] The imaginative insight thus evoked has universal significance

---

16. Cf. Reis, "Remembrance of Things Past," 9.
17. Jasper, "From Theology to Theological Thinking," 293–305.
18. Jones, *Art and Trust of the Parables*, 130–31.

and the capacity to transform whoever takes up the challenge *of reading religiously*. Reading religiously does not mean that one should deny that having developed his art in a period of moral and political disquiet against the background of racial activism in the United States of America, Baldwin cannot be read polemically. He was indeed a moral spokesperson for the oppressed and the marginalised. But, in Detweiler's words, religious reading, like parables, resist all conclusive analysis. Hence, Baldwin's works do not become irrelevant once the political issues he addressed are resolved. The short stories reverberate beyond American sociopolitical questions and embrace matters of universal religious significance such as personal identity, scapegoatism, tragedy, role-playing, and pilgrimage.

As he blends autobiographical memory with history in "The Rockpile" and "The Outing," Baldwin successfully grapples with the antiseptic holiness of shopfront Churches of his childhood. He cuts the figure of the scapegoat in "The Man Child," the outcast in "Previous Condition," before moving on to filial love and acceptance of differences in "Sonny's Blues." In all these, Baldwin functions within the tradition of ancient and modern visionaries searching for a better world. This throws light on how "Going to Meet the Man" is a testimony that, despite the human condition, evil cannot defeat the human spirit. Finally, driven by a universal vision, Baldwin connects his life and American experience with all humankind in "This Morning, This Evening, So Soon." One is, on the whole, persuaded that his has been a successful effort to move narrative art beyond entertainment to the level where it becomes an instrument for articulating moral questions that are fundamental to what it means to be human.

Works and Interview by James Baldwin

Baldwin, James. *The Amen Corner*. New York: Dial, 1968.
———. *Another Country*. New York: Dial, 1962.
———. "Are We on the Edge of Civil War?" In *The Americans*. Interview by David Frost, 145–50. New York: Stein & Day, 1970.
———. *Blues for Mr Charlie*. New York: Dial, 1964.
———. *The Devil Finds Work*. New York: Dial, 1976.
———. "Disturber of the Peace: James Baldwin." Interview by Eve Auchincloss and Nancy Lynch, in *The Black American Writer*, edited by C. W. E. Bigsby, vol. 1, 199–216. Deland, FL: Everett/Edwards, 1969.
———. *Evidence of Things Not Seen*. New York: Holt, 1985.
———. *The Fire Next Time*. New York: Dial, 1963.
———. *Giovanni's Room*. New York: Dell, 1956.
———. *Going to Meet the Man*. New York: Dial, 1965. Reprint, London: Penguin, 1991.
———. *Go Tell It on the Mountain*. London: Joseph, 1954.
———. *If Beale Street Could Talk*. New York: Dial, 1974.
———. "An Interview with a Negro Intellectual." In *The Negro Protest: Talks with James Baldwin, Malcolm X, Martin Luther King*, Kenneth B. Clarke, 1–14. Boston: Beacon, 1963.
———. "James Baldwin." In *King, Malcolm, Baldwin: Three Interviews*, interviewed by Kenneth B. Clarke. Middletown, CT: Wesleyan University Press, 1985.
———. "James Baldwin: The Art Fiction/LXXVIII." Interview by Jordan Elgrably. *Paris Review* 91 (Spring 1984).
———. "James Baldwin . . . in Conversation." Interview by Dan Georgakas in *Black Voices: An Anthology of Afro-American Literature*, edited by Abraham Chapman, 660–68. New American Library, 1968.
———. *Jimmy's Blues: Selected Poems*. London: Joseph, 1983. Reprint, New York: St. Martin's, 1986.
———. *Just Above My Head*. New York: Dial, 1979.
———. *Little Man, Little Man: A Story of Childhood*. Illustrated by Yoran Cazac. New York: Dial, 1976.
———. *Nobody Knows My Name: More Notes of a Native Son*. New York: Dial, 1961.
———. *No Name on the Street*. New York: Dial, 1972.
———. *Notes of a Native Son*. Boston: Beacon, 1955.
———. *Nothing Personal*. Photographs by Richard Avedon. New York: Atheneum, 1964.

———. *One Day When I Was Lost*. A Scenario Based on Alex Haley's *The Autobiography of Malcolm X*. London: Joseph, 1971.
———. *Price of a Ticket: Collected Non-fiction*. New York: St Martin's, 1985.
———. *Tell Me How Long the Train's Been Gone*. New York: Dial, 1968.
———. "Why I Left America. Conversations: Ida Lewis and James Baldwin." In *New Black Voices*, edited by Abraham Chapman, 409–19. New York: New American Library, 1972.
Baldwin, James, and Margaret Mead. *A Rap on Race*. Philadelphia: Lippincott, 1973.
Gates, Henry L., Jr. "An Interview with Joseph Baker and James Baldwin (1973)." In *James Baldwin: The Legacy*, edited by Quincy Troupe, 161–72. New York: Simon & Schuster, 1989.

General Bibliography

Abrams, Meyer H. *Glossary of Literary Terms*. New York: Holt, Rinehart & Winston, 1988.
———. "The Transformation of English Language: 1930–1995." *Daedalus: Journal of the American Academy of Arts and Sciences* 126 (1997) 105–31.
Achtemeier, Paul J., ed. *Harper's Bible Dictionary*. San Francisco: Harper & Row, 1985.
Albert, Richard N. "The Jazz-Blues Motif in James Baldwin's 'Sonny's Blues.'" *College Literature* 11.2 (1984) 178–85.
Allen, Clifford J., ed. *Broadman Bible Commentary*. Vol. 2. Nashville: Broadman, 1969.
Allen, Shirley S. "Religious Symbolism and Psychic Reality in Baldwin's *Go Tell It on the Mountain*." In *Critical Essays*, edited by Fred L. Standley and Nancy V. Burt, 166–88. Reprinted from *College Language Association Journal* 19 (1975) 173–99.
———. "The Ironic Voice in James Baldwin's *Go Tell It on the Mountain*." In *James Baldwin: A Critical Evaluation*, edited by Therman B. O'Daniel, 30–46. London: Donker, 1977.
Alter, Robert. *The Art of Biblical Narrative*. New York: Basic Books, 1981.
Aristotle, "Poetics." In *The Basic Works of Aristotle*. Edited by Richard McKeon. Translated by Ingram Bywater. New York: Random House, 1941.
Arnold, Matthew. "The Study of Poetry." In *English Literature and Irish Politics*, edited by R. H. Super, 161–188. Ann Arbor: University of Michigan Press, 1973.
Aulén, Gustaf. *Christus Victor: An Historical Study of the Three Main Types of the Idea of Atonement*. Translated by A. G. Hebert. 1911. Reprinted, Eugene, OR: Wipf & Stock, 2003.
Austin, J. L. *How to Do Things with Words*. Cambridge: Harvard University Press, 1962.
Austin, Michael. "Art and Religion as a Metaphor." *British Journal of Aesthetics* 35.2 (1995) 146.
Ayer, A. J. *Language, Truth and Logic*. London: Gollancz, 1936.
Bader, A. L. "The Structure of Modern Short Story." In *Short Story Theories*, edited by Charles E. May, 107–15. Athens: Ohio University Press., 1976.
Bal, Mieke. *Narratology: Introduction to the Theory of Narrative*. Translated by Christine van Boheemen. Toronto: University of Toronto Press, 1985.
Baldwin, James. "The Artist's Struggle for Integrity." In *Seeds of Liberation*, edited by Paul Goodman, 380–87. New York: Braziller, 1964.
———. "As Much Truth as One Can Bear." In *Opinions and Perspectives* from *The New York Times Book Review*, edited by Francis Brown, 207–15. Boston: Houghton Mifflin, 1964.

General Bibliography

———. "Black Boys Look at White Boys." In *Smiling through the Apocalypse*, edited by Harold Hayes, 713–30. New York: McCall, 1969.

———. "Compressions: L'Homme et La Machine." In *Cesar: Compression d'or*, edited by Cesar Baldaccini, 9–16. Paris: Hachette, 1973.

———. "The Creative Process." In *Creative America*, 17–21. New York: Ridge, 1962.

———. "East River Downtown." In *First Person Singular: Essays for the Sixties*, edited by Herbert Gold, 38–45. New York: Dial, 1963.

———. "Easy Rider." In *An Annual of Fiction*, 3–26. New York: Dial, 1962.

———. "Envoi." In *A Quarter Century of Un-Americana 1938-63: A Tragico Comical Memorabilia of HUAC*, edited by Charlotte Pomerantz, New Amsterdam: Marzani & Munsell, 1963.

———. "Fifth Avenue Uptown: A Letter from Harlem." In *First Person Singular: Essays for the Sixties*, edited by Herbert Gold, 27–38. New York, Dial, 1963. Reprinted in *For Our Times: 24 Essays by 8 Contemporary Americans*, edited by Barry Gross, 33–42. New York: Dodd, Mead, 1970.

———. "Foreword." In *Freedom Ride* by Jim Peck. New York: Simon & Schuster, 1962.

———. "Foreword." In *Lonely Rage: The Autobiography of Bobby Seale*. New York: Times Books, 1978.

———. "From Dreams of Love to Dreams of Terror." *Natural Enemies: Youth and Clash of Generations*, edited by Alexander Klein, 274–79. New York: Lippincott, 1969.

———. "Gabriel's Prayer." In *Black Insights: Significant Literature by Black Americans –1960 to the Present*, edited by Nick Aaron Ford, 196–219.Waltham, MA: Ginn, 1971.

———. "The Highland to Destiny." In *Martin Luther King, Jr.: A Profile*, edited by C. Eric Lincoln, 90–112. New York: Hill & Wang, 1970.

———. "In Search of a Basis for Mutual Understanding and Racial Harmony." In *The Nature of Human Society*, edited by H. Ober Hess, 231–40. Philadelphia: Fortress, 1967.

———. "Introduction." In *The Chasm: The Life and Death of a Great Experiment in Ghetto Education*, by Robert Campbell. Boston: Houghton Mifflin, 1974.

———. "Introduction." In *We Are Everywhere: Narrative Accounts of Rhodesian Guerrilla*, by Michael Raeburn. New York: Random House, 1978.

———. "James Baldwin on the Negro Actor." In *Anthology of the American Negro in the Theatre*, edited by Lindsay Patterson, 127–30. New York: Publishers Co., 1967.

———. "The Language of the Streets." In *Literature and the Urban Experience: Essays on the City and Literature*, edited by Chalmers Watts, 133–37. New Brunswick, NJ: Rutgers University Press, 1981.

———. "Mass Culture and Creative Artists: Some Personal Notes." In *Culture for the Millions?*, edited by Jacob Norman, 120–23. Princeton: Van Nostrand, 1961.

———. "My Dungeon Shook." In *The Outnumbered: Stories Essays, and Poems About Minority Groups by America's Leading Writers*, edited by Charlotte Brooks, 148–53. New York: Delacorte, 1967.

———. "Ray's Wounds." In *New World Writings*, Vol. 2, 109–16. New York: New American Library, 1952.

———. "A Report from Occupied Territory." In *Law and Resistance: American Attitudes Toward Authority*. New York: Harper and Row, 1970 318–28.

———. "The Search for Identity." In *American Principles and Issues*, edited by Oscar Handlin, 459–67. New York: Holt, Rinehart and Winston, 1961.

General Bibliography

———. "Sonny's Blues." In *Best American Short Story*, edited by Martha Foley and David Burnet, 21–53. Boston: Houghton Mifflin, 1958. Reprinted in John Gordon and L. Rust Hills, eds., *New York: The City as Seen By Masters of Art and Literature*, 365–93. New York, Shorecrest, 1965. Also in *The Loners: Short Stories about the Young and Alienated*, 160–202. New York: Macmillan, 1970.

———. "Stranger in the Village." In *For Our Times: 24 Essays by 8 Contemporary Americans*, edited by Barry Gross, 21–33. New York: Dodd, Mead, 1970.

———. "A Talk to Harlem Teachers." In *Harlem USA*, edited by John Henrik Clarke, 171–80. Rev. ed. New York: Collier, 1971.

———. "The Threshing Floor." In *Cavalcade: Negro American Writing from 1760 to the Present*, edited by Arthur P. Advise and Saunders Redding, 572–82. Boston: Houghton Mifflin, 1971.

———. "Unnameable Objects, Unspeakable Crimes." In *The White Problem in America*, edited by the editors of Ebony, 173–81. Chicago: Johnson, 1966.

———. "The Uses of the Blues." In *The Twelfth Anniversary Playboy Reader*, edited by Hugh M. Hefner, 150–59. Los Angeles: Playboy Press, 1965.

———. "We Can Change the Country." In *Seeds of Liberation*, edited by Paul Goodman, 341–45. New York: Braziller, 1964.

———. "The White Problem." In *100 Years of Emancipation*, Robert A. Goldwin, 80–88. Chicago: Rand McNally, 1964, p. 80–88.

———. "A Word from Writer Directly to Reader." In *Fictions of the Fifties*, Herbert Gold, 18–19. New York: Double Day, 1959.

Baldwin, James, et al., in *Perspective: Angels of African Art*, edited by Michael Weber. New York: Abrams, 1987.

Balibar, Etienne, and Macherey, Pierre. "On Literature as an Ideological Form." In *Untying the Text: A Post-Structuralist Reader*, edited by Robert Young, 79–99. London: Routledge & Kegan Paul, 1981.

Barbour, John D. *Tragedy as a Critique of Virtue: The Novel and Ethical Reflection*. Scholars Press Studies in the Humanities Series 2. Chico, CA: Scholars, 1984.

Barclay, Craig R. "Schematization of Autobiographical Memory." In *Autobiographical Memory*, edited by David C. Rubin, 82–99. New York: Cambridge University Press, 1986.

Bates, H. E. "The Modern Short Story: Retrospect." In *Short Story Theories*, edited by Charles E. May, 72–79. Athens: Ohio University Press, 1976.

Bayley, John. *The Short Story: Henry James to Elizabeth Bowen*. Brighton, UK: Spires, 1988.

Berlin, Adele. "The Role of the Text in the Reading Process." *Semeia* 62 (1993) 143–47.

Berry, Donald. *The Psalms and Their Readers: Interpretative Strategies for Psalm 18*. Journal for the Study of the Old Testament Supplements 153. Sheffield: JSOT Press, 1993.

Bieganowski, Ronald. "James Baldwin's Vision of Otherness in 'Sonny's Blues' and *Giovanni's Room*." *College Language Association Journal* 32.1 (1988) 69–80.

Bigsby, C. W. E. "The Divided Mind of James Baldwin." In *Critical Essays on James Baldwin*, edited by Fred L. Standley and Nancy V. Burt, 94–110. Boston: Hall, 1988.

Bloom, Harold. *The Book of J*. Translated by David Rosenberg. New York: Grove Weidenfeld, 1990.

Bluefarb, Sam. "James Baldwin's 'Previous Condition': A Problem of Identification." In *James Baldwin: A Critical Evaluation*, edited by Therman B. O'Daniel, 151–62. London: Donker, 1977.

GENERAL BIBLIOGRAPHY

Bonhoeffer, Dietrich. *Letters and Papers from Prison*. Translated by R. H. Fuller etal. New York: Macmillan, 1967.
Bouchard, Larry D. *Tragic Method and Tragic Theology: Evil in Contemporary Drama and Religious Thought*. University Park: Pennsylvania State University Press, 1989.
Boucher, Madeleine. *The Mysterious Parables: A Literary Study*. Catholic Biblical Quarterly Monograph Series 6. Washington, DC: Catholic Biblical Association of America, 1977.
———. *The Parables*. New Testament Message 7. Wilmington, DE: Glazier, 1981.
Bowen, Elizabeth. "The Faber Book of the Modern Short Story." In *Short Story Theories*, edited by Charles E. May, 152–58. Athens: Ohio University Press, 1976.
Brewer, William F. "What Is Autobiographical Memory?" In *Autobiographical Memory*, edited by David C. Rubin, 25–49. New York: Cambridge University Press, 1988.
Brink, Andrew. *Bertrand Russell: A Psychobiography of a Moralist*. Atlantic Highlands, NJ: Humanities Press International, 1989.
Broad, C. D. *Five Types of Ethical Theory*. London: Kegan Paul, Trench & Trubner, 1930. 9th ed., 1967.
Brown, Joseph A. "I, John, Saw the Holy Number: Apocalyptic Visions in *Go Tell It on the Mountain* and *Native Son*." *Religion and Literature* 27.1 (1995) 53–74.
Buber, Martin. *I and Thou*. Translated by Walter Kaufman. Edinburgh: T. & T. Clark, 1970.
Budd, Malcolm. "Music and the Communication of Emotion." *The Journal of Aesthetics and Art Criticism* 47.2 (1989) 129–38.
Butterworth, Robert. "Pohier's Liberation of God." *The Month* (June 1986) 191–93.
Buttlar, Annemarie. "Problems of African American History: Some Thoughts on the Need for Interdisciplinary Co-operation." In *History and Tradition in Afro-American Culture*, edited by Gunter H. Lenz, 17ff. Campus Forschung 407. Frankfurt: Campus, 1984.
Byerman, Keith. "Words and Music: Narrative Ambiguity in 'Sonny's Blues.'" *Studies in Short Fiction* 19.4 (1982) 367–72.
Cameron, James. *A Time of Terror: A Survivor's Story*. London: Writers & Readers, 1995.
Campbell, James. *Talking at the Gates: A Life of James Baldwin*. London: Faber & Faber, 1991.
Carey, John. "An End to Evaluation." *Times Literary Supplement* 4013 (22 February 1980) 204.
Carr, David. *Time, Narrative and History*. Studies in Phenomenology and Existentialist Philosophy. Bloomington: Indiana University Press, 1986.
Carrasco, David. "Those Who Go on a Sacred Journey: The Shapes and Diversity of Pilgrimages." *Concilium* 4 (1996) 13–24.
Cavell, Stanley. *Disowning Knowledge in Six Plays of Shakespeare*. Cambridge: Cambridge University Press, 1987.
Champion, James. "The Parable as an Ancient and a Modern Form." *Journal of Literature and Theology* 3.1 (1989) 16–39,
Chapman, Clarke H., Jr. "Black Theology and the Theology of Hope: What Have they to Say to Each Other?" In *Black Theology: A Documentary History, 1966–1979*, edited by Gayraud S. Wilmore and James H. Cone, 193–219. Maryknoll, NY: Orbis, 1979.
Chatman, Seymour. *Story and Discourse: Narrative Structure in Fiction and Film*. Ithaca, NY: Cornell University Press, 1978.
Clarke, Michael. "James Baldwin's Sonny's Blues. Childhood, Light and Life." *College Language Association Journal* 29.2 (1985) 197–205.

General Bibliography

Cleaver, Eldridge. "Notes on a Native Son." In *James Baldwin: A Collection of Critical Essays*, edited by Kenneth Kinnamon, 66–76. Englewood Cliffs, NJ: Prentice-Hall, 1974.

Cohn, Dorrit. "The Encirclement of Narrative." *Poetics Today* 2.2 (1981) 157–82.

Cone, James H. *Black Theology and Black Church*. New York: Seabury, 1969.

———. *The Spirituals and the Blues: An Interpretation*. 1972. Reprint, Maryknoll, NY: Orbis, 1991.

Cottingham, John. *A Descartes Dictionary*. Oxford: Blackwell, 1993.

Courage, Richard A. "Baldwin's *Go Tell It on the Mountain*: Voices of a People." *College Language Association Journal* 32.4 (1989) 401–25.

Coverley, Merlin. *Psychogeography*. Harpenden, UK: Pocket Essentials, 2010.

Crane, R. S. "The Concept of Plot." In *The Theory of the Novel*, edited by Philip Stevick, 141–45. New York: Free Press, 1967.

———. "The Concept of Plot and the Plot of Tom Jones." In *Critics and Criticism: Ancient and Modern*, edited by R. S. Crane, 616–47. 5th ed. Chicago: University of Chicago Press, 1952.

Crellin, Innes. "The Anachronism of Morality." *Philosophy Now* 14 (1995/96) 9–12.

Crossan, John Dominic. *In Parables: The Challenge of the Historical Jesus*. New York: Harper &Row, 1973. 2nd ed. Eagle Books. Sonoma, CA: Polebridge, 1992.

———. *Raid on the Articulate: Comic Eschatology in Jesus and Borges*. 1976. Reprint, Eugene, OR: Wipf & Stock, 2008.

Curran, Charles E. "Utilitarianism and Contemporary Moral Theology: Situating the Debate." *Louvain Studies* 6 (1977) 239–55.

Curran, Charles E., and Richard A. McCormick, eds. *Moral Norms and Catholic Tradition*. Readings in Moral Theology 1. New York: Paulist, 1979.

———. *New Directions in Fundamental Moral Theology*. Notre Dame: University of Notre Dame Press, 1985.

Currie, Gregory. *The Nature of Fiction*. Cambridge: Cambridge University Press, 1990.

Daly, Gabriel. "Interpreting Original Sin." *Priest and People* 10 (1996) 87–91.

Danto, Arthur. *Analytical Philosophy of History*. Cambridge: Cambridge University Press, 1965.

Davidson, Donald. "What Metaphors Mean." *Critical Inquiry* 5 (1978) 31–47.

Debord, Guy. "Introduction to a Critique of Urban Geography." In *Situationist International Anthology*, edited and translated by Ken Knabb. Berkeley CA: Bureau of Public Secrets, 1981.

Descartes, René. *Philosophical Writings*. Translated by Norman Kemp Smith. London: Macmillan, 1952.

De Schrijver, Georges. "From Theodicy to Anthropodicy: The Contemporary Acceptance of Nietzsche and the Problem of Suffering." In *God and Human Suffering*, edited by Jan Lambrecht and Raymond F. Collins, 95–119. Louvain Theological & Pastoral Monographs 3. Louvain: Peeters, 1990.

———. "Hermeneutics and Tradition." In *Authority in the Church*, edited by Piet Fransen, 32–47. Annua Nuntia Lovaniensia 26. Leuven: Peeters, 1983.

Detweiler, Robert, and Glenn Meeter, eds. *Faith and Fiction: The Modern Short Story*. Grand Rapids: Eerdmans, 1979.

———. *Breaking the Fall: Religious Reading of Contemporary Fiction*. San Francisco: Harper &Row, 1989.

———. "What Is a Sacred Text?" *Semeia* 31 (1985) 213–30.

General Bibliography

Dillistone, F. W. *Christianity and Symbolism*. London: Collins, 1955.
———. *The Christian Understanding of Atonement*. Philadelphia: Westminster, 1968.
Dinsmore, Charles Allen. *Atonement in Literature and Life*. London: Constable, 1906.
Dodd, C. H. *The Parables of the Kingdom*. New York: Scribner, 1961.
Douglas, Frederick. *Life and Times of Frederick Douglas*. New York: Collier, 1962.
Dulles, Avery. *Revelation Theology: A History*. New York: Herder & Herder, 1969.
Dumouchel, Paul, ed. *Violence and Truth: On the Work of René Girard*. London: Athlone, 1978.
Eaton, Marcia. "A Strange Kind of Sadness." *Journal of Aesthetics and Art Criticism* 41 (1982) 51–63.
Eckman, Fern Marja. *The Furious Passage of James Baldwin*. London: Joseph, 1966.
Edmiston, William F. "Focalization and the First-person Narrator: A Revision of the Theory." *Poetics Today* 10.4 (1989) 729–44.
Eldridge, Richard. "How Can Tragedy Matter for Us?" *Journal of Aesthetics and Art Criticism* 52.3 (1994) 287–97.
Elizondo, V. "Pilgrimage: An Enduring Ritual of Humanity." *Concilium* 4 (1996) vii–x.
Ellenberger, Henri F. "The Concept of Creative Illness." *Psychoanalytic Review* 55 (1968) 442–56.
———. *The Discovery of the Unconscious: The History and Evolution of Dynamic Psychiatry*. London: Penguin, 1970.
Elliot, T. S. "Religion and Literature." In *Selected Essays*. London: Faber & Faber, 1932.
Eslinger, Lyle. *Into the Hands of the Living God*. Journal for the Study of the Old Testament Supplements 84. Sheffield: Almond, 1989.
Fabre, Michael. "Fathers and Sons in Go Tell it on the Mountain." In *James Baldwin: A Collection of Critical Essays*, 120–38. Englewood Cliffs, NJ: Prentice-Hall, Inc., 1974.
Farrer, Austin. "Revelation." In *Faith and Logic: Oxford Essays in Philosophical Theology*, edited by Basil Mitchell, 84–107. London: Allen & Unwin, 1957.
Feagin, Susan L. "The Pleasure of Tragedy." *American Philosophical Quarterly* 20 (1983) 95–104.
Fiddes, Paul S. *Past Event and Present Salvation: The Christian Idea of Atonement*. London: Darton, Longman & Todd, 1989.
———. *Freedom and Limit: A Dialogue Between Literature and Christian Doctrine*. London: Macmillan, 1991.
Forsman, Rodger. "Revelation and Understanding: A Defence of Tradition." In *Hermeneutics, the Bible and Literary Criticism*, edited by Ann Loades and Michael McLain, 46–78. London: Macmillan, 1992.
Fowl, John. *Daniel Martin*. London: Cape, 1977.
Frazer, J. G. *The Golden Bough*. Vol. 1, abridged. New York: Macmillan, 1963.
Friedman, Norman. "What Makes a Story Short?" In *Short Story Theories*, edited by Charles E. May, 131–46. Athens: Ohio University Press, 1976.
Frye, Northrop. *Anatomy of Criticism: Four Essays*. Princeton: Princeton University Press, 1957.
Funk, Robert W. *The Poetics of Biblical Narrative*. Foundations & Facets. Sonoma, CA: Polebridge, 1978.
Gadamer, Hans Georg. *Truth and Method*. 2nd rev. ed. Translation revised by Joel Weinsheimer and Donald G. Marshall. New York: Crossroad, 1993.

General Bibliography

Gardner, Sebastian. "Aesthetics." In *The Blackwell Companion to Philosophy*, edited by Nicholas Bunnin and E. P. Tsui-James, 229-55. Blackwell Companions to Philosophy 1. Oxford: Blackwell, 1996.

Gaster, T. H. "Azazel." In *Interpreter's Dictionary of the* Bible, edited by George Arthur Buttrick, 1:325-26. New York: Abingdon, 1962.

Gates, Henry L., Jr. "An Interview with Joseph Baker and James Baldwin (1973)." In *James Baldwin: The Legacy*, edited by Quincy Troupe, 161-72. New York: Simon & Schuster, 1989.

Gatewood, Esther L. "An Experimental Study of the Nature of Musical Enjoyment." In *The Effects of Music*, edited by Max Schoen, 78-130. London: Kegan Paul, Trench & Trubner, 1927.

Genette, Gérard. *Narrative Discourse: An Essay in Method*. Translated by Jane E. Lewin. Ithaca, NY: Cornell University Press, 1980.

Girard, René. "'The Ancient Trail Trodden by the Wicked': Job as a Scapegoat." *Semeia* 33 (1985) 13-42.

———. *Deceit, Desire and the Novel: Self and Other in Literary Structure*. Baltimore: John Hopkins University Press, 1966.

———. "Generative Scapegoating." In *Violent Origins*, edited by Robert G. Hamerton-Kelly, 73-105. Stanford, CA: Stanford University Press, 1987.

———. *The Scapegoat*. London: Athlone, 1986.

———. *Things Hidden Since the Foundation of the World*. London: Athlone, 1987.

———. *"To Double Business Bound": Essays on Literature, Myth, Mimesis, and Anthropology*. Baltimore: John Hopkins University Press, 1978.

———. *Violence and the Sacred*. Translated by Patrick Gregory. Baltimore: John Hopkins University Press, 1972.

Goehr, Lydia. "Political Music and Politics of Music." *Journal of Aesthetics and Art Criticism* 52.1 (1994) 99-112.

Goldman, Alan. "Emotion in Music (A Postscript)." *Journal of Aesthetics and Art Criticism* 53.1 (1995) 59-69.

Gollwitzer, Helmut. "What Is Black Theology?" In *Black Theology: A Documentary History, 1966-1979*, edited by Gayraud S. Wilmore &James H. Cone, 152-80. Maryknoll, NY: Orbis, 1979.

Gordimer, Nadine. "The Flash of Fireflies." In *Short Story Theories*, edited by Charles E. May, 178-81. Athens: Ohio University Press, 1976.

Graham, Gordon. "The Value of Music." *Journal of Aesthetics and Art Criticism* 53.2 (1995) 135-53.

Grisez, Germain. *The Way of the Lord Jesus*, Vol. 1: *Christian Moral Principles*. Chicago: Franciscan Herald, 1983.

Gruner, Rolf. *Philosophies of History: A Critical Essay*. Avebury Series in Philosophy. Aldershot, UK: Gower, 1985.

Gullason, Thomas A. "The Short Story: An Underrated Art." In *Short Story Theories*, edited by Charles E. May, 13-31. Athens: Ohio University Press, 1976.

Gunn, Janet Varner. *Autobiography: Toward a Poetics of Experience*. Philadelphia: University of Pennsylvania Press, 1982.

Gunton, Colin. "Sacrifice and the Sacrifices: From Metaphor to Transcendental?" In *Trinity, Incarnation, and Atonement: Philosophical and Theological Essays*, edited by Ronald J. Fenstra and Cornelius Plantinga, 210-29. Library of Religious Philosophy 1. Notre Dame: University of Notre Dame Press, 1989.

General Bibliography

Gustafson, James. *Ethics from a Theocentric Perspective*. Vol. 2 Chicago: University of Chicago Press, 1984.

Hagopian, John V. "James Baldwin: The Black and the Red-White-and-Blue." In *James Baldwin: A Critical Evaluation*, edited by Therman B. O'Daniel, 156–62. London: Donker, 1977.

Hamerton-Kelly, Robert G. "A Girardian Interpretation of Paul: Rivalry, Mimesis and Victimage in the Corinthian Correspondence." *Semeia* 33 (1985) 65–82.

———. "Sacred Violence and the Curse of the Law (Galatians 3:13): The Death of Christ as a Sacrificial Travesty." *New Testament Studies* 36 (1990) 98–118.

———. *Sacred Violence: Paul's Hermeneutics of the Cross*. Minneapolis: Fortress, Press, 1992.

———. "Sacred Violence and 'Works of Law': Is Christ Then an Agent of Sin?" *Catholic Biblical Quarterly* 52 (1992) 55–75.

Harding, Vincent. "Religion and Resistance among Antebellum Negroes 1800–1860." In *Making of Black America: Essays in Negro Life & History*, edited by August Meier and Elliott Rudwick, 1:179–97. Studies in American Negro Life. New York: Atheneum, 1969.

Hargreaves, John. *A Guide to the Parables*. London: SPCK, 1968.

Head, Dominic. *The Modernist Short Story*. Cambridge: Cambridge University Press, 1992.

Heidegger, Martin. *Being and Time*. Translated by John Macquarrie and Edward Robinson. New York: Harper & Row, 1962.

Heimes, Klaus F. "Interdisciplinary and Intercultural Aspects of Music." *South African Journal of Philosophy* 14.1 (1995) 24–28.

Henderson, Carol. "Knee Bent, Body Bowed: Re-Memory's Prayer of Spiritual Re(new)al in Baldwin's *Go Tell It on the Mountain*." *Religion and Literature* 27.1 (1995) 75–88.

Hendrickx, Herman. *The Parables of Jesus*. San Francisco: Harper & Row, 1986.

Henn, T. R. *The Harvest of Tragedy*. London: Methuen, 1956.

Herrnstein-Smith, Barbara. *Contingencies of Values: Alternative Perspectives for Critical Theory*. Cambridge: Harvard University Press, 1988.

Hesla, David. "Religion and Literature: The Second Stage." *Journal of the American Academy of Religion* 46.2 (1987) 181–92.

Hill, Eric. "Hume and the Delightful Tragedy Problem." *Philosophy* 57 (1982) 319–32.

Hospers, John. *Human Conduct: An Introduction to the Problems of Ethics*. New York: Harcourt, Brace & World, 1961.

Hume, David. *Enquiry Concerning Human Understanding*. Edited by L. A. Selby-Bigge, Oxford: Oxford University Press, 1893.

———. "Of the Standard of Taste." In *Of the Standard of Taste and Other Essays*. New York: Bobbs-Merrill, 1965 [original publication, 1757].

———. "Of Tragedy." In *Philosophical Works*, 237–47. Edinburgh: Adam & Charles Black, 1854.

Ijsseling, Samuel. "Deconstruction and Ethics." *Ethical Perspective* 2.2 (1995) 91–103.

Iser, Wolfgang. *The Act of Reading: A Theory of Aesthetic Response*. Baltimore: Johns Hopkins University Press, 1978.

Jackson, Bruce. "The Afro-American Toast and Worksong: Two Dead Genres." In *History and Tradition in Afro-American Culture*, edited by Gunter H. Lenz, 244–55. Campus Forschung 407. Frankfurt: Campus, 1984.

General Bibliography

Jameson, Fredric. *The Prison-House of Language: A Critical Account of Structuralism and Russian Formalism*. Princeton: University Press, 1972.
Janssens, Louis. "Norms and Priorities in Love Ethics." *Louvain Studies* 6 (1977) 207–38.
———. "Ontic Good and Evil: Premoral Values and Disvalues." Translated by Joseph A. Selling. *Louvain Studies* 12 (1987) 62–82.
Jasper, David. "The Bible in Arts and Literature: Sources of Inspiration for Poets and Painters." *Concilium* 1 (1995) 47–60.
———. *Coleridge as Poet and Religious Thinker*. Pittsburgh Theological Monograph Series n.s. 15. Allison Park, PA: Pickwick Publications, 1985.
———. "The Death and Rebirth of Religious Language." *Religion and Literature* 28.1 (1996) 5–19.
———. "From Theology to Theological Thinking: The Development of Critical Thought and Its Consequence for Theology." *Literature and Theology* 9.3 (1995) 293–305.
———, ed. *Images of Belief in Literature*. London: Macmillan, 1984.
———. "Literature and Theology." In *The Blackwell Encyclopedia of Modern Christian Thought*, edited by Alistair McGrath, 335–39. Oxford: Blackwell, 1993.
———. *The New Testament and Literary Imagination*. London: Macmillan, 1987.
———. "On Reading Scripture as Literature." *History of European Ideas* 3 (1982) 311–34.
———. *Postmodernism, Literature and the Future of Theology*. London: Macmillan, 1993).
———. *Readings in the Canon of Scripture: Written for Our Learning*. Studies in Literature and Religion. London: Macmillan, 1995.
———. *The Study of Literature and Religion: An Introduction*. Studies in Literature and Religion. Basingstoke, UK: Macmillan, 1989.
———. "Violence and Post-Modernism." *History of European Ideas* 20.4–6 (1995) 801–6.
Jasper, David, and Colin Crowder. *European Literature and Theology in the Twentieth Century: Ends of Time*. Studies in Literature and Religion. London: Macmillan, 1990.
Jasper, David, and T. R. Wright. *The Critical Spirit and the Will to Believe: Essays in Nineteenth Century Literature and Religion*. Basingstoke, UK: Macmillan, 1989.
Jeanrond, Werner G.. *Theological Hermeneutics: Development and Significance*. London: Macmillan, 1994.
Jenkyns, Marina. *The Play's the Thing: Exploring Text in Drama and Therapy*. London: Routledge, 1996.
Jones, Geraint V. *The Art and Truth of the Parables: A Study in the Literary Form and Modern Interpretation*. London: SPCK, 1964.
Jones, Harry L. "Style, Form and Content in the Short Fiction of James Baldwin." In *James Baldwin: A Critical Evaluation*, edited by Therman B. O'Daniel, 143–50. London: Donker, 1977.
Kant, Immanuel. "Critique of Aesthetic Judgement." Part 1 of *Critique of Judgement*, trans. W. S. Pluhar, Indianapolis: Hackett, 1987 [Original publication, 1790].
Kaufmann, Walter. *Tragedy and Philosophy*. Garden City, NY: Doubleday, 1968.
Kelly, Gerald. *Medico-Moral Problems*. St. Louis: Catholic Hospital Association, 1958.
Kent, George E. "Baldwin and the Problem of Being." In *James Baldwin: A Critical Evaluation*, edited by Therman B. O'Daniel, 19–29. London: Donker, 1977.
Kermode, Frank. *The Genesis of Secrecy: On the Interpretation of Narrative*. Cambridge: Harvard University Press, 1979.
Kinnamon, Kenneth, ed. *James Baldwin: A Collection of Critical Essays*. Englewood Cliffs, NJ: Prentice-Hall, 1974.

General Bibliography

Kivy, Peter. "Auditor's Emotions: Contentions, Concessions and Compromise." *British Journal of Aesthetics and Art Criticism* 51.1 (1993) 1–12.

———. *The Corded Shell*. Princeton: Princeton University Press, 1980.

———. *Music Alone: Philosophical Reflection on the Purely Musical Experience*. Ithaca, NY: Cornell University Press, 1990.

———. *Sound Sentiment: An Essay on the Musical Emotions, Including the Complete Text of The Corded Shell*. The Arts and Their Philosophies. Philadelphia: Temple University Press, 1989.

Kjargaard, Mogens Stiller. *Metaphor and Parable: A Systematic Analysis of the Specific Structure and Cognitive Function of the Synoptic Similes and Parables qua Metaphor*. Acta Theologica Danica 20. Leiden: Brill, 1986.

Klaus, F. "Interdisciplinary and Intercultural Aspects of Music." *South African Journal of Philosophy* 14.1 (1995) 24–28.

Knauer, Peter. "A Good End Does not Justify an Evil Means—Even in A Teleological Ethics." In *Personalist Morals: Essays in Honour of Louis Janssens*, edited by Joseph A. Selling, 71–85. Bibliotheca Ephemeridium Theologicarum Lovaniensium 83. Leuven: Leuven University Press, 1988.

Kong, Lily. "Popular Music in Geographical Analysis." *Progress in Geography* 19.2 (1995) 183–98.

Kort, Wesley A. *Take, Read: Scripture, Textuality, and Cultural Practice*. University Park: Pennsylvania State University, 1996.

Kostelanetz, Richard. "Notes on the American Short Story Today." In *Short Story Theories*, edited by Charles E. May, 215–25. Athens: Ohio University Press, 1976.

Krieger, Murray. *The Tragic Vision: Variations on a Theme in Literary Interpretation*. New York: Holt, Rinehart & Winston, 1960.

Krook, Dorothea. *Elements of Tragedy*. New Haven: Yale University Press, 1969.

Lakoff, George. "The Contemporary Theory of Metaphor." In *Metaphor and Thought*, edited by Andrew Ortony, 202–51. 2nd ed. Cambridge: Cambridge University Press, 1993.

Lamarque Peter, ed. *Philosophy and Fiction: Essays in Literary Aesthetics*. Aberdeen: Aberdeen University Press, 1983.

Lamarque, Peter, and Stein Haugom Olsen. *Truth, Fiction, and Literature: A Philosophical Perspective*. Oxford: Clarendon, 1994.

Lancelot, James. "Music as Sacrament." In *The Sense of the Sacramental: Movement and Measure in Art and Music, Place and Time*, edited by David Brown and Ann Loades, 179–85. London: SPCK, 1995.

Landy, Robert J. *Drama Therapy: Concepts and Practices*. Springfield, IL: Thomas, 1986.

Lash, John S. "Baldwin Beside Himself: A Study in Modern Phallicism." In *James Baldwin: A Critical Evaluation*, edited by Therman B. O'Daniel, 47–55. London: Donker, 1977.

Ledbetter, Mark. "Revisiting Old Friends, Making New Enemies: How Reading Religiously Changes My Life." *Literature and Theology* 9.5 (1995) 279–92.

Leonard, Joan. "Loitering with Intent: Muriel Spark's Parabolic Technique." *Studies in Literary Imagination* 18.1 (1985) 65–77.

Levi, A. H. T. "The Relationship between Literature and Theology: An Historical Reflection." *Journal of Literature and Theology* 1.1 (1987) 11–18.

Levin, Lawrence W. *Black Culture and Black Consciousness*. New York: Oxford University Press, 1977.

General Bibliography

Levin, Samuel R. "Language, Concepts, and World: The Domain of Metaphor." In *Metaphor and Thought*, edited by Andrew Ortony, 112–23. 2nd ed. Cambridge: Cambridge University Press, 1993.

Lévinas, Emmanuel. *Collected Philosophical Papers*. Translated by Alphonso Lingis. Phaenomenologica 100. Dordrecht: Nijhoff, 1987.

———. "Ethics as First Philosophy." In *The Levinas Reader*, edited by Sean Hand, 75–87. Oxford: Blackwell, 1989.

———. "God and Philosophy." In *Collected Philosophical Papers*, 153–74. Translated by Alphonso Lingis. Dordrecht: Nijhoff, 1987.

———. *Otherwise Than Being or Beyond Essence*. Translated by Alphonso Lingis. The Hague: Nijhoff, 1981.

———. *Totality and Infinity: An Essay on Exteriority*. Translated by Alphonso Lingis, Philosophical Series 24. The Hague: Nijhoff, 1979.

Levine, Baruch. "René Girard on Job: The Question of the Scapegoat." *Semeia* 33 (1985) 125–35.

Licht, Jacob. *Storytelling in the Bible*. Jerusalem: Magnes, 1978.

Lloyd, G. E. R. *Aristotle: The Growth and Structure of His Thought*. London: Cambridge University Press, 1968.

Lloyd, Peter. "The Danger of Moral Certainty." *Philosophy Now* 15 (Spring/Summer 1996) 23–25.

Lohafer, Susan. *Coming to Terms with the Short Story*. Baton Rouge: Louisiana State University Press, 1983.

Lunden, Rolf. "The Progress of a Pilgrim: James Baldwin's Go Tell It on theMountain." *Studia Neophilologica: A Journal of Germanic and Romance Languages and Literature* 63 (1981) 113–26.

Lynch, Michael F. "Beyond Guilt and Innocence: Redemptive Suffering and Love in Baldwin's Another Country." *Obsidian II: Black Literature in Review* 7 (1992) 1–19.

———. "The Everlasting Father: Mythic Quest and Rebellion in Baldwin's Go Tell It on the Mountain." *College Language Association Journal* 37 (December 1993) 156–75.

———. "A Glimpse of the Hidden God: Baldwin's Dialectical Christianity in Go Tell It on the Mountain." In *New Essays on Go Tell It on the Mountain*, edited by Trudier Harris, 181–95. The American Novel. New York: Cambridge University Press, 1995.

———. "Just Above My Head: James Baldwin's Quest for Belief." *Literature & Theology* 11.3 (1997) 284–98.

Macdonald, James E., and Caryn L. Beck-Dudley. "Are Deontology and Teleology Mutually Exclusive?" *Journal of Business Ethics* 13 (1994) 615–23.

Macebuh, Stanley. *James Baldwin: A Critical Study*. Third Press Library of Criticism 1. New York: Third Press, 1973.

Mack, Burton L. "The Innocent Transgressor: Jesus in Early Christian Myth and History." *Semeia* 33 (1985) 135–65.

Mangan, Joseph T. "An Historical Development of the Principle of Double Effect." *Theological Studies* 10 (1949) 41–61.

Marcus, Laura. *Auto/biographical Discourses: Theory, Criticism and Practice*. Manchester: Manchester University Press, 1994.

Margolin, Uri. "Reference, Coreference, Referring and the Dual Structure of Literary Narrative." *Poetics Today* 12.3 (1991) 517–42.

Matthews, Brander. "The Philosophy of the Short Story." In *Short Story Theories*, edited by Charles E. May, 60–71. Athens: Ohio University Press, 1976.

Mertens, Herman-Emiel. "His Very Name Is Beauty: Aesthetic Experience and Christian Faith." *Louvain Studies* 20 (1995) 316–31.
Martin, Graham D. "A New Look at Fictional Reference." *Philosophy* 57 (1982) 223–36.
Martin, Wallace. *Recent Theories of Narrative*. Ithaca, NY: Cornell University Press, 1986.
McCormick, Richard A. "Ambiguity in Moral Choice." In *Doing Evil to Achieve Good: Moral Choice in Conflict Situations*, edited by Richard A. McCormick and Paul Ramsay, 7–53. Chicago: Loyola University Press, 1978.
McFague, Sallie. *Metaphorical Theology: Models of God in Religious Language*. Philadelphia: Fortress, 1982.
———. "The Parabolic in Faulkner, O'Connor, and Percy." *Notre Dame English Journal* 40 (1983) 49–66.
———. *Speaking in Parables: A Study in Metaphor and Theology*. Philadelphia: Fortress Press, 1975.
McInerny, Ralph. *Aquinas on Human Action: A Theory of Practice*. Washington, DC: Catholic University of America Press, 1992.
McKenna, Andrew. "Introduction." *Semeia* 33 (1985) 1–12.
Metz, Johan Baptist. "Suffering unto God." Translated by Matthew Ashley. *Critical Inquiry* 20.4 (1994) 611–22.
Meyer, Leonard. *Emotion and Meaning in Music*. Chicago: Chicago University Press, 1956.
Milbank, John. "Stories of Sacrifice." *Modern Theology* 12.1 (1996) 27–56.
Miller, Hillis J. "The Problematic of Ending in Narrative." *Nineteenth Century Fiction* 3 (1978) 3–7.
Milne, Pamela J. "Folktales and Fairy Tales: An Evaluation of Two Proppian Analyses of Biblical Narratives." *Journal for Study of Old Testament* 34 (1986) 35–60.
Mlakuzhyil, George. *The Christocentric Literary Structure of the Fourth Gospel*. Analecta Biblica 117. Rome: Editrice Pontificio Institutio Biblico, 1987.
Moller, Karen. *The Theme of Identity in the Essays of James Baldwin*. Gothenburg Studies in English 32. Gothenburg: Acta Universitatis Gothoburgensis, 1975.
Moravia, Alberto. "The Short Story and the Novel." In *Short Story Theories*, edited by Charles E. May, 147–51. Athens: Ohio University Press, 1976.
Mosher, Marlene. "James Baldwin Blues." *College Language Association* 26 (1982) 112–24.
Mossman, James. "Race, Hate, Sex, and Color: A Conversation with James Baldwin and Colin MacInnes." In *Conversation with James Baldwin*, edited by Fred L. Stanley and Louis H. Pratt, 48–58. Jackson: University of Mississippi Press, 1989.
Motlhabi, Mokgethi. "The Historical Origins of Black Theology." In *The Unquestionable Right to Be Free: Black Theology from South Africa*, edited by Itumeleng J. Mosala and Buti Tlhagel, 37–56. Maryknoll, NY: Orbis, 1986.
Nelson, Emmanuel S. "James Baldwin's Vision of Otherness and Community." In *Critical Essays on James Baldwin*, edited by Fred L. Standley and Nancy V. Burt, 121–24. Boston: Hall, 1988.
Nichols, Charles H. "Color, Conscience and Crucifixion: A Study of Racial Attitudes in American Literature and Criticism." *Jahrbuch für Amerikastudien* 6 (1961) 37–47.
Novak, Michael. "Editorial: Future-Hating." *Journal of Ecumenical Studies* 8 (Summer 1971) 622–26.
Novitz, David. "Art, Narrative, and Human Nature." *Philosophy of Literature* 13 (1989) 57–74.
O'Connor, Frank. *The Lonely Voice*. London: Macmillan, 1965.

General Bibliography

Ortmann, Otto. "Types of Listeners: Genetic Considerations." In *The Effects of Music*, edited by Max Schoen, 38–77. London: Keagan Paul, Trench & Trubner, 1927.

Ostendorf, Bernhard. "Black Poetry, Blues and Folklore: Double Consciousness in Afro-American Oral Culture." *Jahrbuch für Amerikastudien / American Studies* 20.2 (1975) 209–59.

Packer, Mark. "Dissolving the Paradox of Tragedy." *Journal of Aesthetics and Art Criticism* 47.3 (1989) 209–19.

Parker, David. *Ethics, Theory and the Novel*. Cambridge: Cambridge University Press, 1994.

Paton, Margaret. "Hume on Tragedy." *British Journal of Aesthetics* 13 (1973) 121–32.

Pattyn, Bart. "The Emotional Boundaries of Our Solidarity." *Ethical Perspectives* 3 (1996) 101–8.

Peperzak, Adriaan. "The One for the Other: The Philosophy of Emmanuel Levinas." *Man and World* 24 (1991) 427–59.

Petrie, Hugh G., and Rebecca S. Oshlag. "Metaphor and Learning." In *Metaphor and Thought*, edited by Andrew Ortony, 577–609. 2nd ed. Cambridge: Cambridge University Press, 1993.

Pickering, George. *Creative Malady*. London: Allen & Unwin, 1974.

Poe, Edgar Allen. "Review of Twice-Told Tales." In *Short Story Theories*, edited by Charles E. May, 45–51. Athens: Ohio University Press, 1976.

Pohier, Jacques. *God: In Fragments*. London: SCM, 1985.

Post, Paul. "The Modern Pilgrim: A Christian Ritual between Tradition and Post-Modernity." *Concilium* 4 (1996) 1–9.

Purcell, Michael. "The Ethical Significance of Illeity (Emmanuel Levinas)." *Heythrop Journal* 37 (1996) 125–38.

Putschogl, Gerhard. "Black Music—Key Force in Pro-American Culture: Archie Shepp on Oral Tradition and Black Culture." In *History and Tradition in Afro-American Culture*, edited by Gunter H. Lenz, 262–76. Campus Forschung 407. Frankfurt: Campus, 1984.

Quinton, Anthony. "Tragedy." In *Thoughts and Thinkers*. London: Duckworth, 1982.

Radford, Colin. "Emotions and Music: A Reply to Cognitivists." *Journal of Aesthetics and Art Criticism* 47 (1989) 69–76.

Reid, Ian. *The Short Story*. Critical Idiom 37. London: Methuen, 1977.

Ricoeur, Paul. "Biblical Hermeneutics." *Semeia* 4 (1975) 27–148.

———. "The Hermeneutical Function of Distanciation." *Philosophy Today* 17.2–4 (1973) 129–41.

———. *The Symbolism of Evil*. Translated by Emerson Buchanan. Religious Perspectives 17. New York: Harper & Row, 1967.

Ries, John. "Introduction." *Ethical Perspectives* 3 (1996) 73–75.

———. "Remembrance of Things Past, Remembrance of Things Future: The Exile of Indigenous People." *Inter-Sections* 3 (1995) 8–14.

Rigali, Norbert J. "Reimaging Morality: A Matter of Metaphors." *Heythrop Journal* 35 (1994) 1–14.

Rimmon-Kenan, Shlomith. *Narrative Fiction: Contemporary Poetics*. New Accents. London: Routledge, 1983.

Robinson, J. A. "Autobiographical Memory: A Historical Prologue." In *Autobiographical Memory*, edited by David C. Rubin, 19–24. Cambridge: Cambridge University Press, 1988.

General Bibliography

Robinson, Jenefer. "The Expression and Arousal of Emotion in Music." *Journal of Aesthetics and Art Criticism* 52.1 (1994) 13–22.

Rohrberger, Mary. "The Short Story: A Proposed Definition." In *Short Story Theories*, edited by Charles E. May, 80–82. Athens: Ohio University Press, 1976.

Salzman, Todd. *Deontology and Teleology: An Investigation of the Normative Debate in Roman Catholic Moral Theology*. Bibliotheca Ephemeridum theologicarum Lovaniensium 120. Leuven: Leuven University Press, 1995.

Sandall, Robert. "I Woke Up This Morning . . . Happier." In *Sunday Times*, 23 July 1996, sec. 10, 16–17.

Savery, Pancho. "Baldwin, Bebop, and Sonny's Blues." In *Understanding Others: Cultural and Cross-Cultural Studies and the Teaching of Literature*, edited by Joseph Trimmer and Tilly Warnock, 165–76. Urbana, IL: National Council of Teachers of English, 1992.

Scheler, Max. "On the Tragic." Translated by Bernard Stambler. In *Tragedy: Vision and Form*, edited by Robert Corrigan, 3–18. San Francisco: Chandler, 1965.

Schier, Flint. "The Claim of Tragedy: An Essay in Moral Psychology and Aesthetic Theory." *Philosophical Papers* 18.1 (1989) 7–26.

———. "Tragedy and the Community of Sentiment." In *Philosophy and Fiction: Essays in Literary Aesthetics*, edited by Peter Lamarque, 73–92. Aberdeen: Aberdeen University Press, 1983.

Schleiermacher, Friedrich D. E. *Hermeneutics: The Hand-written Manuscripts*. Edited by Heinz Kimmerle. Translated by James Duke and Jack Forstman. American Academy of Religion Text and Translation Series 1. Atlanta: Scholars, 1986.

Schon, David A. "Generative Metaphor: A Perspective on Problem-setting in Social Policy." In *Metaphor and Thought*, edited by Andrew Ortony, 137–63. 2nd ed. Cambridge: Cambridge University Press, 1993.

Schwager, Raymund. "Christ's Death and the Prophetic Critique of Sacrifice." Translated by Patrick Riordan. *Semeia* 33 (1985) 100–121.

Searle, John R. "Metaphor." In *Metaphor and Thought*, edited by Andrew Ortony, 83–111. 2nd ed. Cambridge: Cambridge University Press, 1993.

———. *Speech Acts: An Essay in the Philosophy of Language*. Cambridge: Cambridge University Press, 1969.

Self, Will. *Psychogeography*. London: Bloomsbury, 2007.

Selling, Joseph. "Moral Questioning and Human Suffering: In Search of a Credible Response to the Meaning of Suffering." In *God and Human Suffering*, edited by Jan Lambrecht and Raymond F. Collins, 155–82. Louvain Theological & Pastoral Monographs 3. Louvain: Peeters, 1990.

Sewall, Richard B. *The Vision of Tragedy*. New Haven: Yale University Press, 1959.

Shaw, Valerie. *The Short Story: A Critical Introduction*. London: Longman, 1983.

Shelley, P. B. *A Defence of Poetry*. 1821. Reprinted in *English Critical Essays: Nineteenth Century*, edited by Edmund D. Jones, 102–38. Oxford: Oxford University Press, 1968.

Shepp, Archie. "Innovations in Jazz." In *History and Tradition in Afro-American Culture*, edited by Gunter H. Lenz, 256–61. Campus Forschung 407. Frankfurt: Campus, 1984.

Simon, Ulrich. *Pity and Terror: Christianity and Tragedy*. New York: St. Martin's, 1989.

Sparshott, Francis. "Music and Feeling." *The British Journal of Aesthetics and Art Criticism* 52.1 (1994) 23–35.

General Bibliography

Standley, Fred L., and Nancy V. Burt, ed. *Critical Essays on James Baldwin*. Boston: Hall, 1988.
Steiner, George. *The Death of Tragedy*. London: Faber & Faber, 1961.
———. *Real Presences*. Chicago: University of Chicago Press, 1989.
Stiver, Dan R. *The Philosophy of Religious Language: Signs, Symbols & Story*. London: Blackwell, 1996.
Stott, William. *Documentary Expression and Thirties America*. New York: Oxford University Press, 1976.
Strong, L. A. G. "The Story: Notes at Random." *Lovat Dickson's Magazine*, March 1934 281–82.
Stroup, George W. *The Promise of Narrative Theology*. London: SCM, 1981.
Suites, David B. "Fictional Characters Are Just Like Us." *Philosophy and Literature* 18.1 (1994) 105–8.
Suleiman, Susan Rubin. *Authoritarian Fictions: The Ideological Novel as a Literary Genre*. Princeton: Princeton University Press, 1983.
Swarns, Rachel L. "272 Slaves Were Sold to Save Georgetown: What Does It Owe Their Descendants?" *New York Times*, April 16, 2016. http://www.nytimes.com/2016/04/17/us/georgetown-university-search-for-slave-descendants.html?_r=0
Syreeni, Kari. "Metaphorical Appropriation: (Post) Modern Biblical Hermeneutic and the Theory of Metaphor." *Literature and Theology* 9.3 (1995) 321–38.
Talbot, Mary M. *Fiction at Work: Language and Social Practice in Fiction*. London: Longman, 1995.
Taylor, Mark. "Denegating God." *Critical Inquiry* 20.4 (1994) 592–610.
Thomas, Terence, and Elizabeth Manning. "The Iconic Function of Music." In *The Sense of the Sacramental: Movement and Measure in Art and Music, Place and Time*, edited by David Brown and Ann Loades, 159–71. London: SPCK, 1995.
Tolstoy, Leo. *What Is Art?* Translated by A. Maud. Indianapolis: Hackett, 1960.
Traylor, Eleanor. "I Hear Music in the Air: James Baldwin's *Just Above My Head*." In *James Baldwin: The Legacy*, edited by Quincy Troupe, 95–106. New York: Simon & Schuster, 1989.
Trilling, Lionel. *Beyond Culture: Essays on Literature and Learning*. New York: Harcourt Brace Jovanovich, 1965.
Trin, T. Minh-ha. *When the Moon Waxes Red: A Presentation, Gender and Cultural Politics*. New York: Routledge, 1991.
Troupe, Quincy, ed. *James Baldwin: The Legacy*. New York: Simon & Schuster, 1989.
Turner, Victor, and Edith Turner. *Image and Pilgrimage in Christian Culture*. New York: Columbia University Press, 1978.
Ugorji, Lucius Iwejuru. *The Principle of Double Effect: A Critical Appraisal of Its Traditional Understanding and Its Modern Interpretation*. European University Studies. Series XXIII, Theology 245. New York: Lang, 1985.
van Inwagen, Peter. "Fiction and Metaphysics." *Philosophy and Literature* 6–7 (1982–1983) 67–77.
Via, Dan. *The Parables: Their Literary and Existential Dimensions*. 1967. Reprint, Eugene, OR: Wipf & Stock, 2007.
Wallace, Mark I. "Postmodern Biblicism: The Challenge of René Girard for Contemporary Theology." *Modern Theology* 5.4 (1989) 309–35.
Walton, Kendall L. "How Marvellous! Toward a Theory of Aesthetic Value." *Journal of Aesthetics and Art Criticism* 51.3 (1993) 499–510.

———. *Mimesis as Make-Believe: On the Foundations of the Representative Arts.* Cambridge: Harvard University Press, 1990.

———. "What Is Abstract about the Art of Music?" *Journal of Aesthetics and Art Criticism* 46 (1988) 351–64.

Werth, Paul. "Extended Metaphor: A Text-World Account." *Language and Literature* 3.2 (1994) 77–103.

Westermann, Claus. *The Parables of Jesus in the Light of the Old Testament.* Translated by Friedemann W. Golka and Alastair H. B. Logan. Edinburgh: T. & T. Clark, 1990.

Whittle, Roger. "Baldwin's *Going to Meet the Man*: Racial Brutality and Sexual Gratification." In *Critical Essays on James Baldwin*, edited by Fred L. Standley and Nancy V. Burt, 194–204. Boston: Hall, 1988.

Wiener, P. P. *Dictionary of the History of Ideas.* New York: Scribner, 1973.

Wieser, Thomas. "Community: Its Unity, Diversity and Universality." *Semeia* 33 (1985) 83–95.

Wilder, Amos N. *Early Christian Rhetoric: The Language of the Gospel.* 1964. Reprint, Eugene, OR: Wipf & Stock, 2014.

———. "Story and Story-World." *Interpretation* 57 (1983) 353–64.

———. "The Uses of a Theological Criticism." In *Literature and Religion*, edited by Giles B. Gunn, 37ff. Forum Books. London: SCM, 1971.

Wilder, Craig Steven. "War and Priests: Catholic Colleges and Slavery in the Age of Revolution." In *Slavery's Capitalism: A New History of America's Economic Development*, edited by Sven Beckert and Seth Rockman, 227–42. Philadelphia: University of Pennsylvania Press, 2016.

Williams, Sherley Anne. *Give Birth to Brightness: A Thematic Study in Neo-Black Literature.* New York: Dial, 1972.

Wilshire, Bruce. *Role Playing and Identity: The Limits of Theatre as Metaphor.* Studies in Phenomenology and Existential Philosophy. Bloomington: Indiana University Press, 1982.

Wimmer, Reiner. "What Makes Experience Revelatory?" In *Revelation and Experience*, edited by Vincent Brummer and Marcel Sarot, 9–25. Utrechte Theologische Reeks 33. Utrecht: Faculteit der Godgeleerdheit 1996.

Wittgenstein, Ludwig. *Philosophical Investigations.* Translated by G. E. M. Anscombe, Oxford: Blackwell, 1976.

Worton, Michael, and Judith Still, ed. *Intertextuality: Theories and Practice.* Manchester: Manchester: University Press, 1990.

X, Malcolm. *The Autobiography of Malcolm* X. With the assistance of Alex Haley. 1965. Reprint, New York: Ballentine, 1973.

Index

acting
  autobiographical memory, 107–9
  communication as, 100n43
  identity paradox, 97–100, 98nn31–35
  mimetic sympathy, 99n36, 99n41, 100–102
  morality, 102–4
  projection of alternate worlds, 116, 116n97
  proportionality, 105–7
  truth in fiction, 101n50
aesthetics
  appreciation of, 136n70
  artistic sensibility, 55–56, 55n91
  link between theology and, 28–29, 119
  literary, 141n97
  moral dimension, 135–37, 136n71, 136nn73–74, 137n75, 137n78
  musical experiences, 141n95
  new experiences, 156
  paradox of tragedy, 69–72
  standards of, 125, 125n19
  transformation of ordinary things, 92
African American church
  historical sketch, 13–15
  influence on JB, 153
  music of collective sorrow, 134n60
  sin and death at center, 17–22
  Spirituals, 113–16, 115n93, 116n97, 132
African Americans
  civil rights movement, 62–64, 63n14, 63n17, 94–95, 94n14
  freedom and, 14–15, 115n95
  JB's identity, 23–24, 26, 94n14, 95n15, 118–19
  musical culture, 119, 120n5, 131–35, 133nn55–57, 134n59, 144n108
  problematic relationship to Christianity, 11–12
alienation, 49–50, 49n62. *See also* selfhood
Aquinas, Thomas, 103
Aristotle, 33, 60, 60–61n4, 65, 65n24, 69n43, 71–72, 87
Arnold, Matthew, 47n57
arts. *See* acting; literature; music
atonement doctrine. *See also* sacrifice
  crucifixion of Christ, 51–52
  historical background, 45–48, 46n55, 47n56
  literature as scripture, 53–54
  necessity of repetition, 51n72, 56
  reconciliation, 56–57
  representation through fiction, 54
  salvation, 51–52, 52n77
Aulén, Gustaf, 52n77
autobiographical memory
  actors' use of, 101, 107–9
  exploration of race, 94–95, 97
  fictional qualities, 72–76, 74nn67–68
  selfhood in context of, 22–24, 24n85, 26, 101, 101n49, 153
  shifting attention from personal to universal, 28, 119, 119n3, 158

Index

"Autobiographical Memory" (Robinson), 24n85
Aza'zel, 35–36, 36–37n22

Baldwin, David (stepfather). *See also* father-son relationships
    inability to establish contact with others, 107–8
    relationship with JB, 8, 24, 101n49, 108n75, 112, 114
Baldwin, Emma Berdis Jones (mother), 8
Baldwin, James. *See specific works for more information*
    American identity, 95–97, 96–97n26
    biographical sketch, 7–11
    birth of, 8
    career of, 10–11
    as child preacher, 8–9
    "creative illness," 9–10
    critical readings of, 1, 11–12
    education of, 8
    ethnic writer label, 94n14, 95n15, 118–19, 158
    identity problem, 92–93, 92–93nn6–7
    in Paris, 91–92, 93n7, 94–97, 110–11, 113, 117
    relationship with stepfather, 8, 24, 101n49, 107–8, 108n75, 112, 114
    religious experiences, 153
    sexuality of, 10
    short stories as intertexts of corpus, 17–22, 25–27
    works
        "Going to Meet the Man," 27, 59–89, 154–55
        Go Tell It on the Mountain, 17, 21–22, 108n75
        Just Above My Head, 120n5
        Nobody Knows My Name, 96–97
        Notes of a Native Son, 107, 117, 118
        "Previous Condition," 6–7, 153, 158
        "Sonny's Blues," 28–29, 118–51, 158
        "The Man Child," 27, 30–58, 154, 158
        "This Morning, This Evening, So Soon," 28, 90–117, 156–57, 158
Barbour, John, 82, 84–86
Bates, H. E., 16
beauty. *See* aesthetics
being, as desire, 33–34
Benjamin, Walter, 75n70
The Bible. *See also* scriptures
    as critical lens, 4–5, 12, 12n35
    as divine message, 116, 156
    as literature, 47, 47n57
    critique of violence, 46n55, 56–57, 58
    historicity, 31n3
    imagery from, 146–50
    revelation theology, 138, 139n87
    tragedy, 62n11
    Leviticus, 31, 35–37, 51
    Job, 44n47
    Jeremiah, 148
    Ezekiel, 148
    Zechariah, 148
    Enoch, 36
    Mark, 88
    Revelations, 148
    Old Testament, 138
    New Testament, 138
Bieganowski, Ronald, 131, 140
Bigsby, C. W. E., 119n3
black Christianity
    historical sketch, 13–15
    influence on JB, 153
    music of collective sorrow, 134n60
    sin and death at center, 17–22
    Spirituals, 113–16, 116n97, 132
blues
    cultural-historical context, 119, 120n5, 131–35, 133n57
    emotional pain, 131, 131n47, 134, 134nn59–61
    innovation, 134, 134n62, 144n108
    storytelling, 135, 135n64
Booth, Wayne, 152
Bouchard, Larry, 60, 76
Brereton, Geoffrey, 65nn24–25, 68n41

Index

"brother's keeper" motif, 120–21, 120n5, 141–44, 150, 158
Buber, Martin, 77n81, 78n84
Budd, Malcolm, 128
Byerman, Keith B., 142n101, 149n132

Cameron, James, 73, 75, 88, 88–89n124
Carrasco, David, 110n81, 112
catharsis, 68–69, 68n41, 69n43, 135n68
Cavell, Stanley, 61
Chapman, G. Clarke, 14
Christ figures. *See also* Jesus Christ
   atonement doctrine, 36–37, 37n24, 45–48, 46n55, 47n56, 50–53
   godforsakenness, 62
   imperfect resolution, 56–57, 58
Christianity. *See also* Bible; morality
   African American church, 13–15, 17–22, 113–16, 116n97, 132, 134n60, 153
   apartheid exigesis, 11–12, 12n34
   atonement doctrine, 27, 45–48, 46n55, 47n56
   defining mythology, 31
   JB's rejection of, 11–12
   revelation theology, 137–40, 137nn79–80, 138n83, 139n87
   solidarity, 100n42
civil rights movement
   depictions of, 62–64, 63n14, 63n17
   intensity of, 91, 92–95
   literature of, 94n14
   segregation, 11–12, 12n33
Clarke, Michael, 149
cognitivism, 125–26, 125–26n21, 125n17, 126nn24–25, 128, 135n66
collective responsibility, 84–87
colonisation, 12, 12n34
communication
   attempts at, 100n43, 122–23
   revelation of self, 140–41
   through music, 123–31, 131n43, 131n45, 132, 135n64, 157
communitas, 111–12
Cone, James H., 15, 115n95
contrast experiences, 28, 90n1, 94–97, 95n16, 114, 156–57
creative illness, 9–10, 9n28

culture texts, 119, 120n5, 131–35, 132n52, 133nn55–57
cup of trembling imagery, 148–50
Curran, Charles, 106n69

Daly, Gabriel, 86
darkness imagery, 144–48
Day of Atonement, 35–38, 36–37n22, 36nn20–21, 37n24
Democritus, 32–33
deontology, 104, 104n57
Descartes, Rene, 77n82
desire
   competition for, 34n15
   for knowledge, 68
   mimetic, 30–33, 34n14, 34n16, 49–50, 57–58
Detweiler, Robert, 158
Dickens, Charles, 74
Dillistone, F.W., 36, 36n20
Dinsmore, Charles Allen, 53, 54, 56
Dionysian rites, 32, 32n7
disabilities, 44
distancing, 100–101, 142n102
documentaries, 73n65
Douglass, Frederick, 115n95
Dulles, Avery, 137n79, 138, 139–40

Eckman, Fern Marja, 112
Eldridge, Richard, 60n3, 67
Elizondo, V., 111
Ellenberger, Henri, 9
emotivism, 126–28, 127n28, 128, 135n66, 141n95
Enlightenment period, 48
Enoch, 36
eschatology, 80
ethics, 76–80, 78nn84–85, 79n87. *See also* morality
   Christian solidarity, 100n42
   exploration through tragedy, 84–89
   relationality-responsibility, 106n69
   responsibilities, 68
ethnic writer label, 94n14, 95n15, 118–19, 119n3, 158
evil
   human condition, 27, 62, 64, 88–89, 88–89n124

Index

evil *(continued)*
  lesser, 105n64
  means with good ends, 102–4
  moral *vs.* physical, 105n65
  proportionalism, 105–7, 105nn64–66, 106n71, 106nn68–69
  reconciliation to, 72
exile, self, 49–50, 49n62. *See also* pilgrimage
Exum, J. Cheryl, 61n7
eye contact, 76–80, 78n83
Ezekiel, 148

fantasy, 62n13
father-son relationships. *See also* scapegoat motif
  autobiographical elements, 8, 24, 101n49, 107–8, 108n75, 112, 114
  burden of illegitimacy, 17, 108n75
  fears of being a bad father, 109
  hatred between sons and, 17–20, 101, 107–8, 108n75
  knowledge of human nature, 63, 66–68, 79, 86
  sons as doubles of fathers, 143–44, 143n107
Feagin, Susan L., 71
fiction, exploration of history through, 12n33, 72–76, 74nn67–68, 75n70, 101n50, 158. *See also* literature
Fiddes, Paul, 36, 47, 50, 53, 136, 137n78
fire imagery, 147–48
flashback device, 62–64
folklore, 132
Forsman, Rodger, 139n87
France. *See also* "This Morning, This Evening, So Soon"
  contrast experience, 28, 95n16, 156
  JB in, 91–92, 93n7, 94–97, 110–11, 113, 117
  as sacred site, 111, 113
Frazer, James, 31, 40
freedom, 14–15, 115n95
Fugitive Slave Act (1850), 115n95

Gadamer, Hans Georg, 131n43
Girard, René

alienation, 49–50
historicity of gospels, 31n3
on Job, 44n47
"Monstrous Double," 50
moral monstrosity, 39
scapegoat mechanism, 27, 30–35, 40–45, 43, 57–58
God. *See also* atonement doctrine; sacrifice
  immediacy of, 21, 22n74
  love of, 106n69
  mystery of, 57, 77n82, 136–37n74
  nature of, 58, 80, 116, 136, 138–39, 139n87, 154, 156
  negativity towards, 11, 11n31, 12, 25
  role in suffering, 19, 27, 36n20, 64, 89, 148, 149
God: In Fragments (Pohier), 22
"Going to Meet the Man" (Baldwin), 59–89
  human condition, 27, 62
  moral sensitivity in, 69–72
  otherness, 155
  overview, 62–64
  redemption, 155
  sacrifice, 154
  self as other, 76–80
  tragic elements, 65–69
  tragic heroes, 80–84
Goldman, Alan, 141n95
Gollwitzer, Helmut, 13n39
Gordimer, Nadine, 5n13
gospels
  critique of violence, 46n55, 56–57, 58
  as divine message, 116, 156
  historicity, 31n3
  tragedy, 62n11
Go Tell It on the Mountain (Baldwin), 17, 21–22, 108n75
Gunn, Janet V., 23

hamartia, 65n26, 81
Hamerton-Kelly, Robert, 31n2, 33n11, 34n14, 40, 46n55
hedonism, 104n60
heroes, tragic, 65n26, 80–84
history

Index

African American church, 13–15
atonement doctrine, 45–48, 46n55, 47n56
biblical, 31n3
cultural contexts, 119, 120n5, 131–35, 133n57
fictional qualities, 72–76, 74nn67–68, 101n50, 158
significance to identity, 150n138
homosexuality, 10
human condition
  affirmation of life, 68–69, 72
  evil, 27, 62, 64, 72, 88–89, 88–89n124
  functions of tragedy, 60n3, 61n9, 71–72n57, 75n70
  man's inhumanity to man, 60–61
  revelation, 137nn79–80
  role of experience, 84–87
  significance of past and future, 150n138
  suffering, 64, 66–67, 88–89
  vulnerability, 153
Hume, David, 69–70, 125

identity. *See also* race; selfhood
  American, 95–97, 95n18, 96–97n26, 114
  determination, 28
  doubles, 143n107
  paradox of, 92
  pilgrimages, 79n109, 90–92, 110–13, 114
  revelatory events, 140n92
  self-discovery, 140–41n94, 153
  significance of past and future, 150n138
Ijsseling, Samuel, 148–49, 148n130
illegitimacy, burden of, 17
imagery, 123n11, 140n92, 144–50, 144n110
imagination
  as both activity and attitude, 43n45
  emotional arousal, 126n25, 127n28, 128–30, 129n40
  as extension of real world, 55, 55n91
  fantasy, 62n13
  musical composition, 127–28
  projection of alternate worlds, 116, 116n97
  revelatory events, 140n92
  sexuality, 62n13
innovation, musical, 134, 134n62
instrumental music, 125n17
intentions, 102–7, 106n71
intertextuality, 17–22, 25–27, 135n66, 148–49, 148nn129–30
Isaacs, Marie E., 51n72
Isaiah, 148

Janssens, Louis, 105
Jasper, David, 53, 74, 83n101, 139n88, 154
jazz blues
  cultural-historical context, 119, 120n5, 131–35, 133n57
  emotional pain, 131, 131n47, 134, 134nn59–61
  innovation, 134, 134n62, 144n108
  storytelling, 135, 135n64
Jeremiah, 148
Jesus Christ
  resurrection, 22n74
  revelation theology, 138
  sacrificial death of, 36–38, 37n24, 38n28, 45–48, 46n55, 47n56, 50–53
Job, 44n47
Jones, Emma Berdis (later Baldwin), 8
Just Above My Head (Baldwin), 120n5

Kant, Immanuel, 136
Kaufmann, Walter, 60
Kivy, Peter, 125–26n21, 126n24
Knauer, Peter, 106
knowledge, as tragic element, 66–67, 67–68n37, 67n30
Kong, Lily, 132n52, 134n60
Kort, Wesley A., 46n53
Krieger, Murray, 83n102
Krook, Dorothea, 65–69

Lamarque, Peter, 43n45, 74
Landy, Robert J., 100
language, poetic, 144–48
Leibniz, Gottfried Wilhelm, 80

Index

Lévinas, Emmanuel, 27, 62, 76–80, 76n78, 79
Leviticus 16, 31, 35–37, 51
lightness imagery, 144–48, 144n110
listener-response theories, 124–31, 125–26n21, 125n17, 126nn24–25, 127n28, 135n66, 141n95
literature. *See also* aesthetics
  beneficial aspects of tragedy, 60n3
  deception through, 40, 40n34
  exploration of history through, 72–76, 74nn67–68, 75n70, 101n50, 158
  folklore, 132
  form as distinct from subject matter, 73
  functions of, 1–4, 5
  moral dimension, 136n71, 152
  poetic language, 144–48
  poetry, 47, 47n57, 53
  projection of alternate worlds, 116, 116n97
  reading religiously, 157–58
  relative complexity of novels and short stories, 5–6
  as scripture, 47, 47n57, 53–54
  short stories, 4–7, 16–22, 25–27, 37
  social protest, 94n14, 95n15
  theological dimension, 4–5, 12, 12n35, 152–58
  toasts, 133, 133n55
Lloyd, Peter, 69n43
Lynch, Michael F., 11–12, 119n3
lynching, 63n17

"The Man Child" (Baldwin)
  alienation of Jamie, 49–50
  as parable, 37
  scapegoat motif, 27, 31–32, 154, 158
  victimhood, 42–45
Manning, Elizabeth, 131n48
Mark, 88
Martin, Graham D., 74
McKenna, Andrew, 34n16
Mertens, Herman-Emiel, 136–37, 137n75
metanarrative, 98n34
Meyer, Leonard, 127

Middle Ages, 47
Miller, Arthur, 60–61n4
Millican, Arthenia Bates, 63n17, 76n76, 85
mimetic desire
  alienation, 49–50
  in classical Greece, 32–33
  Girard's scapegoat hypothesis, 30–32, 34n14, 57–58
  role of disciple, 34n16
mimetic sympathy, 99n36, 99n41, 100–102
"The Modern Short Story: Retrospect" (Bates), 16
Möller, Karen, 97n26
"Monstrous Double," 50
mood, 126n24
morality. *See also* ethics
  duties, 105n62
  justifications, 102–4
  "Monstrous Double," 50
  moral monstrosity, 39
  moral *vs.* physical evil, 105n65
  proportionalism, 105–6n66, 105–7, 105n64, 106n71, 106nn68–69
  responsibilities, 68
moral sensitivity, 69–72
music
  cognitive theory of listener response, 125–26, 125–26n21, 126nn24–25, 128, 135n66
  communication through, 123–31, 131n43, 131n45, 132, 135n64, 157
  as culture text, 119, 120n5, 131–35, 132n52
  emotivist theory of listener response, 126–28, 127n28, 128, 135n66, 141n95
  imagery, 123n11
  innovation, 134, 134n62, 144n108
  instrumental, 125n17
  interdisciplinary aspects, 132n50
  intertextuality, 135n66
  as mechanism for reaching unconscious, 28–29, 119, 120n5, 123–25, 151
  religious, 122, 131n48, 132–33n53
  revelatory experience, 140–41

Index

social function of, 128–31, 129nn39–40, 131n43, 131n48, 134n60
Spirituals, 113–16, 115n93, 116n97, 132, 156
mythology, 30–31, 31n4, 38–40, 39n31, 46–47

Nelson, Emmanuel S., 140–41n94
New Testament
  gospels, 31n3, 46n55, 56–57, 58, 62n11, 116, 156
  revelation, 138
  Mark, 88
  Revelations, 148
Nichols, Charles H., 12n33
Nietzsche, Friedrich, 82, 89
Nobody Knows My Name (Baldwin), 96–97
Notes of a Native Son (Baldwin), 107, 117, 118
novels, complexity of, 5–6. *See also* literature

"Ode: Intimations of Immortality" (Wordsworth), 144n110
Oedipus Rex (Socrates), 39
Old Testament, 138
Oliver Twist (Dickens), 74
Olsen, Stein Haugom, 43n45, 74
"On the Standard of Taste" (Hume), 125
ontological gaps, 16
original sin, 86
otherness
  actor paradox, 98–99, 98nn31–35, 99n36, 99n41, 100n44
  distancing, 100–101, 142n102
  exile from self, 49–50, 49n62
  eye contact, 76–80, 78n83
  obligations to, 78n85, 79n87
  openness to, 28, 131
  race and, 108–9, 155
  self as, 76–77n78, 76–80, 77n79, 77n81, 88, 88nn122–23, 155
"The Outing" (Baldwin)
  autobiographical memory, 158
  guilt, 153–54

religion in, 25–26
sin in, 17–19, 21–22

Packer, Mark, 71
parables, short stories as, 6–7, 37
Paris. *See also* "This Morning, This Evening, So Soon"
  contrast experience, 28, 95n16, 156
  JB in, 91–92, 93n7, 94–97, 110–11, 113, 117
  as sacred site, 111, 113
Pattyn, Bart, 100n42
Pentecostalism. *See* African American church
Peperzak, Adriaan, 76–77n78, 78n85
persecution texts, 42–45
pilgrimage
  communitas, 111–12
  contrast experiences, 28, 90n1, 94–97, 95n16, 114, 156–57
  of JB, 91–92, 93n7, 94–97, 110–11, 113, 117
  journey into the past, 109n79
  sites of, 110n81, 113
  value of, 90–92
Plato, 33
pleasure paradox, 69–72
poesis, 76
Poetics (Aristotle), 65
poetry, 47, 47n57, 53, 133, 133nn55–57
Pohier, Jacques, 22, 22n74
Post, Paul, 92
poverty, 8, 15, 21, 44
"Previous Condition" (Baldwin), 153
  human condition, 153
  otherness, 158
  structure of, 6–7
proportionalism, 105–7, 105nn64–66, 106n71, 106nn68–69
psychogeography, 90–92, 90n1, 109–14, 109n79. *See also* pilgrimage
Purcell, Michael, 78n83
purification
  atonement doctrine, 45–48, 46n55, 47n56, 51–57, 51n72, 52n77
  catharsis, 68–69, 68n41, 69n43, 135n68

Index

purification *(continued)*
  through sacrifice, 35–38, 36nn20–21, 37n24, 38n28
Putschogl, Gerhard, 133n57

Quinton, Anthony, 60–61n4, 71–72n57

race. *See also* identity
  civil rights movement, 62–64, 63n14, 63n17, 94–95, 94n14
  contrast experiences, 114
  ethnic writer label, 94n14, 95n15, 118–19, 119n3
  European experiences of, 91–92, 95–97
  otherness and, 108–9, 155
  perceptions of Sweden, 96n21
  portrayal in fiction, 12n33, 75, 85, 108
  sexuality and, 62n13
  social protest fiction, 94n14, 95n15
  treatment of minorities, 93n7
  in United States, 91–95, 95n18, 113
reconciliation. *See* salvation
  in tragedy, 82
Reformation period, 47–48
religion. *See also* Christianity; theology
  aesthetic dimension, 136–37, 136n71, 136nn73–74
  as critical lens, 17–21, 25–26
  cultural connections of, 131n48
  links to literature, 75n70
  music, 132–33n53
  sacredness, 39–40n33
religious revivalism, 122, 146–47
revelation, 137–41, 137nn79–80, 139n87, 140–41n93, 140n92
Revelations, 148
Ries, John C., 150n138
Robertson, Patricia, 122, 149
Robinson, J. A., 24n85
Robinson, Jenefer, 126–27, 126n25
"The Rockpile" (Baldwin)
  autobiographical memory, 158
  guilt, 153–54
  religion in, 25–26
  sin in, 19–22
role-playing

  autobiographical memory, 107–9
  communication, 100n43
  identity paradox, 97–100, 98nn31–35
  mimetic sympathy, 99n36, 99n41, 100–102
  morality, 102–4
  projection of alternate worlds, 116, 116n97
  proportionality, 105–7
  truth in fiction, 101n50
Role Playing and Identity (Wilshire), 92

sacrifice. *See also* atonement doctrine; scapegoat motif
  death of Jesus as, 36–38, 37n24, 38n28, 45–48, 46n55, 47n56, 50–53
  definition of, 37
  necessity of repetition, 51n72, 56
  purification through, 35–38, 36nn20–21, 37n24, 38n28
  salvation through, 51–52, 52n77, 154, 155
Salzman, Todd, 106n69
Sandall, Robert, 134n59
scapegoat motif. *See also* sacrifice
  alienation stage, 49–50
  in biblical literature, 35–38
  Girard, 27, 30–35, 40–45, 43, 57–58
  Girard's theory of desire, 30–35
  mirror of Passion narrative, 27, 31–32, 154
  in mythology, 39–40
  social anthropological viewpoint, 40–42, 84
  victimisation, 42–45, 43n44
Schier, Flint, 61n9, 67–68n37, 67n30, 68n38, 70n49, 72, 75
Schwager, Raymund, 37n24
scriptures
  as critical lens, 4–5
  as literature, 47, 47n57
  defining, 46n53
  imagery from, 146–50
  literature as, 53–54
  revelation theology, 138, 139n87
  Leviticus, 31, 35–37, 51

Index

Job, 44n47
Jeremiah, 148
Ezekiel, 148
Zechariah, 148
Enoch, 36
Mark, 88
Revelations, 148
Old Testament, 138
New Testament, 138
segregation, 11–12, 12n33
selfhood
   actor paradox, 98–99, 98nn31–35, 99n36, 99n41, 100n44
   in context of autobiographical memory, 22–24, 24n85, 26
   distinguished from other, 78, 78n84, 100–101
   exile from self, 49–50, 49n62
   obligations to other, 78n85, 79, 79n87
   as other, 76–77n78, 76–80, 77n79, 77n81, 88, 88nn122–23, 155
Selling, Joseph, 64, 103
Sewall, Richard, 60n1
sexuality, 10, 62n13, 63n17
shame, as tragic element, 65
Shepp, Archie, 133, 133n53
Ship of Zion, 146–47
short stories, 4–7, 16–22, 25–27, 37
sin
   atonement doctrine, 27
   guilt, 153–54
   Hebrew Bible nature of, 35–36, 36n20
   original sin, 86
   preoccupation with, 17–22
   tragic flaws, 84
slavery
   Christian justification for, 11–12
   freedom from, 115n95
   music, 134n59
   religious conversion of slaves, 13–14, 13n39
   Spirituals, 113–16, 116n97, 132, 156
societal contradictions, 28
solidarity, 98n33, 100n42
"Sonny's Blues" (Baldwin), 118–51
   biblical imagery, 148–49
   "brother's keeper" motif, 120–21, 120n5, 141–44, 150, 158
   communication through music, 123–31, 131n43, 131n45, 132, 135n64, 157
   functions of narrator, 147n125, 149n132
   link between theology and aesthetics, 28–29
   overview, 119–23
sons. *See* father-son relationships
Sparshott, Francis, 125n17, 128–29
Spirituals, 113–16, 115n93, 116n97, 132, 156
Stroup, George W., 140n92
suffering
   as part of human condition, 64, 66–67, 88–89
   role of God in, 19, 27, 36n20, 64, 89, 148, 149
   sensitivity to, 70
   as tragic element, 65–69, 66n27, 82n95
Sweden, 96n21
Sykes, John, 51

teleology, 104
theology
   as critical lens, 4–5, 12, 12n35
   link between aesthetics and, 28–29, 119
   literature as platform for, 4–5, 12, 12n35, 152–58
"This Morning, This Evening, So Soon" (Baldwin), 90–117
   autobiographical memory in, 28, 101, 101n49, 107–9
   morality, 102–4
   overview, 90–91, 93–94
   pilgrimage, 156–57, 158
Thomas, Terrence, 131n48
toasts, 133, 133n55
Totality and Infinity (Lévinas), 79
tragedy
   Aristotelian, 60, 60–61n4, 69–72, 87
   beneficial aspects in literature, 60n3
   categorization of, 82–83
   elements of, 61n7, 65–69, 65n24

tragedy *(continued)*
   fictional quality of history, 72–76
   functions of, 60–61, 61n9
   heroes, 65n26, 80–84
   as metaphor, 65n25
   otherness, 76–80
   paradox of, 69–72
tragic heroes, 65n26, 80–84
transference, 100n45
Trilling, Lionel, 119n3, 136n71, 152
Turner, Victor, 109–10, 111

United States. *See also* African American church; African Americans; slavery
   civil rights movement, 62–64, 63n14, 63n17, 91, 92–95, 94n14
   embrace of, 114–17
   racial tensions, 91–95, 92n7, 113, 158
   segregation, 11–12, 12n33
utilitarianism, 104, 104n61

victimhood, 42–45, 43n44, 65–66. *See also* scapegoat motif

violence. *See also* scapegoat motif
   calming effects, 50n67
   intrinsic to human condition, 27, 40–42, 64, 72
   Monstrous Double, 49–50
   persecution texts, 43

Wallace, Catherine, 5
Walton, Kendall, 126n25, 127, 136n70
When I Say God (Pohier), 22n74
White, Hayden, 73
Wilder, Amos N., 46n53
Wilshire, Bruce, 92, 98, 98–99n35, 98n32, 99n36, 99n41, 100n42, 101n50
Wittgenstein, Ludwig, 61
Wordsworth, William, 144n110
worksong, 133, 133nn55–57

Yom Kippur, 35–38, 36–37n22, 36nn20–21, 37n24
Young, Norman H., 51n72

Zechariah, 148

www.ingramcontent.com/pod-product-compliance
Lightning Source LLC
Chambersburg PA
CBHW051744230426
43670CB00012B/2152